C
GRAPHICS & PROJECTS

C
Graphics & Projects

By

B.M. HAVALDAR

ANMOL PUBLICATIONS PVT. LTD.
NEW DELHI - 110 002 (INDIA)

ANMOL PUBLICATIONS PVT. LTD.
4374/4B, Ansari Road, Daryaganj
New Delhi - 110 002
Ph.: 23261597, 23278000
Visit us at: www.anmolpublications.com

C Graphics and Projects

First Published, 2005

ISBN 81-261-2310-9

PRINTED IN INDIA

Published by J.L. Kumar for Anmol Publications Pvt. Ltd., New Delhi and Printed at Mehra Offset Press, Delhi.

Dedicated To
My Well Wishers

K.K. Misal
V.S. Manavade
Dr. Ram Kulkarni

CONTENTS

FOREWORD

Just to remind you that still I was enjoying the ride on the previous work on C programming and I am asked to continue the ride on the next level with C graphics and projects. Though it took me for a while to adjust to the new environment but it is fascinating.

Let me come to the point I have gone through the earlier work of this author and mentioned that the work was good. In a short time I have a copy of his another work on C graphics and projects. The title of the edition looks very unconventional because most of the editions covered on C have got standard narration of topics. Here the author tries to look the whole concept in a different manner. As the name suggests C graphics and projects the focus is more on actual usage of the power of C in graphics which is complemented with certain good projects with live examples..

Here I am trying to explore the best possible usage of graphics in real environments. Let me share my experience with you while surfing the topics in a sequential manner.

In the first two chapters as per the students are concerned I see a good amount of information is covered on basic fundamentals on graphics, the role of C in graphics and other relevant details along with sufficient examples, which will give a nice feeling to start the further exploration in the ocean of graphics.

In the 3rd and 4th chapter the stage is set for exploring the graphics. The author has covered simple animation techniques; drawing of uni dimensional diagrams along with related good amount of examples. By this time students/users start getting the concept and grip of the graphics, which is a stepping-stone to explore the next level of graphics by using C language. The Digital differential analyzer, spiral generations are the classic examples in the above chapters.

The chapter 5 opens up the real power of graphics. I have observed the author has covered the substantial information about two dimensional and 3 dimensional graphics. He has also covered most of the fundamentals as well as some complex examples in this chapter. I can see really what I can do in the imaginative world of graphics, which is a wonderful experience to learn with the examples. However I felt some more explanations are needed with respect to the beginning of the topics.

In the chapter 6 the author touches upon the finer points of display of graphics. It is very essential because what we actually see in the screens should be a perfect views, otherwise distortion of picture on the screen will spoil the whole look of the output. The author teaches us how to control the above aspects with standard algorithms so that we can get a desired output. The line clipping algorithm, southern land Hodge man algorithm are the good examples for references.

As per the part A of C graphics and projects is considered the author has spent lot of his efforts by keeping his focus on the students across all the streams. Most of the above topics are the part of the curriculum prescribed by various universities in India. I strongly feel Students can use this book as part of their studies.

Coming to the part B of this edition the author unleashes the real power of graphics with various projects with live source code demos. I feel this part is useful to various background people apart from vast community of students. These examples can be a very good reference for faculties, software programmers and the people who wanted to explore the ocean of graphics.

In the chapter 1 the author demonstrates all the functions of a computer system graphically with various functionalities. Hypocom, CPU and the functions of the Multiplexer are the good examples. These examples can be used extensively in the classrooms to teach the basic functionality of the computers. Students can tryout various other options by modifying the source code for the desired outputs.

In the Chapter 2 the author explains fundamental concepts and the actual working of LAN functions. The students and the users can get the knowledge of various topologies in LAN with complete implementation details. The complete source code has provided for the examples with live demos.

In the chapter 3 the author explains more functions of CPU in a graphical manner. FIFO, Round robin, priority based CPU scheduling are the interesting examples.

In the chapter 4 the users will get the complete graphical experience of the various searching and sorting methods with lot of examples for each methods along with the source code. Binary search, the merging of sorted lists are the good examples to learn.

Chapter 5 explains complex functions of stacks, queues, various types of linked lists followed by a sufficient amount of various examples backed by the source code. The author is simply at his best to explain the most complex functions of C in an understandable manner to the students as well as the other users.

I have gone through the live demonstrations of various projects in Chapters 6 and chapter 7. These projects simulate the possible ways of usage of graphics. At the same time the author try to give you the real experience of graphics in C through these projects.

In the chapter 8 the author explains various multi-processing tasks schematically with various examples. Disk scheduling is good example followed by the complete source code for the students/users reference perspective.

In my view over all the author tries to keep the students interest in first place and at the same time the interests of the other users also kept in mind. It will be a good users reference edition for the respective users. Let me relax back some time and will come back to you later to share my experience with you, till then enjoy...

D.V. Venkatachalapathy
Chairman & Managing Director
Vikas Global solutions Limited
Bangalore

PREFACE

Dear **readers**, thanks for your support and encouragement that you have shown towards my first work "**Programming Skills Through C**". In that book I have covered the complete concepts, features and syntax of C programming language with numerous examples that teach programming skills to anyone even for beginners, to master C. I got a positive feedback and encouragement from those who have gone through that book and advised me to write a new book that covers the Graphics Programming with C language. In that direction I have come out with a new book that covers the complete Graphical Programming ability of C.

In the world of computer applications Graphics plays an important role. Computers are nothing without graphics. We can take an example of any Graphical User Interface that we use in today's computer applications. What if we compare GUI's with Character User Interfaces? User feels clumsy, uncomfortable and less interesting with CUI's. By this one can understand the importance of 'pixel'. What is a pixel? We will study when we take an interesting and fruitful journey with this book. In the ocean of computer graphics let's explore a small portion of it using C programming language.

The subject '**Computer Graphics**' is included in most of Computer Science courses of Indian Universities and Technical Boards. This book is targeted to students keeping in mind their academic requirements at undergraduate and postgraduate levels.

To start with this book it contains two parts. The first part **'Part A'** deals with introduction to different graphical functions that are available in C and their usage. It consists of six chapters that deal with introduction to Graphics, Bar Graphs and Charts, Animations, Line and Circle Generating Algorithms, 2 Dimensional and 3 Dimensional Transformations and Clipping and Windowing Techniques along with sufficient example programs to illustrate each concept.

'Part B' of this book contains small projects that are implemented using C Graphical Programming. These projects are mainly based on demonstration of different computer related concepts. Namely CPU Scheduling Algorithms, Disk Scheduling Algorithms, LAN Topologies, Data Structures Demonstration, Architectural Demonstration of Working Computers and Searching, Sorting and Merging algorithms.

The other projects include Petrol Bunk Simulation and Buildesigner (the complete solution for residential house plan).

Appropriate Comments are included in the source code wherever necessary to make the readers feel comfortable in understanding each and every line of the source code. This makes the coding self explanatory. Each and every module is tested and executed in **Turbo C** compiler on **DOS** environment. It is required for the readers of this book to be familiar with the C programming language. The user should first read the information provided in the explanation part of each project about what that the project actually does and how it is implemented and what are the modules that are included and their functionality. All modules are self explanatory about the function they are intended to perform.

Bangalore-76

15th Oct. 2004

B. M. Havaldar

ACKNOWLEDGEMENTS

I will be ungrateful if I forget to thank all those who supported me in bringing out this work. This work is not instantaneous and I took many years to be able to produce this book. During this time I haye received help either directly or indirectly from many people.

The material for this book is derived largely from the lectures that I delivered to my students from many years. It is the collection of information over years of my teaching life. I thank all my students without whom I am unable to come out with this work.

I thank Mr. Keshav Srinivas for extending his support for my second work also. He is with me ever since I started working on my first work 'Programming Skills Through C'. He extended his helping hand right from deciding the topics, way of presentation, documentation and his constant support throughout the completion of this project.

I thank Anmol Publications and its staff who came forward to publish my works. My special thanks to Mr. Srinivas Murthy of Anmol Publication Pvt. Ltd. for his constant support to publish my works.

I thank Mr. Girish C. and Mr. Suresh for designing the cover page. I also thank my colleague Shilpa M. N. for her help during editing.

I thank my wife Prathibha Havaldar and my son Shreyas for their kind co-operation during completion of this project.

In spite of my best efforts to give accurate information to the readers, this work may contain the errors that were unnoticed. All suggestions from the readers to improve the quality of this material will be gratefully accepted.

Readers can communicate to my e-mail 'havaldar2k@yahoo.co.uk' or 'kesh_raja@yahoo.co.in' for their valuable suggestions.

B. M. Havaldar

LIST OF PROGRAMS

PART A

GRAPHICS PROGRAMMING

1

INTRODUCTION

Drawing graphs, charts and diagrams with the help of computer programming on the computer screen is called computer graphics. Basically there are two types of computer graphics namely, interactive computer graphics and non-interactive computer graphics. Interactive computer graphics is one in which the user can interact with the image, example playing games in the computer. Non-interactive computer graphics is one in which user is no way interacting with the image, example screen savers.

As a pixel is worth thousand words which means with a small picture one can easily understand the complicated subjects. In our daily life graphics is used in number of different ways. The designers such as textile designer, building construction designer, electronic circuit designer, teachers for explaining the complex theories to the students can use graphics. The different areas of computer graphics are given below.

1.A) Areas of Computer Graphics:

i) **Design and Drawing:** In almost all areas of engineering like civil, mechanical, electronics etc., drawings are important. It is easy for the designer to re-draw or re-generate the images whenever it is present in the computer. Writing on the paper is difficult and even minor changes also become costly. One can simulate the entire design from different angles in computer easily before finalizing them. Computers can store complex drawings and display them according to the user's requirements.

ii) **Animation:** It is an art of moving images on the computer screen. This application of graphics brought the computers pretty close to the average individuals. It is used for number of purposes. Animation in computer graphics is achieved by erasing and redrawing images repeatedly with changing the position of the image on the screen.

iii) **Multimedia applications:** The use of sound cards to make computers produce sound effect led to other uses of graphics. The concept of virtual reality, where in one can be taken through an unreal experience, like going through an unbuilt house (to see how it feels inside, once it is built) are possible by the use of computer graphics technology.

iv) **Simulation:** Creation of virtual environment before it comes into existence and checking how it looks after its completion is simulation. Suppose a boy is provided with a bicycle he can learn himself but if an airplane is provided to the same boy then one can think what happens? In such a situation one can easily create the virtual environments and based on proper simulation of these environments we can make selections or decisions of our own.

1.B) Graphics in C Programming Language:

C is a popular programming language. It supports computer graphics and provides number of standard library functions for drawing regular diagrams and figures on the computer screen. One can use these graphical functions to draw the images easily through computer program. For these we need to initialize the graphics mode and detect the related graphics drivers. The standard library functions are kept in the header file called "graphics.h". For using any of the graphical built-in functions "graphics.h" file must be included.

Before starting with the C language syntax for graphics let us discuss some of the important terms that are used in computer graphics.

a) **Pixel:** It is the smallest recognizable picture part on the computer screen. Each dot(.) we can draw on the computer screen is a pixel and any image or picture we draw is the combinations of pixels.

b) **Resolution:** The maximum number of pixels we can put on the computer screen along x-axis and y-axis is called its resolution. The higher resolution leads to fine quality of an image. Usually it is 640 pixels along x-axis and 480 pixels along y-axis. But these resolution changes from computer to computer based on configuration and operating system as well as applications used.

c) **Co-ordinate system:** Usually the co-ordinate system in C computer graphics considers only positive co-ordinates with integer values. The left top corner of the screen is origin and x keeps on increasing along x-axis horizontally upto right border of the screen and y keeps on increasing vertically down until bottom border of the screen.

d) **Graph driver:** Integer that specifies the graphics driver to be used. We can give graph driver a value using a constant of the 'graphics_drivers' enumeration type available in graphics.h header file.

e) **Graph mode:** Integer that specifies the initial graphics mode (unless graph driver = DETECT is specified). If graph driver = DETECT, initgraph sets graph mode to the highest resolution available for the detected driver. We can give graph mode a value using a constant of the 'graphics_modes' enumeration type available in graphics.h header file.

Let us consider a small program that illustrates graphics initialization.

```
/* Program to initialize the graph and draw a line*/
#include<graphics.h>
#include<conio.h>
void main()
{
int gd=DETECT;          /* Detects the graph driver dynamically*/
int gm;          /* for graph mode */
```

```
initgraph(&gd,&gm,""); /* graph driver, graph mode and path has to be passed as parameters. The
        empty path is specified means the path will be taken dynamically after searching in the
        computer. Otherwise we need to specify the path where bgi directory is stored in the
        computer */
line(10,10,200,200);  /* this function draws a line from starting co-ordinates (10,10) to the target
        co-ordinates (200,200). These co-ordinates are specified in terms of pixels */
getch();
closegraph();              /* closes the graph mode */
}
```

The above program draws a line in between the specified co-ordinates. The syntax of the popular graphical functions are given in the 'Appendix A'. In any of the graphical programs it is essential to detect the graph driver and set the graph mode and path. Once the graphics is initialized it remains in the same mode until closing the graphics mode or terminating the program execution. But it is always advisable to close the graphics mode before terminating the program.

Let us consider the program for drawing a rectangle.

```
/* program to initialize the graph and draw a rectangle */
#include<graphics.h>
#include<conio.h>
void main()
{
int gd=DETECT;             /* Detects the graph driver dynamically*/
int gm;          /* for graph mode */
initgraph(&gd,&gm,"");
rectangle(10,10,200,200);          /* this function draws a rectangle taking co-ordinates (10,10) as
        top left point and target co-ordinates (200,200) as bottom right co-ordinates. These co-
        ordinates are specified in terms of pixels */
getch();
closegraph();              /* closes the graph mode */
}
```

The following program illustrates the combinations of different regular shaped graphical objects. Here we will draw a rectangle and lines along its diagonals. A circle is also drawn inside the rectangle.

```
/* Program to draw a rectangle, lines as its diagonals and a circle */
#include<graphics.h>
#include<conio.h>
void main()
{
int gd=DETECT;
```

```
int gm;
initgraph(&gd,&gm,"");
rectangle(10,10,200,200);        /* draws a rectangle */
line(10,10,200,200);             /* draws a line on the main diagonal*/
line(10,200,200,10);             /* draws a line on off diagonal */
circle(105,105,95);              /* draws a circle taking (105,105)
                                    as centre co-ordinates and 95 as radius
                                    all the dimensions are in pixels */
getch();
closegraph();             /* closes the graph mode */
}
```

By making use of the available library functions we can easily draw such graphics. We can also set the writing colors for drawing by using setcolor() function, which takes color code or color name as its parameter. C graphics supports sixteen colors whose codes range from 0 to 15 (The graphical constants related to colors, styles, patterns etc., are given in Appendix B). When the color name is used as the parameter it must be specified in Capital alphabets. The following program illustrates the circles and ellipses drawn with different colors.

```
/* Program to draw a circle and ellipses */
#include<graphics.h>
#include<conio.h>
void main()
{
int gd=DETECT;
int gm;
initgraph(&gd,&gm,"");
circle(getmaxx()/2, getmaxy()/2,100);          /* draws a circle taking
                              midpoint of the screen as   centre co-ordinates and
                              100 as radius */
setcolor(2);    /* sets the drawing color as green */

ellipse(getmaxx()/2, getmaxy()/2, 0,360,80,50);
        /* draws an ellipse taking centre of the screen as its centre, 0 as starting angle and
    360 as ending angle and 80 pixels as x-radius, 50 pixels as y radius */
setcolor(4);    /* sets the drawing color as red */
ellipse(getmaxx()/2, getmaxy()/2, 90,270,50,80);
        /* draws half the ellipse starting from 90 angle and        ending at 270 angle
    with 50 pixels as x-radius and 80 pixels as y-radius in red color */
getch();
```

```
closegraph();              /* closes the graph mode */
}
```

The different combinations of ellipses and arcs are illustrated in the following program.

```
/* Program to draw ellipses and arcs */
#include<graphics.h>
#include<conio.h>
void main()
{
int gd=DETECT;
int gm;
initgraph(&gd,&gm,"");

setcolor(1);      /* sets the drawing color as blue */
ellipse(getmaxx()/2, getmaxy()/2, 0,360,80,50);
                  /* draws an ellipse taking centre of the screen as its centre, 0 as starting angle and
360 as ending angle and 80 pixels as x-radius, 50 pixels as y radius*/
setcolor(4);      /* sets the drawing color as red */
ellipse(getmaxx()/2, getmaxy()/2, 90,270,50,80);
                  /* draws half the ellipse starting from 90 degree angle and ending at 270 degree
with 50 pixels as x-radius and 80 pixels as y-radius in red color */
setcolor(5);      /* sets the drawing color as pink */
arc(getmaxx()/2,getmaxy()/2, 0,180,100);
                  /* arc with centre of the screen as its center and 100 pixels as radius. It starts at an
angle 0 and ends at an angle 180 degrees, i.e., half circle */
setcolor(9);      /* sets the drawing color as light blue */
arc(300,200, 20,100,70);
                  /* arc with (300,200) as its center and 70 pixels as radius. It starts at an angle 20
and ends at an angle 100 degrees */

getch();
closegraph();              /* closes the graph mode */
}
```

The following program illustrates the putpixel function. It keeps on drawing the pixels throughout the screen until pressing any key from the keyboard. The co-ordinates for drawing the pixel are selected randomly by using rand() library function and taking co-ordinates for x-axis and y-axis randomly within the limits of screen resolution.

```
/* Program to demonstrate put pixel */
#include<graphics.h>
#include<conio.h>
#include<stdlib.h>
#include<dos.h>

void main()
{
int gm, gd=DETECT, i;
initgraph(&gd, &gm,"");
while(!kbhit()) /* until pressing any key this loop continues */
{
putpixel(rand()%getmaxx(),rand()%getmaxy(),rand()%16);
                    /* X and Y co-ordinates and the color are taken randomly*/
delay(2);           /* just to draw the pixels slowly */
}
getch();
closegraph();                /* closes the graph mode */
}
```

The proper combinations of pixels can make any of the graphical objects. The following program shows drawing of lines and rectangles using putpixel () function.

```
/* Program to demonstrate rectangles using putpixel and lines */
#include<graphics.h>
#include<conio.h>
#include<stdlib.h>
#include<dos.h>

void main()
{
int gm,gd=DETECT;
int x1,x2,y1,y2,c,i;

initgraph(&gd,&gm,"");
while(!kbhit()) /* until pressing any key this loop continues */
{
/* for rectangle co-ordinates are taken randomly */
x1=rand()%getmaxx();
```

```
x2=rand()%getmaxx();
y1=rand()%getmaxy();
y2=rand()%getmaxy();

if(x1>x2)
{
c=x1;       /* exchange of x1 and x2 when x1 > x2 */
x1=x2;
x2=c;
}
if(y1>y2)
{
c=y1;       /* exchange of y1 and y2 when y1 > y2 */
y1=y2;
y2=c;
}
c=rand()%16;

/* to draw rectangle using putpixel */
for(i=x1;i<=x2;++i)
{
putpixel(i,y1,c);
delay(1);
}
for(i=y1;i<=y2;++i)
{
putpixel(x2,i,c);
delay(1);
}
for(i=x2;i>=x1;—i)
{
putpixel(i,y2,c);
delay(1);
}
for(i=y2;i>=y1;—i)
{
putpixel(x1,i,c);
delay(1);
}
```

```
delay(200);      /* to draw the pixels slowly */
}
getch();
closegraph();              /* closes the graph mode */
}
```

The closed graphical areas can be filled with different fill effects that can be set using setfillstyle() function. The following program illustrates fill effects for the rectangles which are drawn randomly using putpixel.

```
/* Program to demonstrate rectangles using putpixel and filling them with different fill effects */
#include<graphics.h>
#include<conio.h>
#include<stdlib.h>
#include<dos.h>

void main()
{
int gm,gd=DETECT;
int x1,x2,y1,y2,c,i;

initgraph(&gd,&gm,"");
while(!kbhit()) /* until pressing any key this loop continues */
{
/* to draw rectangle co-coordinates are taken randomly */
x1=rand()%getmaxx();
x2=rand()%getmaxx();
y1=rand()%getmaxy();
y2=rand()%getmaxy();

if(x1>x2)
{
c=x1;     /* exchange of x1 and x2 when x1 is > x2 */
x1=x2;
x2=c;
}
if(y1>y2)
{
c=y1;     /* exchange of y1 and y2 when y1 is > y2 */
```

```
y1=y2;
y2=c;
}
c=rand()%16;
/* for rectangle using putpixel */
for(i=x1;i<=x2;++i)
{
putpixel(i,y1,c);
delay(1);
}
for(i=y1;i<=y2;++i)
{
putpixel(x2,i,c);
delay(1);
}
for(i=x2;i>=x1;—i)
{
putpixel(i,y2,c);
delay(1);
}
for(i=y2;i>=y1;—i)
{
putpixel(x1,i,c);
delay(1);
}
setfillstyle(rand()%12,rand()%8); /* setting the random fill styles and colors */
floodfill(x1+1,y1+1,c);
delay(200);        /* to draw the pixels slowly */
}
getch();
closegraph();              /* closes the graph mode */
}
```

The lines with different lengths and colors are illustrated in the following program.

```
/* Program to demonstrate lines with different colors and co-ordinates */
#include<graphics.h>
#include<conio.h>
#include<stdlib.h>
#include<dos.h>
```

```
void main()
{
int gm, gd=DETECT;
int x1,x2,y1,y2,c,i;

initgraph(&gd, &gm,"");
while(!kbhit()) /* until pressing any key this loop continues */
{
/* to draw rectangle co-ordinates are taken randomly */
x1=rand()%getmaxx();
x2=rand()%getmaxx();
y1=rand()%getmaxy();
y2=rand()%getmaxy();

setcolor(rand()%16); /* to set the line color */
line(x1,y1,x2,y2); /* to draw the line */
delay(200);      /* to draw the pixels slowly */
}
getch();
closegraph();              /* closes the graph mode */
}
```

The viewport is the portion of the screen within the screen. The entire screen is the default viewport. We can make and choose our own viewports according to our requirements. Once the viewport is set the top left co-ordinates of the viewport becomes (0,0) origin and the maximum number of pixels along x-axis and y-axis change according to the size of the view port. Any graphical settings can be unset using graphdefaults() function.

The following program illustrates setting the viewport and clipping the lines. It also sets the different line styles and colors for the lines. The viewport border co-ordinates are taken from the user as input.

```
/* Program to demonstrate viewport, clipping and lines with different colors, line styles and co-ordinates */

#include<graphics.h>
#include<conio.h>
#include<stdlib.h>
#include<dos.h>
#include<stdio.h>
void main()
```

```
{
int gm, gd=DETECT;
int x1,x2,y1,y2,c,i;
clrscr();
printf("enter starting co-ordinates of viewport  (x1,y1)\n");
scanf("%d%d",&x1,&y1);
printf("enter ending co-ordinates of viewport (x2,y2)\n");
scanf("%d%d",&x2,&y2);

initgraph(&gd, &gm,"");

rectangle(x1,y1,x2,y2);/*to show the boundary of viewport */
setviewport(x1,y1,x2,y2,1); /* view port is set and any  drawing now onwards must be drawn
        within the viewports only */

while(!kbhit()) /* until pressing any key this continues */
{
/*  rectangle coordinates are taken randomly */
x1=rand()%getmaxx();
x2=rand()%getmaxx();
y1=rand()%getmaxy();
y2=rand()%getmaxy();
setlinestyle(rand()%10,rand()%10,rand()%20);
setcolor(rand()%16); /* to set the line color */
line(x1,y1,x2,y2); /* to draw the line */
delay(200);
}
getch();
closegraph();                    /* closes the graph mode */
}
```

In computer graphics using C language, we can also display the text and set the different styles for the texts. The following two programs illustrate this.

```
/* Program to demonstrate text and its settings */
#include<graphics.h>
#include<conio.h>
#include<stdlib.h>
#include<dos.h>
#include<stdio.h>
```

```
void main()
{
int gm, gd=DETECT;
initgraph(&gd, &gm,"");

setcolor(5);
settextstyle(4,0,5); /* sets the textstyle with      font, direction and char size */
moveto(100,100); /* takes the CP to 100,100 */
outtext("Bangalore is");

setcolor(4);
settextstyle(3,0,6);
moveto(200,200);
outtext("Silicon ");

setcolor(1);
settextstyle(5,0,6);
moveto(300,300);
outtext("Valley");

setcolor(2);
settextstyle(1,1,5);
outtextxy(150,50,"Bangalore is");

getch();

}

/* Program to demonstrate text and its settings */
#include<graphics.h>
#include<conio.h>
#include<stdlib.h>
#include<dos.h>
#include<stdio.h>
void main()
{
int gm, =DETECT;
initgraph(&gd, &gm ,"");

setcolor(5);
```

```
settextstyle(4,0,5); /* sets the text style with
                               font, direction and char size */
moveto(100,100); /* takes the CP to 100,100 */
outtext("Bangalore is");

setcolor(4);
settextstyle(3,0,6);
moveto(200,200);
outtext("Silicon ");

setcolor(1);
settextstyle(5,0,6);
moveto(300,300);
outtext("Valley");

setcolor(2);
settextstyle(1,1,5);
outtextxy(150,50,"Bangalore is");

getch();
}
```

The set of pixels make lines and a set of continuous lines make surfaces. The following program demonstrates the creation of surfaces using lines and different colors.

```
/* Program to demonstrate surfaces using lines and colors */
#include<graphics.h>
#include<conio.h>
#include<dos.h>
#include<alloc.h>
#include<math.h>

void main()
{
int gm, gd=DETECT, i, j;
initgraph(&gd, &gm,"");
setviewport(100,100,300,300,0);
for(j=0;j<200;j=j+20)
{
for(i=0;i<=200;++i)
```

```
{
if(i%20==0)
setcolor(rand()%16+1);
line(i,j,i,j+20);
}
delay(100);
}
getch();
}
```

Following is a menu driven program that shows different parts of the car.

/* Program to draw a car. The different graphical functions are used to draw different parts of the car */

```
#include<stdio.h>
#include<graphics.h>

main()
{
int x,y,i, choice;
unsigned int size;
void *car;

 int gd=DETECT, gm;
 initgraph(&gd, &gm," ");

do
{
cleardevice();
printf("1:BODY OF THE CAR\n");
printf("2:WHEELS OF THE CAR\n");
printf("3:CAR\n");
printf("4:QUIT");
printf("\nEnter your choice\n");
 scanf("%d",&choice);
switch(choice)
{
case 1:  initgraph(&gd,&gm," ");
         line(135,300,265,300);
```

```
        arc(100,300,0,180,35);
        line(65,300,65,270);
        line(65,270,110,220);
        line(110,220,220,220);
        line(140,220,140,215);
        line(180,220,180,215);
        line(175,300,175,220);
        line(120,215,200,215);
        line(220,220,260,250);
        line(260,250,85,250);
        line(260,250,345,275);
        arc(300,300,0,180,35);
        line(345,300,345,275);
        line(335,300,345,300);
        getch();
        cleardevice();
        break;

case 2: initgraph(&gd,&gm,"");
        circle(100,300,25);
        circle(100,300,13);
        circle(300,300,25);
        circle(300,300,13);
        getch();
        cleardevice();
        break;

case 3: initgraph(&gd,&gm," ");
        outtextxy(150,40,"MARUTI 800");
        circle(100,300,25);
        circle(100,300,13);
        line(135,300,265,300);
        arc(100,300,0,180,35);
        line(65,300,65,270);
        line(65,270,110,220);
        line(110,220,220,220);

        line(140,220,140,215);
        line(180,220,180,215);
        line(175,300,175,220);
```

```
            line(120,215,200,215);
            line(220,220,260,250);
            line(260,250,85,250);
            line(260,250,345,275);
            arc(300,300,0,180,35);
            circle(300,300,25);
            circle(300,300,13);
            line(345,300,345,275);
            line(335,300,345,300);
            getch();
            cleardevice();
            break;

    case 4:   exit(0);
    }
  }
  while(choice!=4);
  closegraph();
  getch();
  }
```

2

BAR GRAPHS AND CHARTS

The computer graphics is used in the business to show the statistics in terms of graphical charts. It is easy for the customers to understand the business statistics by graphs rather than with mere words. In this chapter we will introduce the concept of bar graphs, pie charts, line graphs etc through programs.

The statistics of the products or entities are easily represented with the help of bar charts. Usually in banking sectors the banks can use bar graphs to show their business growth in different successive years, any ERP (enterprise resource planning) is represented using these graphs.

The following program illustrates the bar() function. The bar() function is used to draw 2-Dimensional bars and filling them automatically with the present fill styles and patterns.

```
/* Program to draw 2D bars*/
#include<graphics.h>
#include<conio.h>
void main()
{
int gd=DETECT;
int gm;
initgraph(&gd,&gm,"");
bar(10,10,20,200);          /*draws a 2D bar starting at (10,10) &
                            ending at (20,200). It is same as rectangle ()
                            function, it fills the rectangle with
                            present fill style */
setfillstyle(2,4); /* It sets the fill styles, the first
                            parameter is pattern style (2 is for line
                            fill ) and second parameter is color */


bar(50,10,70,200);


getch();
```

```
closegraph();                /* closes the graph mode */
}
```

In the following program we can create the vertical bars with fixed width but heights according to the user inputs. The maximum number of bars is restricted to 20 because of resolution problems.

```
/* Program to draw a 2D vertical bars */
#include<graphics.h>
#include<stdio.h>
#include<conio.h>
void main()
{
int gm, gd=DETECT, i;
int n, a[20],t;
clrscr();
do
{
t=0;
printf("\n enter n > 0 and <=20 \n");
scanf("%d",&n);
if(n<=0 || n>20)
{
printf(" enter the limit correctly press any key to continue...\n");
getch();
t=1;
}
}while(t==1);
for(i=0;i<n;++i)
{
do
{
t=0;
printf("\n enter value( >0 and <=400) %d : ",i+1);
scanf("%d",&a[i]);
if(a[i]<=0 || a[i]>400)
{
printf(" enter the limit correctly press any key to continue...\n");
getch();
t=1;
}
```

```
}while(t==1);
}
initgraph(&gd, &gm,"");
line(10,400,n*25+20,400);
for(i=0;i<n; ++i)          /* draws n bars with different filling
                           colors and patterns */
        {
        setfillstyle(i+1,i+1);      /* fill pattern and color for each
                                    of the bars changes dynamically*/
        rectangle(i*25+25,400-a[i],i*25+40,400);
                                    /* the y-coordinate of each bars changes dynamically and
                                      between each bars 10 pixels gap is maintained */

        floodfill(i*25+30,399,15);/* fills the rectangular bar with
                                    specified fill styles and colors*/
        }

getch();
closegraph();              /* closes the graph mode */
}
```

The different fill effects can be given for the bar graphs for getting effectiveness in the demonstrations. The following program illustrates this with the help of horizontal graphs.

```
/* Program to draw 2D horizontal bars fill effects */
#include<graphics.h>
#include<stdio.h>
#include<conio.h>
void main()
{
int gm, gd=DETECT, i;
int n, a[20],t;
clrscr();
do
{
t=0;
printf("\n enter n > 0 and <=20 \n");
scanf("%d", &n);
if(n<=0 || n>20)
{
```

```
printf(" enter the limit correctly press any key to continue...\n");
getch();
t=1;
}
}while(t==1);
for(i=0;i<n;++i)
{
do
{
t=0;
printf("\n enter value( > 0 and <= 600) %d : ",i+1);
scanf("%d",&a[i]);
if(a[i]<=0 || a[i]>600)
{
printf(" enter the limit correctly press any key to continue...\n");
getch();
t=1;
}
}while(t==1);
}
initgraph(&gd,&gm,"");
line(40,10,40,n*25+35);
for(i=0;i<n;++i)  /* draws n bars with different filling     colors and patterns */
        {
        setfillstyle(i+1,i+1);        /* fill pattern and color for each of the bars changes
                                      dynamically*/
        rectangle(40,i*25+25,a[i]+40,i*25+40);
                                      /* the x-coordinate of each bars changes dynamically and
                                      between each bars 10 pixels gap is maintained */

        floodfill(41,i*25+30,15);/* fills the rectangular bar with specified fill styles and
                                      colors*/
        }

getch();
closegraph();              /* closes the graph mode */
        }
```

In the following program we are illustrating the pie chart. Here we are considering only four parts in the chart. The user can input the values, which are compared for their part in the 360⁰ circle. According to each values contributions the circle is divided into parts.

```
/* Program to illustrate the pie chart */
#include<stdio.h>
#include<conio.h>
#include<graphics.h>
void main()
{
int gd=DETECT, gm;
int a,b,c,d,s;
clrscr();
printf("\n enter 4 values\n");
scanf("%d%d%d%d",&a,&b,&c,&d);

/* re-calculating the contribution of each value in the circle area */
s=a+b+c+d;
a=a*360/s;
b=b*360/s;
c=c*360/s;
d=d*360/s;
initgraph(&gd, &gm,"");
setfillstyle(1,2);
pieslice(300,250,0,a,100);
setfillstyle(1,4);
pieslice(300,250,a,a+b,100);
setfillstyle(1,6);
pieslice(300,250,a+b,a+b+c,100);
setfillstyle(1,8);
pieslice(300,250,a+b+c,360,100);
getch();
}
```

3

ANIMATION

Animation is defined as the movement of graphical objects on the screen. To get the effectiveness in graphical demonstrations animation is essential. In C programming with graphics, animation is achieved with the help of writing and erasing the images in quick successions by changing their positions. After writing the image we need to give delay for getting effectiveness in image movements. The less delay leads to fast movements and more delay leads to slow movements of objects during animation.

For writing and erasing the images we can use putimage() function. The change in the opcode parameter erases and writes the image. After erasing the image from the screen quickly we need to write it in next location so that image looks like moving. The following program illustrates movement of rectangular object from one side of the screen to the other side.

```
/* Program to demonstrate movement of objects */
#include<graphics.h>
#include<conio.h>
#include<dos.h>
#include<alloc.h>

void main()
{
int gm, gd=DETECT, i;
char *z; /* to get the image */
initgraph(&gd, gm,"");
rectangle(10,10,50,50);
z=malloc(imagesize(10,10,50,50)); /* memory allocation to the variable to store the image */
getimage(10,10,50,50,z); /* gets the image into variable z */
putimage(10,10,z,1);/* erases the image from the original place */
for(i=10;i<=getmaxx()-50;++i)
{
```

```
putimage(i, getmaxy()/2-20,z,2);
delay(5);  /* image will be written and
          after some delay it will be erased and re-written in
          next location based on delay it looks like
          moving fast or slow */
putimage(i, getmaxy()/2-20,z,1);
}
putimage(i, getmaxy()/2-20,z,2);/* write the image in target position*/

getch();
}
```

The following program moves the rectangular image from center of the screen to all four directions as well as all four diagonals of the screen.

```
/* Program to demonstrate movement of objects */
#include<graphics.h>
#include<conio.h>
#include<dos.h>
#include<alloc.h>

void main()
{
int gm, gd=DETECT, i;
char *z; /* to get the image */
initgraph(&gd, &gm,"");
rectangle(10,10,50,50);
z=malloc(imagesize(10,10,50,50)); /* memory allocation to the
                              variable to store the image */
getimage(10,10,50,50,z); /* gets the image into variable z */
putimage(10,10,z,1);/* erases the image from the original place */

for(i=0;i<=getmaxy()/2-50;++i)
{
putimage(getmaxx()/2,getmaxy()/2-i,z,2); /* Vertically up */
putimage(getmaxx()/2,getmaxy()/2+i,z,2); /* Vertically down */
putimage(getmaxx()/2-i,getmaxy()/2,z,2); /*  Horizontally left */
putimage(getmaxx()/2+i,getmaxy()/2,z,2); /* Horizontally right */

putimage(getmaxx()/2-i,getmaxy()/2-i,z,2); /* To top-left corner */
```

```
putimage(getmaxx()/2-i,getmaxy()/2+i,z,2); /* to top-right corner */
putimage(getmaxx()/2+i,getmaxy()/2-i,z,2); /* To bottom-left corner */
putimage(getmaxx()/2+i,getmaxy()/2+i,z,2); /* To bottom-right corner */

delay(5);        /* image will be written and     after some delay it will be erased and re-written
in next location based on delay it looks like moving fast or slow */

putimage(getmaxx()/2,getmaxy()/2-i,z,1);
putimage(getmaxx()/2,getmaxy()/2+i,z,1);
putimage(getmaxx()/2-i,getmaxy()/2,z,1);
putimage(getmaxx()/2+i,getmaxy()/2,z,1);
putimage(getmaxx()/2-i,getmaxy()/2-i,z,1);
putimage(getmaxx()/2-i,getmaxy()/2+i,z,1);
putimage(getmaxx()/2+i,getmaxy()/2-i,z,1);
putimage(getmaxx()/2+i,getmaxy()/2+i,z,1);
}

/* write the image in target position*/

putimage(getmaxx()/2,getmaxy()/2-i,z,2);
putimage(getmaxx()/2,getmaxy()/2+i,z,2);
putimage(getmaxx()/2-i,getmaxy()/2,z,2);
putimage(getmaxx()/2+i,getmaxy()/2,z,2);
putimage(getmaxx()/2-i,getmaxy()/2-i,z,2);
putimage(getmaxx()/2-i,getmaxy()/2+i,z,2);
putimage(getmaxx()/2+i,getmaxy()/2-i,z,2);
putimage(getmaxx()/2+i,getmaxy()/2+i,z,2);

getch();
}
```

The following program illustrate the moving wheel animation. For this we are drawing the wheel using circles and lines. The lines really give the moving effect. The lines are drawn successively by changing their co-ordinates. The line co-ordinates on the wheel are calculated using circle DDA algorithm.

```
/* Program to demonstrate moving wheel */

#include<stdio.h>
#include<dos.h>
#include<math.h>
```

```
#include<conio.h>
#include<graphics.h>
void main()
{
int gd=DETECT,gm,i,x,y,r,j;
float x1,y1;
clrscr();
/* Initialization of center co-ordinates of the circle for wheel */
x1=50;
y1=50;
/* For movement of wheel starting from 500 pixels along x-axis */
j=500;
initgraph(&gd,&gm,""); /* Graphics is initialized */
x=x1;
y=y1;
r=sqrt(x*x+y*y);/* Radius of wheel */
while(1)
{
/* for every circle of the wheel */
for(i=1;i<=360;++i)
{
x=x1*cos(i*3.142/180)+y1*sin(i*3.142/180);/* Calculating the points to draw line */
y=y1*cos(i*3.142/180)-x1*sin(i*3.142/180);
setcolor(4);
/* Wheels outer circle */
circle(j,200,r);
circle(j,200,r+5);
/* Center of the wheel */
circle(j,200,4);
circle(j+x,y+200,2);
circle(j-x,200-y,2);
line(j,200,x+j,y+200);
line(j,200,j-x,200-y);
delay(30);
/* Erasing the line and circle that makes movement effect */
setcolor(0);
circle(j,200,r+5);
circle(j,200,r);
circle(j,200,4);
circle(j+x,y+200,2);
```

```
circle(j-x,200-y,2);
line(j,200,x+j,y+200);
line(j,200,j-x,200-y);
j—;
if(j<=50)
break;
}
if(j<=50)
break;
}
/* Rewriting the wheel at target position */
setcolor(4);
circle(j,200,r);
circle(j,200,4);
circle(j,200,r+5);
circle(j+x,y+200,2);
circle(j-x,200-y,2);
line(j,200,x+j,y+200);
line(j,200,j-x,200-y);

getch();
closegraph();
}
```

The movement of the car is demonstrated in the following program. This is done by drawing the car with the help of circle, arc and line. The image is erased and drawn repeatedly to give the moving effect.

```
/* Program to demonstrate the moving car */

#include<stdio.h>
#include<dos.h>
#include<alloc.h>
#include<stdlib.h>
#include<conio.h>
#include<graphics.h>

void main()
{
```

```
int gd=DETECT,gm,i,x,y,r,j;
void *z;
clrscr();
initgraph(&gd,&gm,"");

/* creation of car image */
circle(30,130,8);
circle(30,130,2);
circle(110,130,8);
circle(110,130,2);
arc(30,130,0,180,11);
arc(30,130,60,180,14);
line(16,130,19,130);

arc(110,130,0,180,11);
arc(110,130,0,120,14);
line(124,130,121,130);

arc(70,130,0,180,30);
arc(70,130,20,160,33);
arc(70,130,40,140,24);

line(41,130,99,130);
/* Getting the image of the car into variable 'z' after allocating memory */
z=malloc(imagesize(15,90,145,140));
getimage(15,90,145,140,z);
/* Erasing the car image from its original position */
putimage(15,90,z,1);
while(!kbhit()) /* This loop continues until pressing any key */
{
/* Movement of car from left to right horizontally */
y=rand()%400+50; /* Y co-ordinate is taken randomly within the screen co-ordinates along
y-axis */

for(i=getmaxx()-100;i>=10;--i)
{
putimage(i,y,z,2);
delay(rand()%5);
putimage(i,y,z,1);
}
```

```
}
putimage(i,y,z,2);
getch();
closegraph();
}
```

The following program demonstrates the popular sorting algorithm 'Shell Sort'.

```
/* Program to demonstrate working of Shell Sort algorithms */
#include<conio.h>
#include<alloc.h>
#include<graphics.h>
#include<dos.h>
#include<stdio.h>

void main()
        {
        int n,a[100],i,d,k,kl,t=0;
        int gd=DETECT,gm;
        void *z,*z1;
        char *s;
        textcolor(5);
        clrscr();
        printf("  Enter number of elements : ");
        scanf("%d",&n);
        for(i=1;i<=n;i++)
        {
        printf("  Enter element %d : ",i);
        scanf("%d",&a[i]);
        }
        initgraph(&gd,&gm,"");
        setcolor(2);
        settextstyle(7,0,6);
        outtextxy(270,50,"Shell Sorting");

        settextstyle(0,0,0);
        for(i=1;i<=n;++i)
        {
        setcolor(1);
        rectangle(100,i*20+50+1,150,i*20+70);
```

```
sprintf(s,"%d",a[i]);
outtextxy(102,i*20+55,s);
}
d=n/2;
z=malloc(imagesize(100,20,150,40));
z1=malloc(imagesize(100,20,150,40));

while(d>0)
{
    t=0;
    for(i=1;i<=n-d;i++)
    if(a[i]>a[i+d])
        {
        k=a[i];
        a[i]=a[i+d];
        a[i+d]=k;
        t=1;

        getimage(100,i*20+50,150,i*20+70,z);
        getimage(100,(i+d)*20+50,150,(i+d)*20+70,z1);

        for(kl=100;kl>=10;—kl)
        {
        putimage(kl,i*20+50,z,2);
        delay(5);
        putimage(kl,i*20+50,z,1);
        }
        putimage(10,i*20+50,z,2);

        for(kl=100;kl<=190;++kl)
        {
        putimage(kl,(i+d)*20+50,z1,2);
        delay(5);
        putimage(kl,(i+d)*20+50,z1,1);
        }
        putimage(190,(i+d)*20+50,z1,2);

        for(kl=i*20+50;kl<=(i+d)*20+50;++kl)
```

```
{
putimage(10,kl,z,2);
delay(5);
putimage(10,kl,z,1);
}
putimage(10,(i+d)*20+50,z,2);

for(kl=(i+d)*20+50;kl>=(i*20)+50;—kl)
{
putimage(190,kl,z1,2);
delay(5);
putimage(190,kl,z1,1);
}
putimage(190,i*20+50,z1,2);

for(kl=10;kl<=100;++kl)
{
putimage(kl,(i+d)*20+50,z,2);
delay(5);
putimage(kl,(i+d)*20+50,z,1);
}
putimage(100,(i+d)*20+50,z,2);

for(kl=190;kl>=100;—kl)
{
putimage(kl,i*20+50,z1,2);
delay(5);
putimage(kl,i*20+50,z1,1);
}
putimage(100,i*20+50,z1,2);
}

if(t==0)
{
if(d==1)
d=0;
d=(d+1)/2;
}

}
```

```
        free(z);
        free(z1);

    getch();
    closegraph();
    }
```

The following program shows animations with more complex images. The flag is made to fly using animation in the program below.

```
/* Program to demonstrate the flag flying image through animation. The program makes use of
function for three different effects in the flag display */

#include <stdio.h>
#include<graphics.h>
#include <conio.h>
#include <dos.h>

void flag1(); /* to display the flag straight */
void flag2(); /*to display the flag little slanting upwards */
void flag3(); /* to display the flag little slanting downwards */
/* displaying flag1,3 and 2 continuously, we get the flag flying image. */

    void main()
    {
     int gd = DETECT, gm;
     int i, stangle, endangle;
     initgraph(&gd, &gm,"");
     while(!kbhit())
     {
      cleardevice();
      flag1();
      delay(250);
      cleardevice();
      flag3();
      delay(300);
      cleardevice();
      flag2();
      delay(300);
     }
```

```
getch();
closegraph();
return;
}

void flag1()
{
int i;
setfillstyle(SOLID_FILL,6);
bar(50,50,300,100);
setfillstyle(SOLID_FILL, WHITE);
bar(50,100,300,150);
setfillstyle(SOLID_FILL, GREEN);
bar(50,150,300,200);
/* the three color bars have been drawn. */
/*drawing the flag pole */
setfillstyle(SOLID_FILL,8);
bar(40,20,50,460);
for(i=0;i<=360;i+=15)
pieslice(175,125,i,i+15,25);
}
void flag2()
{
int i;
int r1[8] = {50,50,300,75,300,125,50,100};
int r2[8] = {50,100,300,125,300,175,50,150};
int r3[8] = {50,150,300,175,300,225,50,200};
setcolor(0);
setfillstyle(SOLID_FILL,6);
fillpoly(4,r1);
setfillstyle(SOLID_FILL, WHITE);
fillpoly(4,r2);
setfillstyle(SOLID_FILL, GREEN);
fillpoly(4,r3);
setfillstyle(SOLID_FILL,8);
bar(40,20,50,460);
setcolor(9);
setfillstyle(SOLID_FILL, WHITE);
for(i=0; i<=360; i+=15)
pieslice(175,137,i,i+15,25);
```

```
}

void flag3()
{
   int i;
   int r1[8] = {50,50,300,25,300,75,50,100};
   int r2[8] = {50,100,300,75,300,125,50,150};
   int r3[8] = {50,150,300,125,300,175,50,200};
   setcolor(0);
   setfillstyle(SOLID_FILL,6);
   fillpoly(4,r1);
   setfillstyle(SOLID_FILL,WHITE);
   fillpoly(4,r2);
   setfillstyle(SOLID_FILL,GREEN);
   fillpoly(4,r3);
   setfillstyle(SOLID_FILL,8);
   bar(40,20,50,460);
   setcolor(9);
   setfillstyle(SOLID_FILL, WHITE);

   for(i=0; i<=360; i+=15)
   pieslice(175,113,i,i+15,25);

   }
```

Program that follows shows a man walking with an umbrella. For this a man skeleton is drawn with the help of lines, arcs and circles. The image of the rectangular area is stored in a pointer variable using getimage function and using putimage function it will be animated.

```
/* Program to animate a man walking with umbrella. */
#include<stdio.h>
#include<dos.h>
#include<conio.h>
#include<graphics.h>
#include<alloc.h>

void main()
{
int gd=DETECT, gm, i;
void *z;
```

```
initgraph(&gd, &gm,"");
/* Construction of man and umbrella in his hand */
circle(50,28,4);
line(50,32,50,56);
line(50,40,42,48);
line(50,40,58,48);
line(50,56,42,64);
line(50,56,58,64);
line(58,48,64,40);
line(64,40,64,11);
arc(64,20,0,180,17);
arc(64,30,30,150,20);

/* getting the image of the man with umbrella in a variable */
z=malloc(imagesize(5,3,90,90));
getimage(5,3,90,90,z);
putimage(5,3,z,1);

/* Making animation of man walk */
for(i=10;i<=getmaxx()-100;++i)
{
putimage(i,100,z,2);
delay(10);
putimage(i,100,z,1);
}
putimage(i,100,z,2);

getch();
closegraph();
}
```

The program that follows shows the effect of rotation of circle along the line horizontally. To get the rotation effect the circle is drawn using putpixel with different colors. The Brasneham's circle drawing algorithm is used to calculate the pixel co-ordinates on the circle

```
/* program to rotate a circle between two ends of a line */
/* It makes use of two functions one for drawing the circle and the other for erasing the circle */
#include<stdio.h>
#include<conio.h>
#include<stdlib.h>
```

```
#include<math.h>
#include<graphics.h>

#define pi 2*3.1457

void draw_circle(int xa, int ya, int r);
void draw_circle2(int xa, int ya,   int r);

void main()
{
 int gd=DETECT, gm;
 float i, color;
 initgraph(&gd, &gm,"");
 setcolor(YELLOW);
 outtextxy(250,50,"ROTATE A CIRCLE ");
 setcolor(RED);

 for(i=50;i<585;i+=2)
{
 line(10,200,640,200);
 draw_circle(i,200,50);
 draw_circle2(i-2,200,50);
}
getch();
}

/* FUNCTION FOR DRAWING THE CIRCLE */
void draw_circle(int xa, int ya, int r)
{
 float theta,x,y;
 int color;
 for(theta=0;theta<pi;theta=theta+0.01)
 {
 x = xa + r * cos(theta);
 y = ya + r * sin(theta);
 color = random(getmaxcolor());
  putpixel((int)x,(int)y, color);
 }
}
/* FUNCTION FOR ERASING THE CIRCLE */
```

```
void draw_circle2(int xa, int ya, int r)
{
 float theta, x, y;
 int color=0;
 for(theta=0;theta<pi; theta=theta+0.01)
 {
  x = xa + r * cos(theta);
  y = ya + r * sin(theta);
  putpixel((int)x,(int)y, color);
 }
 delay(5);
}
```

The Bucket or Radix sort is explained as follows.

The list of positive integers can be arranged in order by using the bucket sort. For this each of the numbers in the list will be rearranged into 10 buckets for 10 digits of our decimal number system. First the numbers will be placed into the buckets according to the last digit and they will be placed back in the list starting from top elements of the 9th bucket to the bottom element of the 0th bucket one by one. Then the elements from this new list will be redistributed into buckets according to 2nd last digits of the numbers or elements and they will be taken back into the original list. This process will continue number of times equivalent to the highest number of digits in the elements of given list. This algorithm is fully demonstrated in the following program using animation.

```
/* Program to demonstrate graphical demo of working of Bucket or Radix sort */
#include<graphics.h>
#include<stdio.h>
#include<conio.h>
#include<dos.h>
#include<alloc.h>
#include<math.h>

void main()
{
int i,n,xx,a[100],b[100],dg0,j,pp,kk=0;
/* for counting elements in each of the 10 buckets 10 counters are used and initialised to Zeros */
int bk0=0,bk1=0,bk2=0,bk3=0,bk4=0,bk5=0,bk6=0,bk7=0,bk8=0,bk9=0,bk;

int gd=DETECT, gm;
char *s;
```

```
void *z,*z1;
int dd;
clrscr();
/* User input of size and elements of the list */
printf("\n enter n\n");
scanf("%d", &n);
printf("\n enter the elements\n");
for(i=1;i<=n;++i)
scanf("%d",&a[i]);

/* Counting the number of digits in the largest number */
for(i=1;i<=n;++i)
{
j=0;
pp=a[i];
while(pp!=0)
{
j++;
pp=pp/10;
}
if(j>kk)
kk=j;
}

/* Graphical demo starts from here */
initgraph(&gd,&gm,"");
dd=kk;
for(xx=1;xx<=dd;++xx)
{
/* Draws 'n' rectangles and puts the elements in each rectangle */
setcolor(14);
for(i=1;i<=n;++i)
{
rectangle(5,i*20+50,55,i*20+70);
sprintf(s,"%d",a[i]);
outtextxy(9,i*20+57,s);
}

/* Creation of 10 buckets for each of the 10 digits 0 to 9 */
```

```
line(getmaxx()-520,350,getmaxx()-2,350);
for(i=0;i<=9;++i)
{
rectangle(i*52+122,355,i*52+170,375);
sprintf(s,"%d",i);
outtextxy(i*52+135,360,s);
}
/* allocates the memory for storing the rectangle with element */
z=malloc(imagesize(5,5,55,25));
for(i=1;i<=n;++i)
{
getimage(5,i*20+50,55,i*20+70,z);

/* moves the element top along the list */
for(j=i*20+50;j>=20;—j)
{
rectangle(5,i*20+50,55,i*20+70);
putimage(5,j,z,2);
delay(2);
putimage(5,j,z,1);
}
putimage(5,20,z,2);

kk=((int)(a[i]/pow(10,xx-1)))%10;
/* increasing the bucket counters according to the element */
switch(kk)
{
case 0: bk0++;break;
case 1: bk1++;break;
case 2: bk2++;break;
case 3: bk3++;break;
case 4: bk4++;break;
case 5: bk5++;break;
case 6: bk6++;break;
case 7: bk7++;break;
case 8: bk8++;break;
case 9: bk9++;break;
}
```

```
/* moving the image of the rectangle with element horizontally right upto the position of the the
corresponding bucket */
for(j=5;j<=120+kk*52;j++)
{
putimage(j,20,z,2);
delay(2);
putimage(j,20,z,1);
}
putimage(120+kk*52,20,z,2);

/* Moving the image down words according to the bucket */
switch(kk)
{

case 0: /* when the corresponding digit is 0 */

for(j=20;j<=325-bk0*22+22;j++)
{
putimage(120+kk*52,j,z,2);
delay(5);
putimage(120+kk*52,j,z,1);
}
putimage(120+kk*52,325-bk0*22+22,z,2);
break;
case 1:  /* when the corresponding digit is 1 */

for(j=20;j<=325-bk1*22+22;j++)
{
putimage(120+kk*52,j,z,2);
delay(5);
putimage(120+kk*52,j,z,1);
}
putimage(120+kk*52,325-bk1*22+22,z,2);
break;

case 2:  /* when the corresponding digit is 2 */

for(j=20;j<=325-bk2*22+22;j++)
{
putimage(120+kk*52,j,z,2);
```

```
delay(5);
putimage(120+kk*52,j,z,1);
}
putimage(120+kk*52,325-bk2*22+22,z,2);
break;

case 3:  /* when the corresponding digit is 3 */

for(j=20;j<=325-bk3*22+22;j++)
{
putimage(120+kk*52,j,z,2);
delay(5);
putimage(120+kk*52,j,z,1);
}
putimage(120+kk*52,325-bk3*22+22,z,2);
break;

case 4:  /* when the corresponding digit is 4 */

for(j=20;j<=325-bk4*22+22;j++)
{
putimage(120+kk*52,j,z,2);
delay(5);
putimage(120+kk*52,j,z,1);
}
putimage(120+kk*52,325-bk4*22+22,z,2);
break;

case 5:  /* when the corresponding digit is 5 */

for(j=20;j<=325-bk5*22+22;j++)
{
putimage(120+kk*52,j,z,2);
delay(5);
putimage(120+kk*52,j,z,1);
}
putimage(120+kk*52,325-bk5*22+22,z,2);
break;

case 6:  /* when the corresponding digit is 6 */
```

```
for(j=20;j<=325-bk6*22+22;j++)
{
putimage(120+kk*52,j,z,2);
delay(5);
putimage(120+kk*52,j,z,1);
}
putimage(120+kk*52,325-bk6*22+22,z,2);
break;

case 7:  /* when the corresponding digit is 7 */

for(j=20;j<=325-bk7*22+22;j++)
{
putimage(120+kk*52,j,z,2);
delay(5);
putimage(120+kk*52,j,z,1);
}
putimage(120+kk*52,325-bk7*22+22,z,2);
break;

case 8:  /* when the corresponding digit is 8 */

for(j=20;j<=325-bk8*22+22;j++)
{
putimage(120+kk*52,j,z,2);
delay(5);
putimage(120+kk*52,j,z,1);
}
putimage(120+kk*52,325-bk8*22+22,z,2);
break;

case 9:  /* when the corresponding digit is 9 */

for(j=20;j<=325-bk9*22+22;j++)
{
putimage(120+kk*52,j,z,2);
delay(5);
putimage(120+kk*52,j,z,1);
}
```

```
putimage(120+kk*52,325-bk9*22+22,z,2);
break;
} /* end of switch(kk) */
}

setcolor(0);
rectangle(5,n*20+50,55,n*20+70);
setcolor(14);

bk=0;

/* Moving the elements from each of the buckets back to the list */

/* for moving elements of 9th bucket back to list */

while(bk9>0)
{
kk=9;
getimage(kk*52+120,325-bk9*22+22,kk*52+170,325-bk9*22+42,z);

for(j=325-bk9*22+22;j>=20;—j)
{
putimage(kk*52+120,j,z,2);
delay(5);
putimage(kk*52+120,j,z,1);
}
putimage(kk*52+120,20,z,2);

for(j=kk*52+120;j>=5;j—)
{
putimage(j,20,z,2);
delay(5);
putimage(j,20,z,1);
}
putimage(5,20,z,2);

for(j=20;j<=(n-bk)*20+50;++j)
{
putimage(5,j,z,2);
delay(5);
```

```
putimage(5,j,z,1);
}
putimage(5,(n-bk)*20+50,z,2);

bk9—;
bk++;
}

/*for moving elements of 8th bucket back to list   */

while(bk8>0)
{
kk=8;
getimage(kk*52+120,325-bk8*22+22,kk*52+170,325-bk8*22+42,z);

for(j=325-bk8*22+22;j>=20;—j)
{
putimage(kk*52+120,j,z,2);
delay(5);
putimage(kk*52+120,j,z,1);
}
putimage(kk*52+120,20,z,2);

for(j=kk*52+120;j>=5;j—)
{
putimage(j,20,z,2);
delay(5);
putimage(j,20,z,1);
}
putimage(5,20,z,2);

for(j=20;j<=(n-bk)*20+50;++j)
{
putimage(5,j,z,2);
delay(5);
putimage(5,j,z,1);
}
putimage(5,(n-bk)*20+50,z,2);

bk8—;
```

```
bk++;
}

/*for moving elements of 7th bucket back to list    */

while(bk7>0)
{
kk=7;
getimage(kk*52+120,325-bk7*22+22,kk*52+170,325-bk7*22+42,z);

for(j=325-bk7*22+22;j>=20;—j)
{
putimage(kk*52+120,j,z,2);
delay(5);
putimage(kk*52+120,j,z,1);
}
putimage(kk*52+120,20,z,2);

for(j=kk*52+120;j>=5;j—)
{
putimage(j,20,z,2);
delay(5);
putimage(j,20,z,1);
}
putimage(5,20,z,2);

for(j=20;j<=(n-bk)*20+50;++j)
{
putimage(5,j,z,2);
delay(5);
putimage(5,j,z,1);
}
putimage(5,(n-bk)*20+50,z,2SW);

bk7—;
bk++;
}

/*for moving elements of 6th bucket back to list    */
```

```
while(bk6>0)
{
kk=6;
getimage(kk*52+120,325-bk6*22+22,kk*52+170,325-bk6*22+42,z);

for(j=325-bk6*22+22;j>=20;—j)
{
putimage(kk*52+120,j,z,2);
delay(5);
putimage(kk*52+120,j,z,1);
}
putimage(kk*52+120,20,z,2);

for(j=kk*52+120;j>=5;j—)
{
putimage(j,20,z,2);
delay(5);
putimage(j,20,z,1);
}
putimage(5,20,z,2);

for(j=20;j<=(n-bk)*20+50;++j)
{
putimage(5,j,z,2);
delay(5);
putimage(5,j,z,1);
}
putimage(5,(n-bk)*20+50,z,2);

bk6—;
bk++;
}

/*for moving elements of 5th bucket back to list    */

while(bk5>0)
{
kk=5;
getimage(kk*52+120,325-bk5*22+22,kk*52+170,325-bk5*22+42,z);
```

```
for(j=325-bk5*22+22;j>=20;--j)
{
putimage(kk*52+120,j,z,2);
delay(5);
putimage(kk*52+120,j,z,1);
}
putimage(kk*52+120,20,z,2);

for(j=kk*52+120;j>=5;j--)
{
putimage(j,20,z,2);
delay(5);
putimage(j,20,z,1);
}
putimage(5,20,z,2);

for(j=20;j<=(n-bk)*20+50;++j)
{
putimage(5,j,z,2);
delay(5);
putimage(5,j,z,1);
}
putimage(5,(n-bk)*20+50,z,2);

bk5--;
bk++;
}

/*for moving elements of 4th bucket back to list   */

while(bk4>0)
{
kk=4;
getimage(kk*52+120,325-bk4*22+22,kk*52+170,325-bk4*22+42,z);

for(j=325-bk4*22+22;j>=20;--j)
{
putimage(kk*52+120,j,z,2);
delay(5);
putimage(kk*52+120,j,z,1);
```

```
}
putimage(kk*52+120,20,z,2);

for(j=kk*52+120;j>=5;j—)
{
putimage(j,20,z,2);
delay(5);
putimage(j,20,z,1);
}
putimage(5,20,z,2);

for(j=20;j<=(n-bk)*20+50;++j)
{
putimage(5,j,z,2);
delay(5);
putimage(5,j,z,1);
}
putimage(5,(n-bk)*20+50,z,2);

bk4—;
bk++;
}

/*for moving elements of 3rd bucket back to list     */

while(bk3>0)
{
kk=3;
getimage(kk*52+120,325-bk3*22+22,kk*52+170,325-bk3*22+42,z);

for(j=325-bk3*22+22;j>=20;—j)
{
putimage(kk*52+120,j,z,2);
delay(5);
putimage(kk*52+120,j,z,1);
}
putimage(kk*52+120,20,z,2);

for(j=kk*52+120;j>=5;j—)
```

```
{
putimage(j,20,z,2);
delay(5);
putimage(j,20,z,1);
}
putimage(5,20,z,2);

for(j=20;j<=(n-bk)*20+50;++j)
{
putimage(5,j,z,2);
delay(5);
putimage(5,j,z,1);
}
putimage(5,(n-bk)*20+50,z,2);

bk3—;
bk++;
}

/*for moving elements of 2nd bucket back to list    */

while(bk2>0)
{
kk=2;
getimage(kk*52+120,325-bk2*22+22,kk*52+170,325-bk2*22+42,z);

for(j=325-bk2*22+22;j>=20;—j)
{
putimage(kk*52+120,j,z,2);
delay(5);
putimage(kk*52+120,j,z,1);
}
putimage(kk*52+120,20,z,2);

for(j=kk*52+120;j>=5;j—)
{
putimage(j,20,z,2);
delay(5);
putimage(j,20,z,1);
}
```

```
putimage(5,20,z,2);

for(j=20;j<=(n-bk)*20+50;++j)
{
putimage(5,j,z,2);
delay(5);
putimage(5,j,z,1);
}
putimage(5,(n-bk)*20+50,z,2);

bk2—;
bk++;
}

/*for moving elements of 1st bucket back to list    */

while(bk1>0)
{
kk=1;
getimage(kk*52+120,325-bk1*22+22,kk*52+170,325-bk1*22+42,z);

for(j=325-bk1*22+22;j>=20;—j)
{
putimage(kk*52+120,j,z,2);
delay(5);
putimage(kk*52+120,j,z,1);
}
putimage(kk*52+120,20,z,2);

for(j=kk*52+120;j>=5;j—)
{
putimage(j,20,z,2);
delay(5);
putimage(j,20,z,1);
}
putimage(5,20,z,2);

for(j=20;j<=(n-bk)*20+50;++j)
{
```

```
putimage(5,j,z,2);
delay(5);
putimage(5,j,z,1);
}
putimage(5,(n-bk)*20+50,z,2);

bk1—;
bk++;
}

/*for moving elements of 0th bucket back to list   */

while(bk0>0)
{
kk=0;
getimage(kk*52+120,325-bk0*22+22,kk*52+170,325-bk0*22+42,z);

for(j=325-bk0*22+22;j>=20;—j)
{
putimage(kk*52+120,j,z,2);
delay(5);
putimage(kk*52+120,j,z,1);
}
putimage(kk*52+120,20,z,2);

for(j=kk*52+120;j>=5;j—)
{
putimage(j,20,z,2);
delay(5);
putimage(j,20,z,1);
}
putimage(5,20,z,2);

for(j=20;j<=(n-bk)*20+50;++j)
{
putimage(5,j,z,2);
delay(5);
putimage(5,j,z,1);
}
putimage(5,(n-bk)*20+50,z,2);
```

```
bk0—;
bk++;
}

if(xx!=dd)
{
dg0=1;

for(j=0;j<=9;++j)
{
for(i=1;i<=n;++i)
{
      if(xx==1)
      {
            if(a[i]%10==j)
            {
            b[dg0]=a[i];
            dg0++;
            }
            }
      if(xx==2)
      {
            if((a[i]/10)%10==j)
            {
            b[dg0]=a[i];
            dg0++;
            }
            }
            if(xx==3)
      {
            if((a[i]/100)%10==j)
            {
            b[dg0]=a[i];
            dg0++;
            }
            }
            if(xx==4)
      {
            if((a[i]/1000)%10==j)
```

```
        {
        b[dg0]=a[i];
        dg0++;
        }
        }
        if(xx==5)
    {
        if((a[i]/10000)%10==j)
        {
        b[dg0]=a[i];
        dg0++;
        }
        }
}
}
for(i=1;i<=n;++i)
a[i]=b[i];
}
closegraph();
}
free(z);
getch();
}
```

Text can be animated and during animation we can change the size of the text or font of the text. When a set of strings needs to be animated they can be stored in an array of strings and are considered for animation one by one. The following program illustrates this with the help of eight strings. The animation of text movement continues until any key from the keyboard is pressed.

```
/* Program to show the text animation on the screen. The texts are made to move from bottom of
the screen to top one by one and they become small at end */

# include<graphics.h>
# include<conio.h>
# include<dos.h>

void main()
{
int gd=0,gm,i,n,j,t,f;
char
```

```
a[20][80]={"PROGRAMMING","SKILLS","THROUGH","C","ANMOL","PUBLICATIONS",
"BY","B.M.HAVALDAR"};
initgraph(&gd,&gm,"");
settextjustify(1,1);
setusercharsize(10,5,1,1);
        i=getmaxy();
        n=i;
        j=0,t=-1,f=26;
        while(!kbhit()) /* Animation continues till pressing any key */
     {
        if (i<=-50)
        {
         i=n;
         j++;
         f=26;
        }
        else i-=1;
        if(j==8)  /* The array of strings pointer is reset to starting */
        j=0;
        ettextstyle(2,0,f);
        setcolor(f);
        outtextxy(getmaxx()/2,i,a[j]);
        delay(5);

        cleardevice();
        if( (i%20==0))
        f=f+t*1;
        if(f<=1)
        t=1;
        if(f>=26)
        t=-1;
        }
        getch();
        closegraph();
        }
```

4

LINE AND CIRCLE DRAWING METHODS

Any picture can be thought of as a combination of points. The idea is to identify the points which form the part of the picture one is trying to draw and by a suitable technique display these points. To do this, the screen is supposed to be made up of a number of pixels, each pixel corresponding to a point. Those pixels which form a part of the picture being drawn are made to light up so that the picture is visible on the screen.

4.A) Point Plotting Techniques

The coordinate systems of the monitor: Point plotting techniques are based on the use of Cartesian coordinate system. Each point is addressed by two points (x,y) which indicate the distance of the point with respect to the origin shown in the figure.

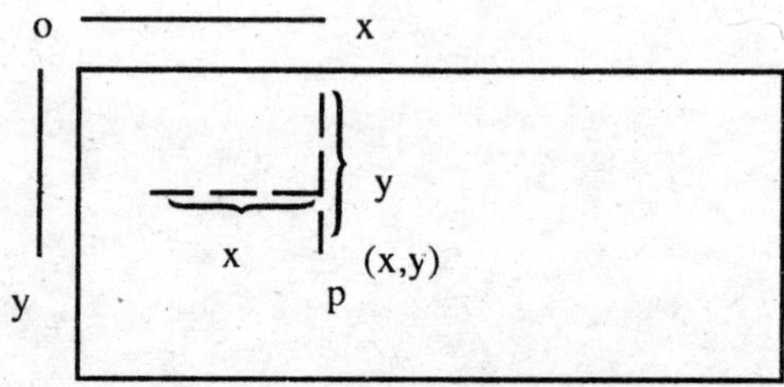

p (x,y) is a pixel at horizontal distance x and vertical distance y from the origin. Any picture to be displayed is to be represented as a combination of points. Though no continuous lines are drawn but only a sense of points are being made bright. Because of the properties of the human eye, we see continuous lines, when the points that are being lighted are fairly close to each other.

4.B) Incremental methods

The concept of incremental methods, as the name suggests, is to draw the picture in stages - incrementally. i.e. from the first point of the picture, we have a method of drawing the second point and from there to the third point etc. They are also sometimes called "iterative methods" because they draw picture in stages or in iterations.

4.C) The Digital Differential Analyzer (DDA)

This includes a class of algorithms which draw lines from their corresponding differential equations. Before we see the actual algorithms, let us see the concept by the example of a simple straight line.

The differential equation of a straight line is given by $\frac{dy}{dx} = \Delta y / \Delta x$

In other words, given a point on the straight line, we can get the next point by adding Δx to the x coordinate and Δy to the y coordinate. So it is an incremental method, where given a starting point we can go on generating points, one after the other each spaced from it's previous point by an additional Δx and Δy, until we reach the final point. The following program makes use of DDA algorithm to draw the line. The two end points of the line are taken from the keyboard and incremental values are calculated.

```
/* Program to Generate a Line using Digital Differential Algorithm (DDA) */
#include <stdio.h>
#include <conio.h>
#include <graphics.h>
#include<math.h>

/* function for plotting the points and drawing the line */
void ddaline(float x1,float y1,float x2,float y2)
{
 int i, color=5;
 float x, y, xinc, yinc, steps;
 steps = abs(x2-x1);
 if (steps < abs(y2-y1))
 steps= abs(y2-y1);
 xinc=(x2-x1)/steps;
 yinc=(y2-y1)/steps;
 x=x1;
 y=y1;
 putpixel((int)x,(int)y, color);
 for (i=1;i<=steps; i++)
 {
 putpixel((int)x,(int)y,color); /*Plots the points with specified color */
 x=x+xinc;
 y=y+yinc;
 }
 }
```

```
/* The main program that inputs line end points and passes them to ddaline() function */
void main()
{
int gd = DETECT, gm, color;
float x1,y1,x2,y2;
printf("\n enter the end points :\n");
scanf("%f %f %f %f",&x1,&y1,&x2,&y2);
clrscr();
initgraph(&gd, &gm, "c:\\tc\\bgi");
ddaline(x1,y1,x2,y2);
getch();
closegraph();
}
```

The main draw back of DDA method is that it generates the line with "stair case" effect. It also needs all parameters as float but C language syntax does not take any floating point values as co-ordinates in computer graphics.

4.D) Bresenham algorithm:

In this algorithm at each stage, one of the coordinate changes by a value 1 other co-ordinate will either change by 1 or will remain constant. This is because, even though the value should change by a small value, because of the rounding off of the values, the value may or may not be sufficient to take the point to the next level. This is decided by value of error factor 'e' which is given by the equation.

e= 'length of less moving axis' / 'length of more moving axis'.

Each and every time actual value of 'e' is added to error term and when it becomes greater than one then the value of less moving axis will be incremented by 1 and 1 is subtracted from error term. The value of more moving axis will be incremented by 1 in every iteration. The following program draws a line using **Bresenham** algorithm for line.

```
/* Program to generate a line using Bresenham's algorithm*/
#include<stdio.h>
#include<conio.h>
#include<stdlib.h>
#include<graphics.h>

void brline(int,int,int,int);

void main()
```

```
{
int gd=DETECT, gmode;
int x1,y1,x2,y2;
printf("\n enter the starting point x1,y1 :");
scanf("%d%d",&x1,&y1);
printf("\n enter the  ending point x2, y2 :");
scanf("%d%d",&x2,&y2);
clrscr();
initgraph(&gdriver, &gmode,"");
brline(x1,y1,x2,y2);
getch();
closegraph();
}

/* Function for Bresenham's line */

void brline(int x1,int y1,int x2,int y2)
{
int e,l,xend;
int color;
float dx,dy,x,y;
dx=abs(x2-x1);
dy=abs(y2-y1);
if(x1>x2)
{
        x=x2;
        y=y2;
        xend=x1;
}
else
{
        x=x1;
        y=y1;
        xend=x2;
}
e=2*dy-dx;

while(x<xend)
{
```

```
            color=random(getmaxcolor());
            putpixel((int)x,(int)y,color);
            if(e>0)
            {
                y++;
            e=e+2*(dy-dx);
}
else
            e=e+2*dy;
            x++;
}
}
```

4.E) Generation of Circles

The above algorithms can always be extended to other curves - the only required condition is that we should know the equations of the curve concerned in a differential form. We discuss few cases below.

4.F) Circle generating DDA:

Circle equation by using polar coordinates is given below.

$$x_{n+1} = x_n \cos q + y_n \sin q$$
$$y_{n+1} = y_n \cos q - x_n \sin q$$

Using these equations the circle can be generated easily. The following program illustrates the circle by using DDA algorithm. The 'q' is the angle and when its steps are small we will get more smooth circle.

```
/* Program to demonstrate circle using DDA algorithm */
#include<graphics.h>
#include<conio.h>
#include<dos.h>
#include<alloc.h>
#include<math.h>

void main()
{
int gm,gd=DETECT,i;
int x,y,x1,y1,j;
initgraph(&gd,&gm,"");
```

```
x=40; /* The co-ordinate values for calculating radius */
y=40;
for(i=0;i<=360;i+=10)
{
        setcolor(i+1);
        x1=x*cos(i*3.142/180)+y*sin(i*3.142/180);
        y1=x*sin(i*3.142/180)-y*cos(i*3.142/180);
        circle(x1+getmaxx()/2,y1+getmaxy()/2,5); /* center of the circle is center
                                                    of the screen */
        delay(10);
}
getch();
}
```

4.G) Spiral generation

A small change in calculating the co-ordinate values (x, y) leads to the formation of spiral instead of circle. This is because in each iteration the changed (new) points are used instead of original input points. The following program draws the spiral.

```
/* Program to demonstrate spiral */
#include<graphics.h>
#include<conio.h>
#include<dos.h>
#include<alloc.h>
#include<math.h>

void main()
{
int gm,gd=DETECT;
float x,y,x1,y1,i;
initgraph(&gd,&gm,"");
x=100;
y=100;
for(i=0;i<=360;i+=0.005)
{
        x=x*cos(i*3.142/180)+y*sin(i*3.142/180);
        y=-x*sin(i*3.142/180)+y*cos(i*3.142/180);
        putpixel((int)x+200,(int)y+200,15);
}
```

```
getch();
}
```

The following program draws the circle using Bresenham's algorithm.

```
/* Program to Implement Bresenham's Circle Drawing Algorithm */

#include <stdio.h>
#include <conio.h>
#include <graphics.h>
#include<math.h>
#include<dos.h>

/* Function for plotting the co-ordinates at four different angles that are placed at equal distances
*/

void plotpoints(int xcentre, int ycentre, int x, int y)
{
int color=5;
putpixel(xcentre+x, ycentre+y, color);
putpixel(xcentre+x, ycentre-y, color);
putpixel(xcentre-x, ycentre+y, color);
putpixel(xcentre-x, ycentre-y, color);

putpixel(xcentre+y, ycentre+x, color);
putpixel(xcentre+y, ycentre-x, color);
putpixel(xcentre-y, ycentre+x, color);
putpixel(xcentre-y, ycentre-x, color);
}

/* Function for calculating the new points for (x ,y) co-ordinates.*/

void cir(int xcentre, int ycentre, int radius)
{
        int x,y,p;
        x=0; y=radius;
        plotpoints (xcentre, ycentre, x, y);
        p=1-radius;
        while(x<y)
        {
```

```
        if (p<0)
        p=p+2*x+1;
        else
        {
            y—;
            p=p+2*(x-y)+1;
        }
        x++;
        plotpoints xcentre, ycentre, x, y);
        delay(100);
        }
}
```

```
/* The main function that takes (x, y) and 'r' the radius from keyboard and activates other
functions for drawing the circle. */
void main()

{
int gd = DETECT, gm, xcentre=200, ycentre=150, radius=50;
printf("\n enter the centre points and radius :\n");
scanf("%d%d%d", &xcentre, &ycentre, &radius);
clrscr();
initgraph(&gd, &gm,"");
putpixel(xcentre,ycentre,5);
cir(xcentre, ycentre, radius);
getch();
closegraph();
}
```

Bresenham specified the algorithm for drawing the ellipse using mid point method. This is illustrated in the following program.

```
/*  BRESENHAM's MIDPOINT ELLIPSE ALGORITHM    */
#include<stdio.h>
#include<conio.h>
#include<math.h>
#include<graphics.h>
int xcenter, ycenter, rx, ry;
int p,px,py,x,y,rx2,ry2,tworx2,twory2;
void drawelipse();
```

```
void main()
{
   int gd=3,gm=1;
   clrscr();
   initgraph(&gd, &gm,"");
   printf("\n Enter X center value : ");
   scanf("%d", &xcenter);
   printf("\n Enter Y center value : ");
   scanf("%d", &ycenter);
   printf("\n Enter X radius value : ");
   scanf("%d", &rx);
   printf("\n Enter Y radius value : ");
   scanf("%d", &ry);
   cleardevice();
   ry2 = ry * ry;
   rx2 = rx * rx;
   twory2 = 2 * ry2;
   tworx2 = 2 * rx2;

   /* REGION first */
   x=0;
   y=ry;
   drawelipse();

   p = (ry2 - rx2 * ry + (0.25 * rx2));
   px = 0;
   py = tworx2 * y;
   while( px < py )
   {
     x++;
     px = px + twory2;
     if(p >= 0)
     {
       y = y - 1;
       py = py - tworx2;
   }
   if(p < 0)
       p = p + ry2 + px;
   else
       {
```

```
            p = p + ry2 + px - py;
            drawelipse();
         }
    }

/*REGION second */
    p = (ry2 * (x + 0.5) * (x + 0.5) + rx2 * (y - 1) * (y - 1) - rx2 * ry2);
    while( y > 0 )
    {
     y = y - 1;
     py = py - tworx2;
     if( p <= 0 )
     {
     x++;
     px = px + twory2;
     }
     if( p > 0 )
          p = p + rx2 - py;
     else
         {
           p = p + rx2 - py + px;
           drawelipse();
         }
 }
  getch();
  closegraph();
}
void drawelipse()
{
  putpixel(xcenter + x, ycenter + y, BROWN);
  putpixel(xcenter - x, ycenter + y, BROWN);
  putpixel(xcenter + x, ycenter - y, BROWN);
  putpixel(xcenter - x, ycenter - y, BROWN);
}
```

5

TRANSFORMATIONS

Changing the size, angle and position of the image on the graphical screen is called its transformation. Basically transformations can be applied for both 2D and 3D graphics. There are mainly three types of transformations namely, 1) Translation, 2) Scaling and 3) Rotation. These three types can be applied for the images of two-dimensions as well as three-dimensions.

5.A) Two Dimensional Transformation

When an image is represented using merely two axes, x-axis and y-axis on a plain then the image is said to be 2D image. The two dimensions indicate the width and height of the image. Consider a rectangle with co-ordinates (10, 10) and (100, 50), the rectangle is having its length 90 units along x-axis and height 40 units along y-axis.

5.B) Three Dimensional Transformation

When an image is represented using three axis, x-axes, y-axis and z-axis on a plain then the image is said to be 3D image. The three dimensions indicate the width height and breadth of the image. Consider a 3D bar with co-ordinates (10, 10) and (100, 50) and breadth 20 then, the bar is having its length 90 units along x-axis and height 40 units along y-axis and breadth 20 units along z-axis.

Whenever we need to change the size of the image or angle of the image or its position then we need to apply transformations on that image. The three main basic transformations are given below.

5.C) Translation:

5.C.I) For 2D image:

Consider a point $P(x_1, y_1)$ to be translated to another point $Q(x_2, y_2)$. If we know the point value (x_2, y_2) we can directly shift to Q by displaying the pixel (x_2, y_2). On the other hand, suppose we only know that we want to shift by a distance of Tx along x axis and Ty along Y axis. Then obviously the coordinates can be derived by the equations

$x_2 = x_1 + T_x$
$y_2 = y_1 + T_y$.

These equations can be represented in the matrix forms as follows:

$$[x2\ y2\ 1] = [x1\ y1\ 1] \begin{bmatrix} 1 & 0 & 0 \\ 0 & 1 & 0 \\ Tx & Ty & 1 \end{bmatrix}$$

Suppose we want to shift a triangle with coordinates at A(20,10), B(30,100) and C(40,70) to 20 units along x-axis and 30 units along y-axis. Then the shifting to be done by 20 units along x axis i.e., Tx is 20 and 30 units along y axis i.e., Ty is 30. Then the new triangle will be at A1 (40, 40), B1 (50, 130) and C1 (60, 110)

5.C.II) For 3D image:

Consider a point $P(x_1, y_1, z_1)$ to be translated to another point $Q(x_2, y_2, z_2)$. If we know the point value (x_2, y_2, z_2) we can directly shift to Q by displaying the pixel (x_2, y_2, z_2). On the other hand, suppose we only know that we want to shift by a distance of Tx along x axis, Ty along Y axis and Tz along z-axis. Then the new co-ordinates are given by the equations

$x_2 = x_1 + T_x$
$y_2 = y_1 + T_y$.
$z_2 = z_1 + T_z$

These equations can be represented in the matrix forms as follows

$$[x1\ y1\ z1\ 1] = [x1\ y1\ z1\ 1] \begin{bmatrix} 1 & 0 & 0 & 0 \\ 0 & 1 & 0 & 0 \\ 0 & 0 & 1 & 0 \\ Tx & Ty & Tz & 1 \end{bmatrix}$$

5.D) Rotation:

5.D.I) For 2D image:

Suppose we want to rotate a point $(x_1\ y_1)$ clockwise through an angle q, about the origin of the coordinate system. Then the new co-ordinates are calculated using circle equations as given below

$x_2 = x_1 \cos q + y_1 \sin q$ and
$y_2 = x_1 \sin q - y_1 \cos q$

These equations can be represented using matrix form as follows.

$$[x2\ y2] = [x1\ y1] \begin{bmatrix} \mathrm{Cos}(\theta) & \sin(\theta) \\ \mathrm{Sin}(\theta) & -\mathrm{Cos}(\theta) \end{bmatrix}$$

5.D.II) 3D Image Rotation

In 3D rotation we need to consider one of the axis as the reference for rotation and accordingly the new co-ordinates for other two axis will be calculated. This is given in the following sections.

Rotation along Z-axis:

Suppose we want to rotate a point (x_1 y_1 z_1) clockwise through an angle q, about the Z-axis of the coordinate system. Then the new co-ordinates are calculated using circle equations as given below

$x_2 = x_1\cos\theta + y_1\sin\theta$
$y_2 = x_1\sin\theta - y_1\cos\theta$ and
$z_2 = z_1$

These equations can be represented using matrix form as follows.

$$[x2\ \ y2\ \ z2] \quad = \quad [x1\ \ y1\ \ z1] \begin{bmatrix} \text{Cos}(\theta) & \sin(\theta) & 0 \\ \text{Sin}(\theta) & -\text{Cos}(\theta) & 0 \\ 0 & 0 & 1 \end{bmatrix}$$

Rotation along Y-axis:

Suppose we want to rotate a point (x_1 y_1 z_1) clockwise through an angle q, about the Y-axis of the coordinate system. Then the new co-ordinates are calculated using circle equations as given below

$x_2 = x_1\cos\theta + z_1\sin\theta$
$y_2 = y1$ and
$z2 = x_1\sin\theta - z_1\cos\theta$

These equations can be represented using matrix form as follows.

$$[x2\ \ y2\ \ z2] \quad = \quad [x1\ \ y1\ \ z1] \begin{bmatrix} \text{Cos}(\theta) & 0 & \sin(\theta) \\ 0 & 1 & 0 \\ \text{Sin}(\theta) & 0 & -\text{Cos}(\theta) \end{bmatrix}$$

Rotation along X-axis:

Suppose we want to rotate a point (x_1 y_1 z_1) clockwise through an angle q, about the X-axis of the coordinate system. Then the new co-ordinates are calculated using circle equations as given below

$x_2 = x_1$
$y_2 = z_1\cos\theta + y_1\sin\theta$ and
$z_2 = z_1\sin\theta - y_1\cos\theta$

These equations can be represented using matrix form as follows.

$$[x2\ \ y2\ \ z2] \quad = \quad [x1\ \ y1\ \ z1] \begin{bmatrix} 1 & 0 & 0 \\ 0 & \text{Cos}(\theta) & \sin(\theta) \\ 0 & \text{Sin}(\theta) & -\text{Cos}(\theta) \end{bmatrix}$$

5.E) Scaling

Scaling is the transformation in which size of the image will be changed. The scale factors are used to change the size. The scale factors may be fractions less than 1 (in such a case the size of the image will be reduced) or it may be any positive value. While specifying the scale factors one should be careful about the possibility of getting the new co-ordinates outside the screen limits. Like translation and rotation the scaling can be applied to both 2D and 3D image as given below.

5.E.I) For 2D image:

Consider a point $P(x_1, y_1)$ to be scaled to get new point $Q(x_2, y_2)$. If we know the point value (x_2, y_2) we can directly shift to Q by displaying the pixel (x_2, y_2). On the other hand, suppose we only know that we want to scale it by the scale factor Sx along x axis and Sy along Y axis. Then obviously the coordinates can be derived by the equations

$x_2 = x_1 * S_x$
$y_2 = y_1 * S_y$.

These equations can be represented in the matrix forms as follows

$$[x2\ y2] \quad = \quad [x1\ y1] \begin{bmatrix} Sx & 0 \\ 0 & Sy \end{bmatrix}$$

Suppose we want to scale a triangle with coordinates at A(20,10), B(30,100) and C(40,70) to 2 units along x-axis and 3 units along y-axis. Then the scaling to be done by 2 units along x axis i.e., Sx is 2 and 3 units along y axis i.e., Sy is 3. Then the new triangle will be at A1 (40, 30), B1 (60, 300) and C1 (80, 210)

5.E.II) For 3D image:

Consider a point $P(x_1, y_1, z_1)$ to be scaled to get new point $Q(x_2, y_2, z_2)$. If we know the point value (x_2, y_2, z_2) we can directly shift to Q by displaying the pixel (x_2, y_2, z_2). On the other hand, suppose we only know that we want to scale by a distance of Sx along x axis, Sy along Y axis and Sz along z-axis. Then the new co-ordinates are given by the equations

$x_2 = x_1 * S_x$
$y_2 = y_1 * S_y$.
$z_2 = z_1 * S_z$

These equations can be represented in the matrix forms as follows

$$[x2\ y2\ z2] \quad = \quad [x1\ y1\ z1] \begin{bmatrix} Sx & 0 & 0 \\ 0 & Sy & 0 \\ 0 & 0 & Sz \end{bmatrix}$$

The transformations can be easily implemented using C language programs. The following programs illustrate different aspects of translation, scaling and rotations on the 2D images.

The following programs implement transformations by taking different graphical objects into consideration.

```
/* Program to draw a rectangle and perform scale with ref to the origin */

#include <graphics.h>
#include <stdio.h>
#include <conio.h>

void rect(int,int,int,int);

void main()
{
        int x,y,len,bre,gd=DETECT,gm;
        float scx,scy;
        clrscr();
        printf("\n\n\tEnter the X of origin ->> ");
        scanf("%d",&x);
        printf("\n\tEnter the Y of origin ->> ");
        scanf("%d",&y);
        printf("\n\n\tEnter the lenth of rectangle ->> ");
        scanf("%d",&len);
        printf("\n\tEnter the breath of rectangle ->> ");
        scanf("%d",&bre);
        initgraph(&gd,&gm,"");/* Graphics is initialized */
        cleardevice();
        rect(x,y,len,bre);
        printf("\n\tEnter the X scaling factor(2-4) ->> ");
        scanf("%f",&scx);
        printf("\n\tEnter the Y scaling factor(2-4) ->> ");
        scanf("%f",&scy);
        rect(x,y,(int)(len*scx),(int)(bre*scy));/* Draws the rectangle */
        getch();
}

void rect(int x,int y,int len,int bre)
{
        line(x,y,x+len,y);
```

```
        line(x,y,x,y-bre);
        line(x+len,y,x+len,y-bre);
        line(x,y-bre,x+len,y-bre);
}
```

```
/* program to draw a rectangle and perform scale with ref to arbitrary point */

#include <graphics.h>
#include <stdio.h>
#include <conio.h>
void rect(int,int,int,int);
void main()
{
        int x,y,len,bre,nx,ny,sx,sy,gd=DETECT,gm;
        float scx,scy;
        clrscr();
        printf("\n\n\tEnter the X of origin ->> ");
        scanf("%d",&x);
        printf("\n\tEnter the Y of origin ->> ");
        scanf("%d",&y);
        printf("\n\n\tEnter the lenth of rectangle ->> ");
        scanf("%d",&len);
        printf("\n\tEnter the breath of rectangle ->> ");
        scanf("%d",&bre);
        initgraph(&gd,&gm,"");
        cleardevice();
        rect(x,y,len,bre);
        printf("\n\n\tEnter the X of arbitary pt ->> ");
        scanf("%d",&nx);
        printf("\n\tEnter the Y of arbitrary pt ->> ");
        scanf("%d",&ny);
        printf("\n\tEnter the X scaling factor(2-4) ->> ");
        scanf("%f",&scx);
        printf("\n\tEnter the Y scaling factor(2-4) ->> ");
        scanf("%f",&scy);
        cleardevice();
        setcolor(8);
        rect(x,y,len,bre);
        setcolor(15);
        sx = abs((int)(x*scx+nx*(1-scx)));
```

```
        sy = abs((int)(y*scy+ny*(1-scy)));
        rect(sx,sy,(int)(len*scx),(int)(bre*scy));
        getch();
        closegraph();
}

/* Function to draw rectangle using line() function */
void rect(int x,int y,int len,int bre)
{
        line(x,y,x+len,y);
        line(x,y,x,y-bre);
        line(x+len,y,x+len,y-bre);
        line(x,y-bre,x+len,y-bre);
}
```

/* program to draw a triangle and show its scaling and rotation. This program makes use of functions to get the new points after scaling and rotation. Reference variables are used to get the newly calculated co-ordinate values from the functions. The triangle co-ordinates are static in nature */

```
#include<stdio.h>
#include<conio.h>
#include<math.h>
#include<stdlib.h>
#include<graphics.h>

/* FUNCTIONS DECLARATIONS */
void scale(int *,int *,float,float,int,int);
void rotate(int *,int *,float,int,int);
void translate(int *,int *,int ,int);

void main()
{
  int gd=DETECT,gm,ch;
  int x1,y1,x2,y2,x3,y3,tx,ty;
  float refx,refy,theta,sx,sy;
  initgraph(&gd,&gm,"");
  do
  {
```

x1=150,y1=300,x2=250,y2=300,x3=200,y3=200,refx=200,refy=250; /* co-ordinate values for triangle to be transformed */

```
cleardevice();
/* Draws the triangle */
line(x1,y1,x2,y2);
line(x2,y2,x3,y3);
line(x1,y1,x3,y3);

/* Menu creation */
setcolor(YELLOW);
outtextxy(140,30,"Main Menu");
outtextxy(140,50," 1. Scale");
outtextxy(140,70," 2. Rotate");
outtextxy(140,90," 3. Translate");
outtextxy(140,110," 4. Exit");
outtextxy(100,150," Enter Your choice : ");
scanf("%d",&ch); /* user choice */
switch(ch)
{
  case 1 :
        outtextxy(10,10," Enter sx and sy : ");
        scanf("%f%f",&sx,&sy); /* scale factors */
        cleardevice();
        /* triangle before scaling */
        line(x1,y1,x2,y2);
        line(x2,y2,x3,y3);
        line(x1,y1,x3,y3);

        /* Scaling to get new points */
        scale(&x1,&y1,sx,sy,refx,refy);
        scale(&x2,&y2,sx,sy,refx,refy);
        scale(&x3,&y3,sx,sy,refx,refy);
        /* Triangle after scaling */
        line(x1,y1,x2,y2);
        line(x2,y2,x3,y3);
        line(x1,y1,x3,y3);

        getch();
        break;
```

```
case 2 :
        outtextxy(100,180," Enter Angle of Rotation : ");
        scanf("%f",&theta); /* Angle of rotation */
        cleardevice();

        /* Triangle before rotation */
        line(x1,y1,x2,y2);
        line(x2,y2,x3,y3);
        line(x1,y1,x3,y3);

        /* Getting the new co-ordinates after rotation */
        rotate(&x1,&y1,theta,refx,refy);
         rotate(&x2,&y2,theta,refx,refy);
        rotate(&x3,&y3,theta,refx,refy);

        /* Triangle after rotation */
        line(x1,y1,x2,y2);
        line(x2,y2,x3,y3);
        line(x1,y1,x3,y3);

        getch();
        break;

case 3 :
        outtextxy(100,180,"Enter tx and ty : ");
        scanf("%d%d",&tx,&ty);
        cleardevice();

        /* Triangle before translation */
        line(x1,y1,x2,y2);
        line(x2,y2,x3,y3);
        line(x1,y1,x3,y3);

        /* To get the Translated co-ordinates */
        translate(&x1,&y1,tx,ty);
        translate(&x2,&y2,tx,ty);
        translate(&x3,&y3,tx,ty);

        /* Triangle after translation */
        line(x1,y1,x2,y2);
```

```
                line(x2,y2,x3,y3);
                line(x1,y1,x3,y3);
                getch();
                break;

        case 4 :
                break;
    }

  }while(ch!=4);
  getch();
  closegraph();
}
/* Function to find the new co-ordinate values for scaling */
void scale( int *xnew,int *ynew,float sx,float sy,int refx,int refy)
{
  translate(xnew,ynew,-refx,-refy);
  *xnew=*xnew*sx;
  *ynew=*ynew*sy;
  translate(xnew,ynew,refx,refy);
}

/* Function to find the new co-ordinate values for rotation */
void rotate(int *xnew,int *ynew,float angl,int refx,int refy)
{
  int *xold,*yold;
  translate(xnew,ynew,-refx,-refy);
  *xold=*xnew;
  *yold=*ynew;
  angl=angl*3.14159/180; /* Angle converted to radians */
  *xnew=*xold*cos(angl)-*yold*sin(angl);
  *ynew=*yold*cos(angl)+*xold*sin(angl);
  translate(xnew,ynew,refx,refy);
}

/* Function to find the new co-ordinate values for translation */
void translate(int *xnew,int *ynew,int tx,int ty)
{
  *xnew=*xnew+tx;
  *ynew=*ynew+ty;
}
```

6

CLIPPING AND WINDOWING

In this chapter we are introducing the concepts of handling pictures that are larger than the available display screen size, since any part of the picture that lies beyond the confines of the screen can not be displayed. We compare the screen to a window, which allows us to view only that portion of the scene outside as the limits of the window would permit. Any portion beyond that gets simply blocked out. But in graphics, this "blocking out " is to be done by algorithms that decide point beyond which the picture should not be shown. This concept is called clipping. Thus, we are "clipping" a picture so that it becomes viewable on a "window".

Since all these operations are done at run time, it is necessary that the algorithms will have to be very fast and efficient. We introduce few clipping and windowing algorithms, in this chapter.

6.A) Need for Clipping and Windowing

The size of a CRT terminal on which the pictures are displayed is limited – both the physical dimensions and it's resolution. The physical dimensions limit the maximum size of the picture that can be displayed on the screen and the resolution limits the amount of district details that can be shown.

The clipping of an image or picture on the screen is handled by number of algorithms that are shown below with programs

6.B) A Line Clipping Algorithm

This algorithm cuts the portion of the line that falls outside of the selected window or viewport.

The rectangle indicates the screen in which they are to be displayed. How to decide which of the lines, or more precisely which part of every line is to be displayed. The concept is simple. Since we know the coordinates of the screen,

i) any line whose end points lie within the screen coordinate limits will have to displayed
ii) Any line whose end points lie totally outside the screen coordinates will have to examined to see if any intermediate point is inside the screen boundary.

iii) Any line whose one end point lies inside the boundary will have to be identified.

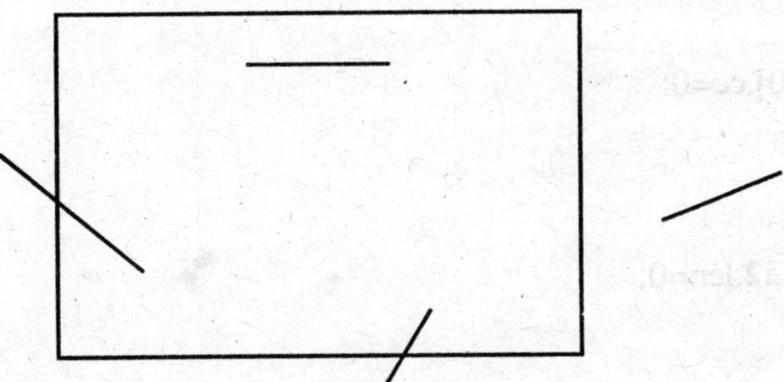

6.C) The Midpoint subdivision algorithm for line clipping

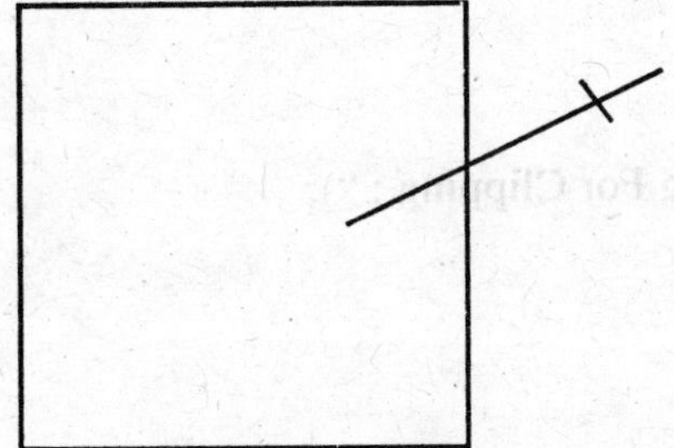

The algorithm processes by dividing the line at the middle. Hence the name mid point division. Now check whether each of these line segment lies inside the viewport completely then retain that line segment, if the line segment is completely outside then erase it. In case if the line segment lies on the border in such a way that some portion of the line is inside the viewport and the other portion is outside then apply the algorithm for that line segment. This will continues until all the portions of the lines that are outside the selected area must be removed.

6.D) Suther land - Hodgeman algorithm for line clipping

The basis of the Suther land Hodgeman algorithms is that it is relatively easy to clip a line against one single edge of the screen at a time i.e. given a complete line, clip the entire line against one edge and take the resultant line to clip against a second edge and so on until all the four edges are covered.

Te following program implements this algorithm.

```
/* Program to implement the cohen-sutherland line clipping algorithm */
#include<stdio.h>
#include<conio.h>
#include<stdlib.h>
#include<graphics.h>
```

```
void clip(float,float,float,float);
int outcode(float,float);

float xr,xl,yb,yt,xx[50],yy[50],cc=0;

void main()
{
   int gd=DETECT,gm,n,i,i1,i2,len=0;
   float x[50],y[50];
   initgraph(&gd,&gm,"");
   cleardevice();
   setbkcolor(BLACK);
   setcolor(CYAN);
   printf("\n\t\t\t LINE CLIPPING ");
   printf("\n\t\t\t*****************");
   printf("\n\t\tHow Many Lines Are Entering For Clipping : ");
   scanf("%d",&n);
   cleardevice();
   for(i=0;i<2*n;i++)
   {
      printf("\n\t\tEnter Starting point of x[%d]y[%d] :",i,i);
      scanf("%f %f",&x[i],&y[i]);
      i++;
      printf("\n\t\tEnter Ending point of x[%d]y[%d] :",i,i);
      scanf("%f%f",&x[i],&y[i]);
}

  cleardevice();

  /* Window Creation */
  setcolor(MAGENTA);
  outtextxy(100,100,"BEFORE CLIPPING");
  xl=200,xr=400,yt=150,yb=300;
  rectangle(xl,yt,xr,yb);
  outtextxy(xl,yt-15,"200,150");
  outtextxy(xr-50,yt-15,"400,150");
  outtextxy(xl,yb+15,"200,300");
  outtextxy(xr-50,yb+15,"400,300");
```

```
/* draws the given lines */
for(i=0;i<2*n;)
{
   i1=i;
   i2=i1+1;
   line((int)x[i1],(int)y[i1],(int)x[i2],(int)y[i2]);
   i=i+2;
}
/* function call for clipping each of the lines */
for(i=0;i<2*n;)
{
   i1=i;
   i2=i1+1;
   clip(x[i1],y[i1],x[i2],y[i2]);
   i=i+2;
}
getch();
cleardevice();

setcolor(LIGHTBLUE);
outtextxy(100,100,"AFTER CLIPPING");
rectangle(xl,yt,xr,yb);
outtextxy(xl,yt-15,"200,150");
outtextxy(xr-50,yt-15,"400,150");
outtextxy(xl,yb+15,"200,300");
outtextxy(xr-50,yb+15,"400,300");
setcolor(BROWN);

for(i=0;i<cc;)
{
   i1=i;
   i2=i1+1;
   line((int)xx[i1],(int)yy[i1],(int)xx[i2],(int)yy[i2]);
   i=i+2;
}
getch();
closegraph();
}

/* Function for clipping the line */
```

```
void clip(float x1,float y1,float x2,float y2)
{
int code1,code2,chk;
float x,y,m;
code1 = outcode(x1,y1);
code2 = outcode(x2,y2);
while( code1 != 0 | code2 != 0) /* both coordinates are inside the window */
{
  m = (float)(y2-y1)/(x2-x1);
  chk = code1 & code2;
  if(chk != 0)
        return;
  chk=code1;
  if(code1 == 0)
        chk = code2;
  if((chk & 1) != 0) /*take binary no of 1 when insect with left */
  {
        y = yl + m * (xl-x1);
        x = xl;
  }
  if((chk & 2) != 0)
  {
        y = yl + m * (xr-x1);
        x = xr;
  }
  if((chk & 4) != 0)
  {
        x = x1 + (yb-yl) / m;
        y = yb;
  }
  if((chk & 8) != 0)
  {
        x = x1 + (yt-y1) / m;
        y = yt;
  }
  if(chk == code1)
        {
         x1=x;y1=y;
         code1 = outcode(x,y);
```

```
        }
        else if(chk == code2)
            {
                x2=x;y2=y;
                code2 = outcode(x,y);
            }
    }
    xx[cc]=x1;
    yy[cc]=y1;cc=cc+1;
    xx[cc]=x2;
    yy[cc]=y2;cc=cc+1;
    return;
}
/* Function for deleting line when it is outside the selected window. */
int outcode(float x, float y)
{
int temp=0;
if(x < xl)
    temp = temp | 1;
  else if (x > xr)
        temp = temp | 2;
      else if(y > yb)
            temp = temp | 4;
          else if(y < yt)
                temp = temp | 8;
  return temp;
}
```

6.E) Polygon Clipping Algorithm

The following program clips polygon using Cohen Sudher Land polygon clipping algorithm.

```
  /* Program for Cohen Sutherland Hodgeman Polygon Clipping Algorithm */
#include<stdio.h>
#include<conio.h>
#include<graphics.h>

void clip(float, float, float, float);
int outcode(float, float);

float xl, xr, yt, yb;
int poly1[25],cc=0;
```

```
void main()
{
   int gdriver = DETECT, gmode;,
   int poly[10],i,n,i1,i2,i3,i4;
   initgraph(&gdriver, &gmode, "");
   cleardevice();
   printf("\nEnter number of points : ");
   scanf("%d",&n);
   for(i=0;i<2*n-1;)
   {
      printf("Enter The %d Point : ",i);
      scanf("%d",&poly[i]);
      ++i;
      scanf("%d",&poly[i]);
      ++i;
   }
   /* Specifies the viewport */
  xl=200,xr=400,yt=150,yb=300;
  rectangle(xl,yt,xr,yb);
  outtextxy(xl,yt-15,"200,150");
  outtextxy(xl-5,yb+15,"200,300");
  outtextxy(xr-50,yt-15,"400,150");
  outtextxy(xr-50,yb+15,"400,300");
  drawpoly(n,poly);
  /* Clips each line of the polygon */
  for(i=0;i<2*n-1;)
  {
     i1=i;i2=i1+1;i3=i2+1;i4=i3+1;
     clip(poly[i1],poly[i2],poly[i3],poly[i4]);
     i=i+4;
  }
  getch();
  cleardevice();
  outtextxy(100,100,"AFTER CLIPPING");
  rectangle(xl,yt,xr,yb);
  outtextxy(xl,yt-15,"200,150");
  outtextxy(xl-5,yb+15,"200,300");
  outtextxy(xr-50,yt-15,"400,150");
  outtextxy(xr-50,yb+15,"400,300");
```

```
   setcolor(BROWN);
   drawpoly(n,poly1);

   getch();
   closegraph();
}

/* CLIPPING */
void clip(float x1,float y1,float x2,float y2)
{
   int code1,code2,chk;
   float x,y,m;
   code1 = outcode(x1,y1);
   code2 = outcode(x2,y2);
   while( code1 !=0 || code2 !=0) /*do both lies inside window*/
   {
      m = (float)(y2-y1)/(x2-x1);
      chk = code1 & code2;
      if(chk != 0)
            return;
      chk=code1;
      if(code1 == 0)
            chk = code2;
      if((chk & 1) != 0)
      {
            y = y1 + m*(xl -x1);
            x = xl;
      }
      if((chk & 2) != 0)
      {
            y = y1 + m*(xr - x1);
            x = xr;
      }
      if((chk & 4) != 0)
      {
            x = x1 + (yb - y1)/m;
            y = yb;
      }
      if((chk & 8) != 0)
      {
```

```
            x = x1 + (yt - y1)/m;
            y = yt;
        }
            if( chk == code1)
            {
              x1=x;y1=y;
              code1 = outcode(x,y);
            }
              else if( chk == code2)
                  {
                    x2=x;y2=y;
                    code2 = outcode(x,y);
                  }
    }
          poly1[cc]=x1;cc=cc+1;
          poly1[cc]=y1;cc=cc+1;
          poly1[cc]=x2;cc=cc+1;
          poly1[cc]=y2;cc=cc+1;
          return;
}

/* function for cutting outside window portion of the line*/
int outcode(float x,float y)
{
  int temp=0;
  if(x < xl)
  temp = temp | 1;
  else if(x > xr)
        temp = temp | 2;
      else if(y > yb)
            temp = temp | 4;
          else if(y < yt)
                temp = temp | 8;
  return temp;
}
```

PART B

PROJECTS

PROJECT 1

HOW COMPUTER WORKS

1.A) SYNOPSIS:

1.A.I) Aim Of The Project:

Actually through this project we want to give the idea, how the inputs are taken from input devices, how it reaches to the respective destination to be processed, how the processed inputs go to output devices and how the intermediate memories hold them.

1.A.II) Project Description:

This project consists of four main modules namely,

1. HYPOCOM
2. CPU
3. Multiplexer
4. De-Multiplexer

Each of these four modules demonstrate four different concepts related to the architecture of computer and their internal working. Each of these modules are explained in detail as follows,

1.A.III) HYPOCOM

In this module we will try to show how the data passes from input to output. We are going to demonstrate the process that takes place in a hypothetical computer as a model. Before that we will describe what is hypothetical computer. It is consist of CPU and I/O devices. There are six parts in CPU they are

1. M.A.R. [memory address register]
2. M.D.R. [memory data register]
3. C.U. [control unit]
4. I.R. [instruction register]
5. G.P.Rs. [General purpose registers]
6. P.C. [program counter]

Our aim is to show how the flow of data and control take place among the peripheral devices through various busses. (Bus is the electrical and electronic circuits through Memory data register is used to store the data or information. The address of the data that is kept in MDR is stored in MAR. The data pass through the data buses.

3: Instruction Register (I.R):

It holds the address of the instructions that are in execution state. For a program there are number of instructions to be executed whose addresses are kept in instruction register. It consists of two parts: an operation code part known as opcode and an address part.

4. Program Counter (P.C):

Program counter is also called as instruction counter and it holds the total number of instructions, which are already been executed, and the next instruction to be executed.

5. General Purpose Registers (G.P.Rs):

These are the special registers, which hold the intermediate results of the expression of the instruction. There should be at least 7 registers of this type namely accumulator, register B, register C, register D, register E, register H and register L. Here accumulator is most frequently used GPRs. All these registers are one byte in size.

6. Control Unit (C.U):

Control unit controls the instructions of the process.

There are several physical data transfer channels, which are known as buses. It connects the CPU and the memory or I/O devices. There are three types of buses, which are as follows:

1. Address bus:

It connects the memory address register(MAR) with the memory or I/O device. It transfers address of data from CPU to memory or I/O device. The width of this bus depends on the configuration of computer.

2. Data bus:

It connects memory data register(MDR) with memory or I/O device. It transfers data from CPU or memory to I/O device.

3. Control bus:

It connects control unit with memory and transfers control signals between them. which data and instructions are transferred). At first CU responds to input and sends the control signal to the IO/M device to confirm their availability. Then CU passes the signal to M.A.R. MAR gets the address of the IO/M from where data has to be read or to where data has to be written.

It makes use of address bus for its operation. The M.A.R then gives the address of the IO/M to MDR. MDR uses data bus to transfer the data to be read or written to the IO/M and comes back. All these take place in the HYPOCOM. These functions we represent dynamically using graphical simulation.

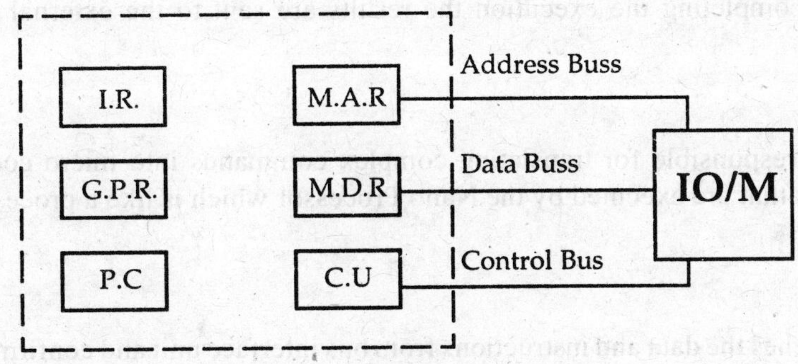

HYPOCOM

The HYPOCOM components are explained in detailed in the following sections.

The registers are describes as follows:

1. Memory Address Register (M.A.R):

Memory address register is used to store the address of the location where data is stored. Usually it is one byte or two bytes register. The address can be transferred with the help of the address buses.

2. Memory Data Register (M.D.R):

1.A.IV) CPU:

In the second module we will describe how the data is processed within the CPU. At first data or instructions enter the bus interface from external world. The Fetch unit fetches the address and confirms its segment and page from the segment unit and paging unit respectively. Once it finds corresponding page and segments then it takes actual data from the bus interface and sends to the decoder unit. Decoder unit decodes the data in such a way that it should be understandable by the processor for subsequent execution. Then data is passed to the execution unit where execution takes place and results are sent back to the external world via bus interface. These different parts are explained in detail in the following sections.

Bus Interface:

The bus inter-face unit (BIU) receives both data and code instructions from the computer's random access memory. The processor is connected to RAM via the PC's mother board circuits, which are known as buses. Data moves from RAM into the processor (number of bits at a time in accordance with the band width of the bus). The bus interface unit sends data and code from external world to the Pre Fetch unit.

Execution Unit:

In this unit the execution of arithmetic and logical expressions takes place. Before the start of execution the data and instructions must be decoded into the language which execution unit can understand. After completing the execution the results are sent to the external world via bus interface unit.

Decoder Unit:

This unit is responsible for translating complex commands into micro code, a series of smaller instructions that are executed by the Nano Processor which is like a processor within the processor.

PreFetch Unit:

This unit fetches the data and instructions from bus interface unit and confirms the page and segment of the respective data and instructions. Then it sends data and instructions to the decoder unit for decoding.

1.A.V) Multiplexer:

Multiplexer is a circuit that takes many numbers of inputs and gives one output. Multi means many and plex means combine. The different gate circuits such as AND, OR, NAND, NOT, XOR,

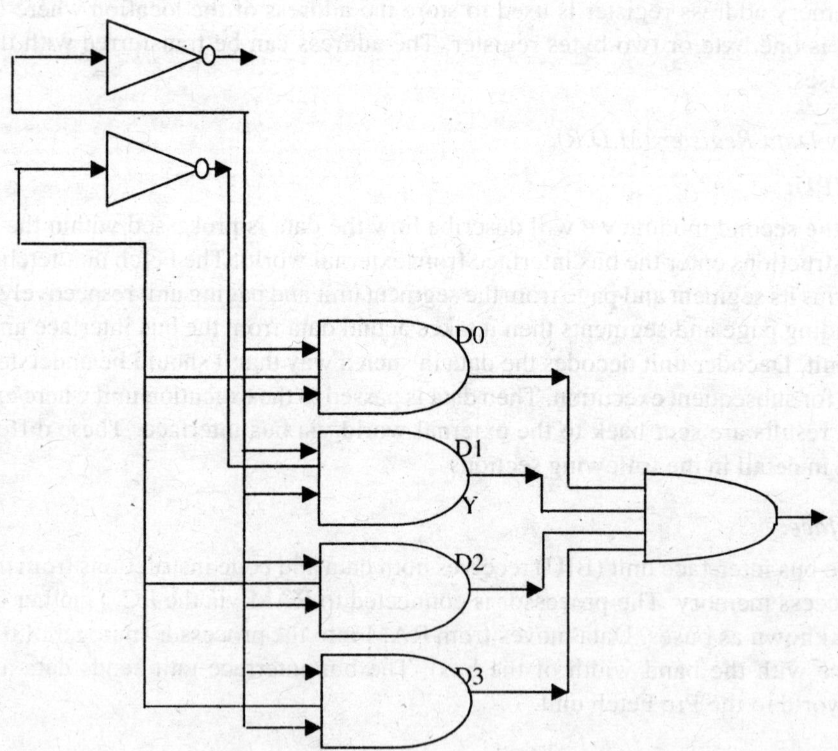

LOGIC DIAGRAM FOR A FOUR-INPUT MULTIPLEXER

XNOR etc. can be used to construct the multiplexer. The output of the intermediate gates can be fed as input to the next successive gates. Finally there must be single output from the entire circuit.

LOGIC GATES:

The following sections describe some of the important Boolean gates which are used in this project to implement multiplexer and de-multiplexer modules.

INVERTER (NOT GATE):

An inverter is a Gate with only one input signal and one output signal, the output state is always the opposite of the input State. An inverter is also called a NOT Gate, because the output is not the same as the input. The output is sometimes called the Compliment (opposite) of the input. The following table summarizes the operation of an Or Gate.

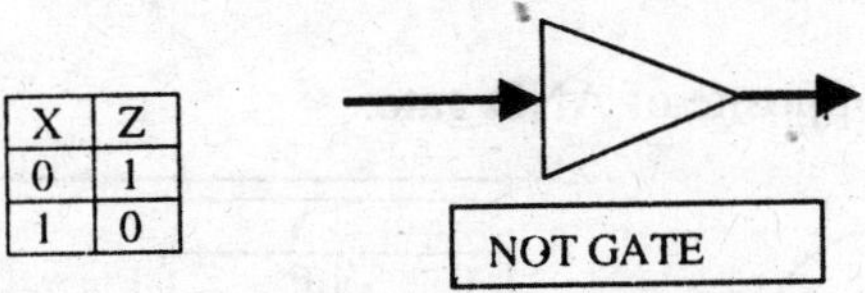

X	Z
0	1
1	0

OR GATE:

The OR gate has two input signals but only one output signal. If both input signals are low then output signal is low or else it remains high.

The following table summarizes the action. A table of this type is called a truth table. It lists all possible inputs with the corresponding outputs.

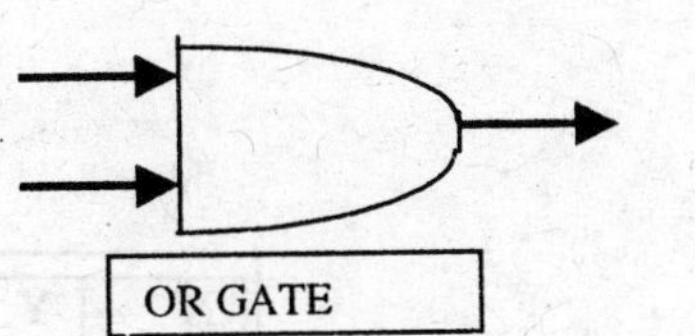

X	Y	Z
0	0	0
0	1	1
1	0	1
1	1	1

AND GATE:

The AND gate has 2 or more input signals but only one output signal. All input must be high to get a high output. The following table summarizes the action.

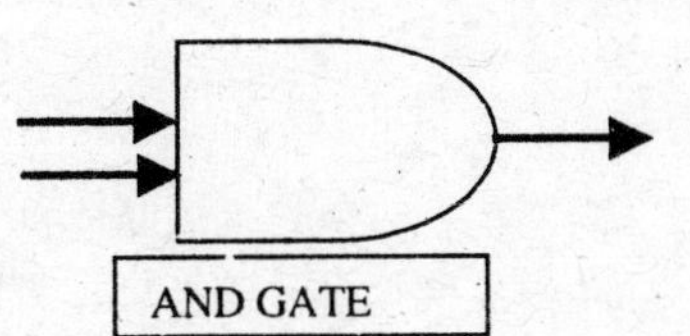

X	Y	Z
0	0	0
0	1	0
1	0	0
1	1	1

NOR GATE:

The NOR gate has two or more input signals but only one output signal. All inputs must be low to get a high output. In other words, the NOR gate recognizes only the input word whose bits are all 0's. The following figure shows the logic structure of a NOR gate, which is an OR gate followed by an inverter.

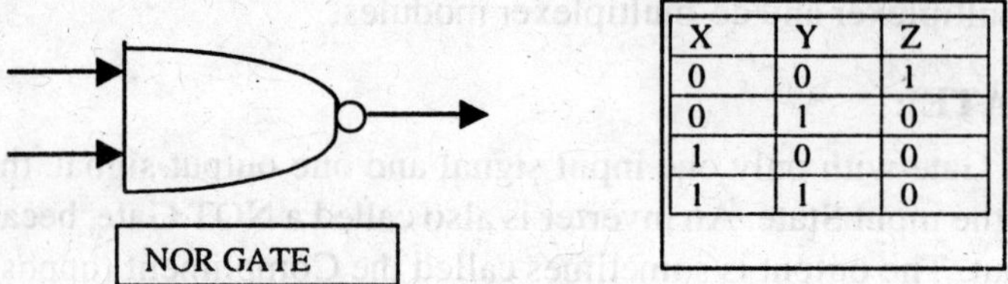

X	Y	Z
0	0	1
0	1	0
1	0	0
1	1	0

NAND GATE:

NAND gate is just the opposite of AND gate.

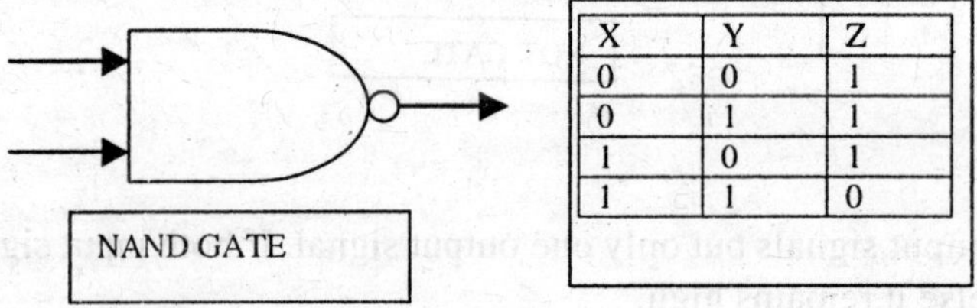

X	Y	Z
0	0	1
0	1	1
1	0	1
1	1	0

EXCLUSIVE-OR GATE(X-OR GATE):

This gate generates a high output when both the inputs are in different levels or else it generates low. The equation is as follows.

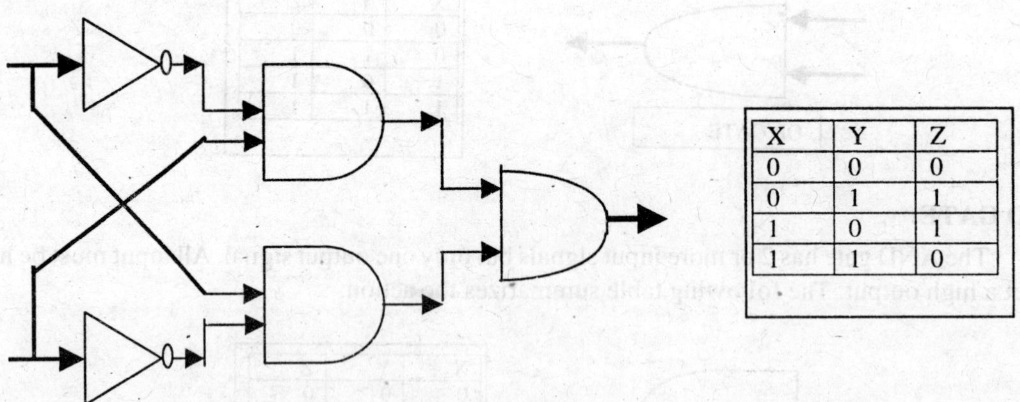

X	Y	Z
0	0	0
0	1	1
1	0	1
1	1	0

EXCLUSIVE –NOR Gate:

This gate is just the opposite of XOR gate.

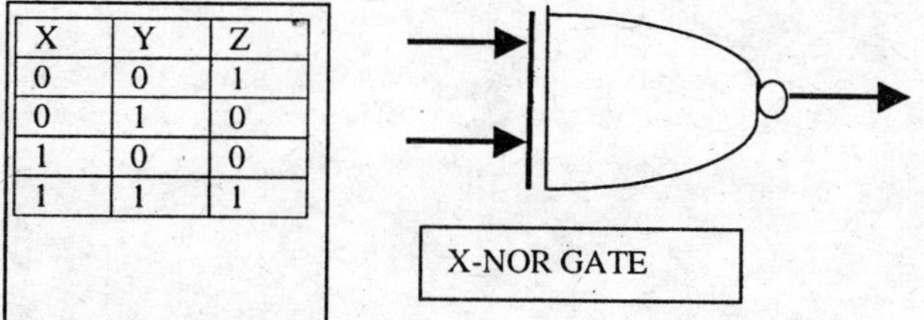

X	Y	Z
0	0	1
0	1	0
1	0	0
1	1	1

1.A. VI) Demultiplexer

This is a logical gate which takes one or more inputs and generates number of possible outputs. As the name indicates it is just the opposite of multiplexer. In this module we have considered two inputs and possible outputs by making use of different gate circuits which are explained above.

1.B) Code Details:

This is completely the menu driven program in which we can choose the menu items using arrow and entry keys. The main module displays the menu with five main items and depending selection the different modules can be activated. When user selects option one the function "hypomain()" is activated and that deals with complete demo of hypothetical computer. This function is defined in the program file "hcwhycom.c". When user selects option two the function "cpumain()" is activated and that deals with complete demo of CPU operations. This function is defined in the program file "hcwcpu.c". When user selects option three the function "multimain()" is activated and that deals with complete demo of multiplexer. This function is defined in the program file "hewmul.c". When user selects option four the function "demulmain()" is activated and that deals with complete demo of de-multiplexer operations. This function is defined in the program file "hcwdemul.c".

1.C) Source Code:

1.C. I) Main module source code.

```
/* This is a main menu module to illustrate how computer works project.
This module displays the menu with 5 menu items, four of them calling other modules, namely
        1)  CPU,
        2)  Hypocom,
        3)  Multiplexer and
        4)  Demultiplexer.
    The last menu item is for terminating the project. The project is self-explainatory and menu
driven. The menu items can be selected through arrow keys from the keyboard. For simplicity all
other modules are made independent and are called from this module. */

/* The header files necessary for the project */

#include<conio.h>
#include<graphics.h>
```

```
#include<stdio.h>
#include<dos.h>
#include<math.h>
#include<alloc.h>
#include<string.h>
#include<ctype.h>

/* Inclusion of other module programs */
#include "hcwcpu.c"
#include "hcwhycom.c"
#include "hcwmul.c"
#include "hcwdemul.c"

/* The function declarations for calling other modules */
void hypomain();
void cpumain();
void multimain();
void demulmain();

/* The project execution starts from here */
void main()
{
 int gd=DETECT,gm,i,j,n,m,kb,chek=0;
 int ch=1;

 initgraph(&gd,&gm,""); /* graphics is initialized */

 setcolor(15);/* sets the foreground color to white */

  /* Draws the rectangular boxes for menu items. */
 for(i=1;i<=5;++i)
        {
        rectangle(150,i*50+50,305,i*50+100);
        }

/* sets the color, style and displays project heading and menu items in the respective boxes */
        setcolor(2);
        settextstyle(0,0,4);
        outtextxy(25,15,"ARCHITECTURAL DEMO");
        setcolor(3);
        outtextxy(25,405," OF COMPUTERS");

        settextstyle(3,0,4);
```

```
        setcolor(12);
        outtextxy(155,105,"HYPOCOM");
        outtextxy(155,155," CPU ");
        outtextxy(155,205,"MULTIPLEX");
        outtextxy(155,255,"DMULPLEX");
        outtextxy(155,305," EXIT");

/* Fills the first menu item, to show that it is selected */
        floodfill(154,ch*50+52,15);

chek=0;
/* The menu selection starts from here */
while(chek==0)
        {
        chek=0;
        setcolor(15);
/* redraws the rectangles for menu items */
        for(i=1;i<=5;++i)
        {
        rectangle(150,i*50+50,305,i*50+100);
        }

/* sets the color, style and displays project heading and menu items in the respective boxes */
        setcolor(2);
        settextstyle(0,0,4);
        outtextxy(25,15,"ARCHITECTURAL DEMO");
        setcolor(3);
        outtextxy(25,405," OF COMPUTERS");

        settextstyle(3,0,4);
        setcolor(12);
        outtextxy(155,105,"HYPOCOM");
        outtextxy(155,155," CPU ");
        outtextxy(155,205,"MULTIPLEX");
        outtextxy(155,255,"DMULPLEX");
        outtextxy(155,305," EXIT");

/* fills the first menu item box */
        setcolor(15);
        floodfill(154,ch*50+55,15);

/* When first menu item is selected, the item name gets erased because of fill effects of the
corresponding item box, so it rewrites menu item after doing the necessary settings */
```

```
if(ch==1)
{
        settextstyle(3,0,4);
        setcolor(12);
        outtextxy(155,105,"HYPOCOM");
        settextstyle(3,0,4);
}
```

/* When second menu item is selected, the item name gets erased because of fill effects of the corresponding item box, so it rewrites menu item after doing the necessary settings */

```
if(ch==2)
{
        settextstyle(3,0,4);
        setcolor(12);
        outtextxy(155,155," CPU ");
        settextstyle(3,0,4);
}
```

/* When third menu item is selected, the item name gets erased because of fill effects of the corresponding item box, so it rewrites menu item after doing the necessary settings */

```
if(ch==3)
{
        settextstyle(3,0,4);
        setcolor(12);
        outtextxy(155,205,"MULTIPLEX");
}
```

/* When fourth menu item is selected, the item name gets erased because of fill effects of the corresponding item box, so it rewrites menu item after doing the necessary settings */

```
if(ch==4)
{
        settextstyle(3,0,4);
        setcolor(12);
        outtextxy(155,255,"DMULPLEX");
}
```

/* When last menu item is selected, the item name gets erased because of fill effects of the corresponding item box, so it rewrites menu item after doing the necessary settings */

```
if(ch==5)
{
     settextstyle(3,0,4);
     setcolor(12);
     outtextxy(155,305," EXIT");
}
```

/* When first menu item is selected, the item name gets erased because of fill effects of the corresponding item box, so it rewrites menu item after doing the necessary settings */

```
if(ch==1)
{
     settextstyle(3,0,4);
     setcolor(12);
     outtextxy(155,105,"HYPOCOM");
}

kb=getche(); /* inputs the key pressed into the variable kb */

switch(kb) /* branching according to the key pressed */
{
```

/* when up arrow is pressed choice position is decreased by one and when choice reaches 0 it will be made to point to last menu item and then clears the graphical screen */

```
case 72:
     ch—;
     if(ch<1)
     ch=5;
     cleardevice();
     break;
```

/* when down arrow is pressed choice position is increased by one and when choice reaches 6 it will be made to point to first menu item and then clears the graphical screen */

```
case 80:
     ch++;
     if(ch>5)
     ch=1;
     cleardevice();
     break;
```

/* when enter key is pressed then based on choice position, we need to call the respective functions for activating respective modules */

```
case 13:
    switch(ch)
    {
```

/* When the choice is 1, call hypocom module. The graphics mode is closed before calling the module and reinitialized after returning back */

```
    case 1: closegraph();
        hypomain();
            initgraph(&gd,&gm,"");
            break;
```

/* When the choice is 2, call CPU module. The graphics mode is closed before calling the module and reinitialized after returning back */

```
    case 2: closegraph();
            cpumain();
            initgraph(&gd,&gm,"");
            break;
```

/* When the choice is 3, call Multiplexer module. The graphics mode is closed before calling the module and reinitialized after returning back */

```
    case 3: closegraph();
            multimain();
            initgraph(&gd,&gm,"");
            break;
```

/* When the choice is 4, call Demultiplexer module. The graphics mode is closed before calling the module and reinitialized after returning back */

```
    case 4: closegraph();
                demulmain();
                initgraph(&gd,&gm,"");
                break;
```

/* When the choice is 5, terminate the project. This is done by setting the chek variable to 1, which leads to termination of outer while loop */

```
case 5:
        chek=1;
        setcolor(2);
        outtextxy(150,400,"SUCCESS");
        break;
    } /* end of inner switch statement, used for calling modules after entry key is
pressed */

  } /* end of outer switch statement, used to check whether up arrow, down arrow or enter
key is pressed */

} /* end of while statement, that terminates when chek variable is having value other 0 */

closegraph(); /* closes the graph mode */

}/* end of main module of How computer works project */
```

1.C.II) The Hypocom Module of the project

```
/* This module shows the demo of activities that takes place in the Hypothetical computer
(HYPOCOM). The CPU consists of MAR, MDR, PC, IR, GPRs AND CU. First the signals from
CU travel through control bus and check the availability of IO/M unit for IO related activity. The
MAR sends the signals through address bus and gets the address of the IO/M unit from where data
has to be read or written. Then the data bus is used by MDR to transfer the data to or from the CPU
to IO/M. The appropriate messages that are displayed during the process make the demo more
understandable. There is no user input during the process. It makes use of functions for horizontal
and vertical movements */

/* This is completely independent module. If user wants to work with this module alone then just
change the function name 'void hypomain()' with 'void main()' and include all necessary header
files. */

/* functions declarations */
void ract_blink(int a,int b,int c,int d,int x);
void hor_rt(int a,int b,int c,int d);
void hor_lt(int a,int b,int c,int d);
void ver_up12(int a,int b,int c,int d);
void ver_dn12(int a,int b,int c,int d);
void drawskeleton();

/* The main of this module starts from here */

void hypomain()
```

```
{
int gd=DETECT,gm,i,x,y;

        initgraph(&gd,&gm,""); /* Graphics is initialized */
        /* to draw the skeleton of the hypocom */
        drawskeleton();
        /* message while showing the demo */
        outtextxy(100,350,"CONTROL UNIT UNDER PROGRESS");
        /* function call to make the respective rectangle to blink */
        ract_blink(180,230,280,270,2);
/* erasing the message before starting the other process. This is done by rewriting the same
message with background color */
        setcolor(0);
        outtextxy(100,350,"CONTROL UNIT UNDER PROGRESS");

/* message while showing the demo */
        setcolor(5);
        outtextxy(100,350," CONTROL SIGNALS PASSING TO IO");
/* The following set of function calls draw the lines and show the movements of signals from
control unit to IO unit */

        ver_up12(210,230,210,222);
        hor_rt(210,222,330,220);
        ver_up12(330,220,330,90);
        hor_rt(330,90,400,90);
        ver_dn12(400,90,400,130);
/* erasing the message before starting the other process. This is done by rewriting the same
message with background color */
        setcolor(0);
        outtextxy(100,350," CONTROL SIGNALS PASSING TO IO");

/* message while showing the demo */
        setcolor(5);
        outtextxy(100,350,"IO IS IN PROGRESS");

        setcolor(5);
        ract_blink(380,130,480,210,6);
/* erasing the message before starting the other process. This is done by rewriting the same
message with background color */
```

```
        setcolor(0);
        outtextxy(100,350,"IO IS IN PROGRESS");

        setcolor(5);
/* to draw the skeleton of the hypocom */
        drawskeleton();
/* message while showing the demo */
        delay(10);
        outtextxy(100,350,"MAR UNDER PROGRESS");
        ract_blink(60,110,140,150,20);
/* erasing the message before starting the other process. This is done by rewriting the same
message with background color */
        setcolor(0);
        outtextxy(100,350,"MAR UNDER PROGRESS");
/* message while showing the demo */
        setcolor(5);
        outtextxy(100,350,"ADRESS SIGNALS TO IO");
/* The following set of function calls draw the lines and show the movements of signals from MAR
unit to IO unit */
        ver_up12(100,110,100,60);
        hor_rt(100,60,430,60);
        ver_dn12(430,60,430,130);
/* erasing the message before starting the other process. This is done by rewriting the same message
    with background color */
        setcolor(0);
        outtextxy(100,350,"ADRESS SIGNALS TO IO");
/* message while showing the demo */
        setcolor(8);
        outtextxy(100,350,"IO IS INSPECTING ADRESS");
        ract_blink(380,130,480,210,6);
/* erasing the message before starting the other process. This is done by rewriting the same
message with background color */
        setcolor(0);
        outtextxy(100,350,"IO IS INSPECTING ADRESS");

/* to draw the skeleton of the hypocom */
        drawskeleton();
        delay(10);
/* message while showing the demo */
```

```
        outtextxy(100,350,"MDR IN PROGRESS");
        ract_blink(180,110,280,150,2);
/* erasing the message before starting the other process. This is done by rewriting the same
message with background color */
        setcolor(0);
        outtextxy(100,350,"MDR IN PROGRESS");

/* message while showing the demo */
        setcolor(5);
        outtextxy(100,350,"MDR SIGNALS TO IO");
/* The following set of function calls draw the lines and show the movements of signals from MDR
unit to IO unit */
        ver_up12(230,110,230,80);
        hor_rt(230,80,410,80);
        ver_dn12(410,80,410,130);
/* erasing the message before starting the other process. This is done by rewriting the same
message with background color */
        setcolor(0);
        outtextxy(100,350,"MDR SIGNALS TO IO");
/* message while showing the demo */
        setcolor(5);
        outtextxy(100,350,"MDR INSPECTING DATA");
        ract_blink(380,130,480,210,6);
/* erasing the message before starting the other process. This is done by rewriting the same
message with background color */
        setcolor(0);
        outtextxy(100,350,"MDR INSPECTING DATA");
/* to draw the skeleton of the hypocom */
        drawskeleton();
/* message while showing the demo */
        setcolor(5);
        outtextxy(100,350,"PLEASE WAIT A WHILE...");
        delay(2000);
}

/* to draw the skeleton of the hypocom */
void drawskeleton()
{
        int i,x,y;
```

```
        outtextxy(160,320,"CPU");
        rectangle(50,100,300,300); /* The border rectangle */
        setcolor(2);
        outtextxy(80,120,"MAR");
        rectangle(60,110,140,150); /* for MAR */
        outtextxy(215,120,"MDR");
        outtextxy(80,180,"GPR");
        outtextxy(80,240,"IR");
        outtextxy(215,180,"PC");
        outtextxy(215,240,"CU");
        outtextxy(415,160,"I/O");
        /* Rectangles for other units */
        rectangle(180,110,280,150);
        rectangle(60,170,140,210);
        rectangle(60,230,140,270);
        rectangle(180,170,280,210);
        rectangle(180,230,280,270);
        setcolor(6);
        rectangle(380,130,480,210);
        setcolor(10);
        /* draws address, data and control buses */
        line(100,110,100,60);
        line(230,110,230,80);
        line(100,60,430,60);
        line(230,80,410,80);
        line(430,60,430,130);
        line(410,80,410,130);
        line(210,230,210,222);
        line(210,222,330,222);
        line(330,222,330,90);
        line(330,90,400,90);
        line(400,90,400,130);
}

/* Function to show the movements of signals horizontally towards right */
void hor_rt(int a,int b,int c,int d)
{
        int i,j,x1,x2;
        if(a>c)
        {
```

```
            x1=a;
            x2=c;
        }
        else
        {
            x1=c;
            x2=a;
        }
        for(i=x2+2;i<x1-2;i++)
        {
            circle(i+1,b,2);/* To indicate the bigger signals circle with radius 2 pixels is
drawn */
            delay(10);
            setcolor(1);
            circle(i+1,b,2);
            delay(5);
        }

        d—;
}

/* Function to show the movements of signals horizontally towards left */ void hor_lt(int a,int b,int
c,int d)
{
        int i,j,x1,x2;
        if(a>c)
        {
            x1=a;
            x2=c;
        }
        else
        {
            x1=c;
            x2=a;
        }
        for(i=x1-2;i>x2+2;i—)
        {
            circle(i+1,b,2);
            delay(10);
            setcolor(1);
```

```
			circle(i-1,b,2);
			delay(5);
		}
		d—;

}

/* Function to show the movements of signals vertically up 12 pixels */
void ver_up12(int a,int b,int c,int d)
{
		int i,j,y1,y2;
		if(b>d)
		{
			y1=b;
			y2=d;
		}
		else
		{
			y1=d;
			y2=b;
		}
		for(i=y1-2;i>y2+2;i—)
		{
			circle(a,i+1,2);
			delay(10);
			setcolor(1);
			circle(a,i-2,2);
			delay(5);
		}
		c—;
}

/* Function to show the movements of signals vertically down 12 pixels */
void ver_dn12(int a,int b,int c,int d)
{
		int i,j,y1,y2;
		if(b<d)
		{
			y1=b;
			y2=d;
```

```
	}
	else
	{
		y1=d;
		y2=b;
	}
	for(i=y1+2;i<y2-2;i++)
	{
		circle(a,i-1,2);
		delay(10);
		setcolor(1);
		circle(a,i+2,2);
		delay(5);

	}
	c—;
}
```

/* Function to show the processing of the particular unit i.e., either CPU or MDR or MAR by making it to blink */

```
void ract_blink(int a,int b,int c,int d,int x)
{
	int i;
	for(i=2;i< 20 ;i+=4)
	{
	setcolor(i);
	rectangle(a,b,c,d);
	delay(1000);
	}
	setcolor(x);
	rectangle(a,b,c,d);
}
```

1.C.III) The CPU activity module

/* This module shows the demo of activities that takes place inside the CPU in any of the computers. The outside data enters into the bus interface, then it will be pre-fetched, checked for segment and page. Once these are identified then, actual data is fetched from bus interface by prefetch unit, the data is decoded, executed and output goes to the outside world through bus interface. There is no user input during the process. It makes use of functions for showing various activities that are needed in the module */

```
/* This is completely independent module. If user wants to work with this module alone then just
change the function name 'void cpumain()' with 'void main()' and include all necessary header
files. */

/* Functions declarations */
void blink(int a,int b,int c,int d);
void horight(int a,int b,int c,int d);
void ver_up(int a,int b,int c,int d);
void horlft(int a,int b,int c,int d);
void ver_dn(int a,int b,int c,int d) ;
void arcmove();
void arcmove1();

/* The CPU activity module starts from here */
void cpumain()
{
        int gd=DETECT,gm;
        initgraph(&gd,&gm,""); /* Graphics is initialized */

        setbkcolor(3); /* sets the background color to CYAN */
        setcolor(10); /* sets the foreground color to light green */
        rectangle(5,5,500,350); /* outer boundary for the entire unit */
        setcolor(4);/* sets the foreground color to RED */
        rectangle(6,6,499,349); /* outer boundary for the entire unit */

/* Draws the segment unit and makes necessary messaging and settings */
        setcolor(10);
        rectangle(7,7,498,348); /* outer boundary for the entire unit */
        setcolor(4);
        rectangle(50,20,150,80); /* rectangle for segment unit */
        outtextxy(55,45,"SEGMENT UNIT");
        setfillstyle(1,2);
        floodfill(55,25,4);/* fills the segment unit */

/* Draws the Decoder unit and makes necessary messaging and settings */
        rectangle(50,270,150,330);
        setfillstyle(1,4);
        floodfill(55,275,4);
        setcolor(10);
        outtextxy(55,295,"DECODER UNIT");
```

```
/* Draws the Prefetch unit and makes necessary messaging and settings */
        setcolor(4);
        rectangle(97,80,103,270);
        rectangle(250,20,350,80);
        setfillstyle(1,5);
        floodfill(255,25,4);
        setcolor(10);
        outtextxy(255,45," PREFETCH ");
        outtextxy(255,55," UNIT");

/* Draws the Paging unit and makes necessary messaging and settings */
        setcolor(4);
        rectangle(250,135,350,195);
        setfillstyle(1,13);
        floodfill(265,145,4);
        outtextxy(255,155," PAGING");
        outtextxy(255,165," UNIT");
        setcolor(4);
        rectangle(297,80,303,135);
        rectangle(297,195,303,250);
        rectangle(150,297,250,303);

/* Draws the Execution unit and makes necessary messaging and settings */
        rectangle(250,250,350,330);
        setfillstyle(1,7);
        floodfill(255,255,4);
        outtextxy(255,280," EXECUTION ");
        outtextxy(255,295," UNIT");

/* Draws the Bus interface unit and makes necessary messaging and settings */
        rectangle(410,105,470,230);
        setfillstyle(1,8);
        floodfill(455,225,4);
        outtextxy(420,140," BUS");
        outtextxy(420,155,"INTER");
        outtextxy(420,170," FACE");
        rectangle(470,164,640,170);

/* Function to draw the arc from execution unit to bus interface unit */
```

```
        arcmove();
        setcolor(4);
        rectangle(97,119,410,125);

/* Function to show the movements horizontally left from outside to bus interface unit */
        horlft(470,164,640,170);

/* Function to make the blinking effect to bus interface unit */
        blink(410,105,470,230);

/* Function to show the movements vertically down */
        ver_dn(297,80,303,125);
        horlft(97,120,303,125);

/* Function to show the movements vertically up */
        ver_up(97,80,103,125);
/* function call to show blinking effect in respective unit */
        blink(50,20,150,80);
        delay(200);

/* Function to show the movements vertically down */
        ver_dn(97,80,103,125);
        horight(97,119,303,125);

/* Function to show the movements vertically down */
        ver_dn(297,119,303,135);
/* function call to show blinking effect in respective unit */
        blink(250,135,350,195);
        delay(200);

/* Function to show the movements vertically up */
        ver_up(297,119,303,125);

/* Function to show the movements horizontally right */
        horight(297,119,410,125);
/* function call to show blinking effect in respective unit */
        blink(410,105,470,230);
        delay(200);
```

```
/* Function to show the movements horizontally left */
            horlft(297,119,410,125);

/* Function to show the movements vertically up */
            ver_up(297,80,303,125);
/* function call to show blinking effect in respective unit */
            blink(250,20,350,80);
            delay(200);

/* Function to show the movements vertically down */
            ver_dn(297,80,303,125);

/* Function to show the movements horizontally left */
            horlft(97,119,303,125);

/* Function to show the movements vertically down */
            ver_dn(97,119,103,270);
/* function call to show blinking effect in respective unit */
            blink(50,270,150,330);
            delay(200);

/* Function to show the movements horizontally right */
            horight(150,297,250,303);
/* function call to show blinking effect in respective unit */
            blink(250,250,350,330);
            delay(200);

/* Function to show the movement of arc from execution unit to bus interface */
            arcmove1();

            delay(2000); /* Waits for 2 seconds before switching to main module */
}

/* Function definition for horizontal left movement in the specified bus */
void horlft(int a,int b,int c,int d)
{
            int x,y,i,r,j;
            if(a<c)
            {
```

```
        x=c;
        y=a;
    }
    else
    {
        x=a;
        y=c;
    }
    r=(d-b)/2;

    for(i=(x-r);i>(y+r);i—)
    {
        setcolor(10);
        circle(i,(b+d)/2,2);
        setcolor(3);
        arc(i,(b+d)/2,270,70,2);
        delay(20);
    }
    for(j=(i+4);j>(y+r);j—)
    circle(j,(b+d)/2,2);
}

/* Function definition for horizontal right movement in the specified bus */
void horight(int a,int b,int c,int d)
{
    int x,y,i,r,j;
    if(a>c)
    {
        x=c;
        y=a;
    }
    else
    {
        x=a;
        y=c;
    }
    r=(d-b)/2;
    for(i=(x+r);i<(y-r);i++)
    {
```

```
            setcolor(10);
            circle(i,(b+d)/2,2);
            setcolor(3);
            arc(i,(b+d)/2,90,260,2);
            delay(20);
        }
        for(j=(i-4);j<(y-r);j++)
        circle(j,(b+d)/2,2);

}

/* Function definition for vertically down movement in the specified bus */
void ver_dn(int a,int b,int c,int d)
{
        int x,y,i,r,j;
        if(b<d)
        {
            x=b;
            y=d;
        }
        else
        {
            x=d;
            y=b;
        }
        r=(c-a)/2;
        for(i=(x+r);i<(y-r);i++)
        {
            setcolor(10);
            circle((a+c)/2,i,2);
            setcolor(3);
            arc((a+c)/2,i,10,170,2);
            delay(20);
        }
        for(j=(i-4);j<(y-r);j++)
        circle((a+c)/2,j,2);

}
```

```
/* Function definition for vertically up movement in the specified bus */
void ver_up(int a,int b,int c,int d)
{
        int x,y,i,r,j;
        if(b<d)
        {
                x=d;
                y=b;
        }
        else
        {
                x=b;
                y=d;
        }
        r=(c-a)/2;
        for(i=(x-r);i>(y+r);i—)
        {
                setcolor(10);
                circle((a+c)/2,i,2);
                setcolor(3);
                arc((a+c)/2,i,190,360,2);
                delay(20);
        }
        setcolor(3);
        for(j=(i+4);j>(y+r);j—)
        circle((a+c)/2,j,2);
}

/* Draws the arc from execution unit to bus interface unit */
void arcmove()
{
        int x,y,i,j=0;
        float x1=32,y1=38;
        setcolor(4);
        for(i=0;i<=100;++i)
        {
                x=x1*cos(i*3.142/180)+y1*sin(i*3.142/180);
                y=-x1*sin(i*3.142/180)+cos(i*3.142/180)*y1;
                setcolor(5);
```

```
                putpixel(x+322+i,y+266,5);
                if(i%14==0)
                {
                        j++;
                }
            putpixel(x+322+i-4+j,y+275-j/2,5);
        }
}

/* function for movements along the arc from execution unit to bus interface */
void arcmove1()
{
        int x,y,i;
        float x1=32,y1=38;
        circle(352,308,2);
        for(i=0;i<=100;++i)
        {
                x=x1*cos(i*3.142/180)+y1*sin(i*3.142/180);
                y=-x1*sin(i*3.142/180)+cos(i*3.142/180)*y1;
                setcolor(5);
                circle(x+322+i,y+270,2);
                circle(x+322+i,y+270,1);
                delay(50);
                setcolor(3);
                circle(x+322+i,y+270,2);
                circle(x+322+i,y+270,1);
        }
        arcmove();
        blink(410,105,470,230);
        horight(470,164,640,170);
        getch();
}

/* function definition for making the rectangular areas of respective units according to the co-
ordinates to blink for a while */
void blink(int a,int b,int c,int d)
{
        setcolor(5);
        rectangle(a,b,c,d);
```

```
        delay(250);
        setcolor(10);
        rectangle(a,b,c,d);
        delay(250);
        setcolor(15);
        rectangle(a,b,c,d);
        setcolor(20);
        rectangle(a,b,c,d);
        delay(250);
        rectangle(a,b,c,d);
        setcolor(25);
        rectangle(a,b,c,d);
        delay(250);
        setcolor(30);
        rectangle(a,b,c,d);
        delay(250);
        setcolor(35);
        rectangle(a,b,c,d);
}
```

1.C. IV) The multiplexer module

/* This module gives demo of multiplexer. The multiplexer, as the name indicates takes many inputs and gives one output. In this module we have considered only OR and AND gates with two inputs at a time. The output of previous gate becomes input to the next gate. This expression in terms of arithmetic expression is taken from the user which in turn consists of only alphabets of character length and only '+' and '.' symbols. The '+' indicates or and '.' indicates and. The input expression is validated and according to the expression the gate circuit of multiplexer is drawn. The sound effect is given to make it more attractive during demo. */

/* This is completely independent module. If user wants to work with this module alone then just change the function name 'void multimain()' with 'void main()' and include all necessary header files. */

```
/* function declarations for drawing AND and OR gates */
void or1(int,int );
void and1(int,int);

/* The function of this module starts here*/
void multimain()
```

```
{

char s[20],s1[20],s2[5]; /* for storing expressions as strings */

int i,l,t=0,gd=DETECT,gm,k2=0;

/* user input of expression with validation starts here */
do
{
        t=0; /* flag is set to 0 */
        clrscr(); /* Clears the text mode screen */

        puts(" enter expression\n");
        gets(s);
        l=strlen(s);

/* Because of screen resolution the expression length is limited to 20 characters long */
if(l>20)
        {
        t=1;
        printf("\n the length of expression should not exceed 20 characters\n");
        }
else
if(l%2!=1) /* when the length of expression is not odd then that should not be the valid expression */
        {
        printf("\n wrong expression\n"); /* message for wrong expression */
        t=1; /* sets the flag variable to 1 */
        }
else
        {
/* checks for each of the odd position characters in the given string is an alphabet or not. if they are not alphabets then the given expression becomes invalid and flag is set to 1 */
        for(i=0;i<l;i=i+2)
        if(!isalpha(s[i]))
                {
                t=1;
                printf("\n wrong expression\n");
                break;
```

```
        }
/* checks for each of the even position characters in the given string is either '+' or '.' or not . if
they are not '+' or '.' then the given expression becomes invalid and flag is set to 1 */
        for(i=1;i<l;i=i+2)
        if(!((s[i]=='.')||(s[i]=='+')))
            {
            t=1;
            printf("\n wrong expression\n");
            break;
            }
        }

        delay(100);
}while(t!=0); /* end of user input. it continues until user enters correct input */

/* Graphical demo starts from here */

initgraph(&gd,&gm,""); /* Initializes the graphics mode */
        s2[0]=s[0];
        s2[1]='\0';

/* displays the first character of the expression */
        outtextxy(70,200,s2);

for(i=1;i<l;i=i+2)
{
        s2[0]=s[i+1];
        s2[1]='\0';
        sound(1000+i*50);
        delay(500);

/* displays the next successive alphabets from the expression in respective positions */

        outtextxy(70+k2*60,200+k2*6+15,s2);
        sound(1500-i*100); /* sound effect */
        delay(500);

/* when the operator part is a '.' it calls and gets the AND gate into the respective position */
if(s[i]=='.')
```

```
        {
        and1(i,k2);
        k2++;
        }
else
        {
/* when the operator part is a '+' it calls and gets the OR gate into the respective position */
        or1(i,k2);
        k2++;
        }
} /* END OF FOR LOOP */

/* Displays the final output message */
        outtextxy(84+k2*60,205+k2*6,"output");
        nosound(); /* turns the internal speaker off */
        delay(2000); /* waits for 2 seconds before switching to main module automatically */
} /* End of multimain() */

/* function for creating and storing the or symbol into void *z variable*/
void and1(int k,int k1)
{
        void *z;

/* AND gate construction */
        line(100,100,100,120); /* line for output of AND gate */
        ellipse(100,110,270,90,15,10); /* Ellipse for AND gate */
        line(82,104,100,104); /* line for first input to AND gate */
        line(82,116,100,116); /* line for second input to AND gate */
        line(115,110,141,110); /* line for closing the half ellipse to AND gate */

/* Allocates the memory and gets the AND gate image into the variable z */
        z=malloc(imagesize(81,99,142,121));
        getimage(81,99,142,121,z);

        putimage(81,99,z,1); /* Erases the original location image */
        putimage(80+k1*60,k*3+200,z,2); /* re-writes the image of AND gate in the respective
        position according expression */
```

```
} /* end of function for AND gate */

/* function for creating and storing the or symbol into void *z variable*/

void or1(int k,int k1)
{
        void *z;

/* OR gate construction */
        line(100,150,130,160);
        line(100,170,130,160);
        line(130,160,150,160);
        ellipse(100,160,270,90,5,10);
        line(90,154,103,154);
        line(90,166,103,166);

/* Allocates the memory and gets the OR gate image into the variable z */
        z=malloc(imagesize(89,150,150,176));
        getimage(89,150,150,176,z);

        putimage(89,150,z,1); /* Erases the original location image */
        putimage(80+k1*60,k*3+200,z,2); /* re-writes the image of AND gate in the respective
        position according to the expression */

}/* end of function for OR gate */
```

1.C. V) The Demultiplexer module

/* This module shows the demo of demultiplexer. In demultiplexer there are one or two inputs and many outputs. Here we have considered two inputs and many outputs. The outputs of all possible gates with one or two inputs are shown. It won't accept any inputs from user. The gates for demo considered are AND, OR, NAND, NOR, XOR, XNOR and NOT. For each of these gates we have used the functions for drawing. The sound effect is also given for effective demo. */

/* This is completely independent module. If user wants to work with this module alone then just change the function name 'void demulmulmain()' with 'void main()' and include all necessary header files. */

/* Function declarations for various functions that draw electronic gate circuits */

```
void and();
void nand();
void or();
void nor();
void not();
void xor();
void xnor();
void makesound(int);

        void *z;        /* Global variable for storing the image of the gate circuit and displaying
them in the respective position in the demultiplexer circuit */

/* The module operation starts here */
void demulmain()
{
  int gd=DETECT,gm,i,x,y;

  initgraph(&gd,&gm," "); /* Graphics is initialized */

  line(389,50,389,355); /* line for demultiplexer main input and output separator */
  makesound(430); /* Function call for sound effect */

  line(389,246,300,246); /* line for second input */
  makesound(730);
  line(389,156,300,156); /* line for first input line */
  makesound(330);

  outtextxy(290,240,"b"); /* second input message */
  makesound(830);
  outtextxy(290,150,"a"); /* first input message */
  makesound(2300);
  makesound(230);

/* AND gate implementation */
        and(); /* function for drawing and getting the AND gate image */
        makesound(450);
        putimage(389,100,z,2); /* Puts the AND gate in respective position in the circuit */
        free(z); /* Frees the memory allocated to global variable z */
        makesound(1500);
```

```
        outtextxy(430,96,"a.b");
        makesound(2830);

/* OR gate implementation */
        or(); /* function for drawing and getting the OR gate image */
        makesound(230);
        putimage(389,130,z,2); /* Puts the OR gate in respective position in the circuit */
        free(z); /* Frees the memory allocated to global variable z */
        makesound(130);
        outtextxy(430,126,"a+b");
        makesound(280);

/* NOT gate implementation */
        not(); /* function for drawing and getting the NOT gate image */
        makesound(1230);
        putimage(389,160,z,2); /* Puts the NOT gate in respective position in the circuit */
        free(z);
        makesound(2030);
        line(447,154,452,154);
        makesound(2300);
        outtextxy(430,156," a");
        makesound(2030);

/* NAND gate implementation */
        nand(); /* function for drawing and getting the NAND gate image */
        makesound(1230);
        putimage(389,190,z,2); /* Puts the NAND gate in respective position in the circuit */
        free(z);
        makesound(230);
        line(430,184,450,184);
        makesound(1230);
        outtextxy(430,186,"a.b");
        makesound(2000);

/* NOR gate implementation */
        nor();
        makesound(300);
        putimage(389,220,z,2);
        free(z);
        makesound(130);
```

```
        line(430,214,450,214);
        makesound(230);
        outtextxy(430,216,"a+b");
        makesound(1230);

/* XOR gate implementation */
        xor();
        makesound(630);
        putimage(389,250,z,2);
        free(z);
        makesound(430);
        outtextxy(430,246,"a + b");
        makesound(2430);
        circle(448,249,5);
        makesound(430);

/* XNOR gate implementation */
        xnor();
        makesound(130);
        putimage(389,280,z,2);
        free(z);
        makesound(230);
        line(430,273,470,273);
        makesound(230);
        outtextxy(430,276,"a + b");
        makesound(2300);
        circle(448,279,5);
        makesound(1230);

 delay(2000); /* waits for 2 seconds before transferring the program control to main */
} /* End of demultiplexer */

/* function for creating and storing the XNOR symbol into void *z variable*/

void xnor()
 {
        line(200,250,230,260);
        line(200,270,230,260);
        line(236,260,250,260);
        circle(233,260,3);
```

```
        ellipse(200,260,270,90,5,10);
        ellipse(197,260,270,90,5,10);
        line(190,255,200,255);
        line(190,265,200,265);
        z=malloc(imagesize(189,249,251,270));
        getimage(189,249,251,270,z);
        putimage(189,249,z,1);
}

/* Function for creating and storing the XOR symbol into void *z variable*/

void xor()
{
        line(100,250,130,260);
        line(100,270,130,260);line(130,260,150,260);
        ellipse(100,260,270,90,5,10);
        ellipse(97,260,270,90,5,10);
        line(90,255,100,255);
        line(90,265,100,265);
        z=malloc(imagesize(89,249,151,270));
        getimage(89,249,151,270,z);
        putimage(89,249,z,1);
}

/* function for creating and storing the NOT symbol into void *z variable*/

void not()
{
        line(100,190,130,200);
        line(100,210,130,200);
        line(136,200,150,200);
        circle(133,200,3);
        line(90,200,100,200);
        line(100,190,100,210);
        z=malloc(imagesize(89,189,151,211));
        getimage(89,189,151,211,z);
        putimage(89,189,z,1);
}
```

```
/* function for creating and storing the NOR symbol into void *z variable*/

void nor()
{
        line(200,150,230,160);
        line(200,170,230,160);
        line(236,160,250,160);
        ellipse(200,160,270,90,5,10);
        line(190,155,203,155);
        line(190,165,203,165);
        circle(233,160,3);
        z=malloc(imagesize(189,150,251,170));
        getimage(189,150,251,170,z);
        putimage(189,150,z,1);
}

/* function for creating and storing the AND symbol into void *z variable*/

void and()
{
        line(100,100,100,120);
        ellipse(100,110,270,90,15,10);
        line(90,105,100,105);
        line(90,115,100,115);
        line(115,110,148,110);
        z=malloc(imagesize(89,99,149,121));
        getimage(89,99,149,121,z);
        putimage(89,99,z,1);
}

/* function for creating and storing the NAND symbol into void *z variable*/

void nand()
{
        line(200,100,200,120);
        ellipse(200,110,270,90,15,10);
        line(190,105,200,105);
        line(190,115,200,115);
        line(221,110,248,110);
        circle(218,110,3);
```

```
        z=malloc(imagesize(189,99,249,121));
        getimage(189,99,249,121,z);
        putimage(189,99,z,1);
}

/* function for creating and storing the OR symbol into void *z variable*/

void or()
{
        line(100,150,130,160);
        line(100,170,130,160);
        line(130,160,150,160);
        ellipse(100,160,270,90,5,10);
        line(90,155,103,155);
        line(90,165,103,165);
        z=malloc(imagesize(89,150,150,170));
        getimage(89,150,150,170,z);
        putimage(89,150,z,1);
}

/* function for sound effect */
void makesound(int k)
{
        sound(k);
        delay(1000);
        nosound();
}
```

PROJECT 2

LAN TOPOLOGIES

2.A) SYNOPSIS

This LAN topology project mainly Concentrates on Simulation of different LAN Topologies such as *BUS ,RING, SERIAL, STAR,* Etc, through which the computer in the LAN gets connected. There will be a number of client systems connected to server. The client initiates the communication or request to server and server response to client's request. In LAN the client can be connected to server in different ways as given below

The menu options are,

BUS

RING

STAR

SERIAL

EXIT

2.A. i) BUS TOPOLOGY

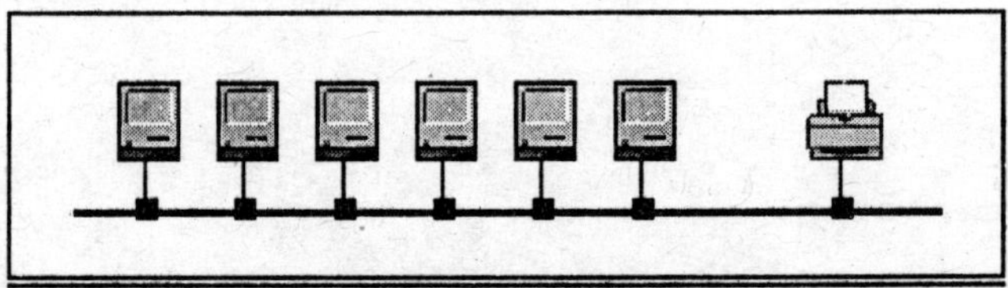

A bus network topology

A bus topology (linear bus) has each station connected to the main cable or backbone using T connection. The backbone is connected to the server at one end and the other end is kept open or it can be connected to a client in the network. Any station can send a packet at any time although only one station at a time can do so. When a server sends a packet(message) the packet header consists of identification about its respective client. The packet is transmitted over a linear bus to its entire length. The destination computer to which the packet is addressed to is also connected to the same linear bus. The transmitted packet is made to reach all the clients connected to the linear bus. Whenever a packet is received by any client address checking is performed to know whether the address to which the packet is destined and the current clients address are matching. If both the address match each other then the client absorbs the message or else it rejects the packet. Bus networks are often used for temporary LANs because the set up is so fast and simple. However if the backbone goes down, the entire LAN goes down. If there is a problem at a station, it may be difficult to isolate it.

2.A.ii) RING TOPOLOGY

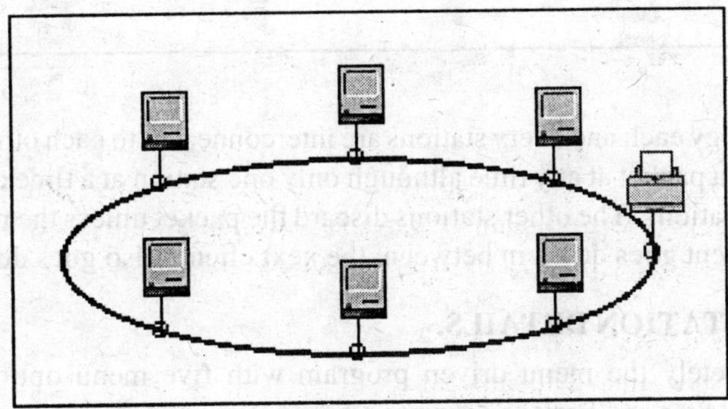

Ring network topology

In this topology all the clients are connected to the server in a ring fashion as shown in the diagram. Here we have to show how data transfer takes place from server to clients and client to server with the help of animation. Any station can send a packet around the ring to the server. When the server sends the message in the form of a packet to the client it traverses the entire ring and each and every client when they come across the packet can check the address on the packet and if a packet belongs to them then only they can accept it. The packet traverses the ring until it gets absorbed by its respective client.

2.A.iii) STAR TOPOLOGY

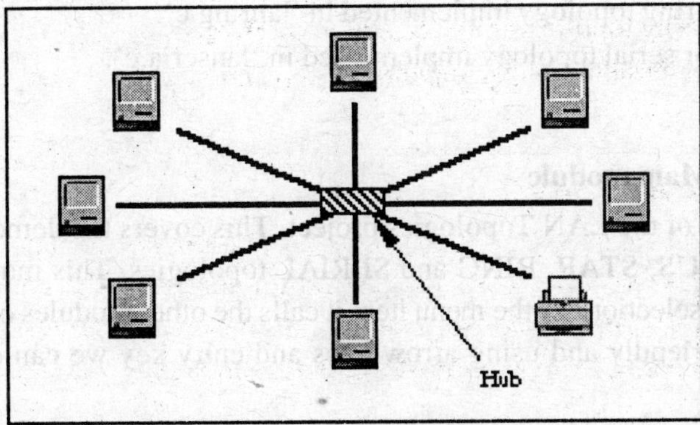

A star topology has each station connected to a central hub. Any station can send a packet at any time although only one station at a time can do so. A packet is sent from a station to the hub. The hub retransmits the packet to the other stations. The other stations discard the packet unless the packet is addressed to it. This is probably the easiest topology to configure although a star topology requires more cabling than either bus or ring topologies. If a station goes down, it does not bring down the entire LAN. However if the hub goes down, then it brings down the entire LAN.

2.A. iv) SERIAL TOPOLOGY

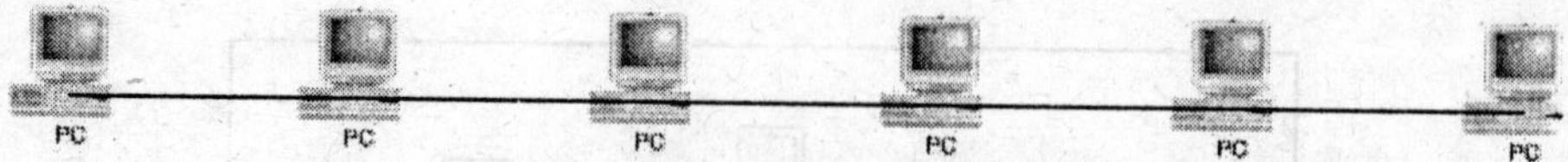

In serial topology each and every stations are interconnected to each other without backbone. Any station can send a packet at any time although only one station at a time can do so. The packet goes to all the other stations. The other stations discard the packet unless the packet is addressed to it. However if any client goes down in between, the next clients also goes down.

2.A. v) IMPLEMENTATION DETAILS.

This is completely the menu driven program with five menu options. For each of the topologies Bus, Ring, Star and Serial a separate module is created. These modules are called from main function based on user's selection to view of the working of different topologies. We have imposed a constraint on number of nodes to be maximum 10 and minimum one which is taken as input before demonstrating any topology. And also the input is taken for which clients are participating in communication from the user and the input is validated for its availability.

In the topologies like Star and Ring different circle drawing algorithms are used to locate the clients and their positions.

The different modules are,

1. busmain() for bus topology implemented in 'lanbus.c'.
2. starmain() for star topology implemented in 'lanstar.c'.
3. ringmain() for ring topology implemented in 'lanring.c'.
4. serialmain() for serial topology implemented in 'lanseria.c'.

2.B) SOURCE CODE

2.B. i) The LAN Project Main module

```
/* This is the main module of the LAN Topologies project. This covers the demonstration of four main topologies namely BUS, STAR, RING and SERIAL topologies. This module displays the menu and according to the selections of the menu item it calls the other modules of the project. The menu is completely user friendly and using arrow keys and entry key we can choose the menu items. */

/* Header files necessary for this project */
#include<conio.h>
#include<graphics.h>
#include<stdio.h>
#include<dos.h>
#include<math.h>
#include<alloc.h>
```

```
/*The modules included in this project */
        #include "lanbus.c"
        #include "lanring.c"
        #include "lanstar.c"
        #include "lanseria.c"

/* The functions of the modules that are called from main module */
        void busmain();
        void ringmain();
        void starmain();
        void serialmain();

/* Main menu module starts from here */

void main()
{
 int gd=DETECT,gm,i,j,n,m,kb,chek=0;
   int ch=1;
   initgraph(&gd,&gm,""); /* graphics is initialized */

/* draws the rectangles for menu items */
   for(i=1;i<=5;++i)
        rectangle(150,i*50+50,305,i*50+100);

   setcolor(2);
   settextstyle(0,0,4); /* setting the styles of the heading of the project */

/* Displays the heading of the project */
        outtextxy(25,15," SIMULATION OF");
        setcolor(3);
        outtextxy(25,405," LAN TOPOLOGIES ");

/* Setting the color and text styles of the menu items */
        settextstyle(3,0,4);
        setcolor(12);

/* Menu items display */
        outtextxy(155,105," BUS");
        outtextxy(155,155," RING ");
        outtextxy(155,205," STAR");
```

```
        outtextxy(155,255," SERIAL");
        outtextxy(155,305," EXIT");

/* filling the first menu item box to indicate its selection */
        floodfill(154,ch*50+52,15);
        chek=0; /* the flag is reset to 0 and when it becomes 1 the program terminates */

/* the main menu selection process starts from here */
while(chek==0)
 {
        chek=0;
        setcolor(15);
        for(i=1;i<=5;++i)
                rectangle(150,i*50+50,305,i*50+100);

/* setting the styles and color of the heading of the project */
        setcolor(2);
        settextstyle(0,0,4);
/* Displays the heading of the project */
        outtextxy(25,15," SIMULATION OF");
        setcolor(3);
        outtextxy(25,405," LAN TOPOLOGIES");

/* Setting the color and text styles of the menu items */
        settextstyle(3,0,4);
        setcolor(12);

        outtextxy(155,105," BUS");
        outtextxy(155,155," RING ");
        outtextxy(155,205," STAR");
        outtextxy(155,255," SERIAL");
        outtextxy(155,305," EXIT");

/* filling the first menu item box to indicate its selection */
        setcolor(15);
        floodfill(154,ch*50+55,15);
        setcolor(12);

/* when the ch variable is 1, then the first menu item is filled and it has to be redrawn */
        if(ch==1)
```

```
    {
        settextstyle(3,0,4);
        setcolor(12);
        outtextxy(155,105," BUS");
    }
/* when the ch variable is 2, then the second menu item is filled and it has to be redrawn */
    if(ch==2)
    {
        settextstyle(3,0,4);
        setcolor(12);
        outtextxy(155,155," RING");
    }
/* when the ch variable is 3, then the third menu item is filled and it has to be redrawn */
    if(ch==3)
    {
        settextstyle(3,0,4);
        setcolor(12);
        outtextxy(155,205," STAR");
    }
/* when the ch variable is 4, then the fourth menu item is filled and it has to be redrawn */
    if(ch==4)
    {
        settextstyle(3,0,4);
        setcolor(12);
        outtextxy(155,255," SERIAL");
    }
/* when the ch variable is 5, then the fifth menu item is filled and it has to be redrawn */
    if(ch==5)
    {
        settextstyle(3,0,4);
        setcolor(12);
        outtextxy(155,305," EXIT");
    }
/* when the ch variable is 1, then the first menu item is filled and it has to be redrawn */
    if(ch==1)
```

```
        {
            settextstyle(3,0,4);
            setcolor(12);
            outtextxy(155,105," BUS");
        }

/* menu selection process starts from here */
        kb=getche(); /* Getting the selection into the variable */
/* when the selection is made using arrow keys, then accordingly menu item selection changes */
        switch(kb)
        {
        case 72: /* checks for upper key pressed */
                ch—; /* decrements the menu item counter by 1 */
                if(ch<1) /* when it goes below 1 it will be set to last menu item */
                ch=5;
                cleardevice(); /* clears the graphical screen */
                break;
        case 80:/* checks for upper key pressed */
                ch++; /* increments the menu item counter by 1 */
                if(ch>5) /* when it goes above 5 it will be set to first menu item */
                ch=1;
                cleardevice();
                break;
        case 13:/* when the pressed key is enter key then according to the menu item counter, it
calls the other modules of the project */

                switch(ch)
                {

                /* When ch is 1, it calls bus topology module of the project */
                case 1:
                        closegraph();
                        busmain();
                        initgraph(&gd,&gm,"");
                        break;

                /* When ch is 2, it calls ring topology module of the project */
                case 2:
                        closegraph();
                        ringmain();
```

```
                initgraph(&gd,&gm,"");
                break;
        /* When ch is 3, it calls star topology module of the project */
        case 3:
                closegraph();
                starmain();
                initgraph(&gd,&gm,"");
                break;
        /* When ch is 4, it calls serial topology module of the project */
        case 4:
                closegraph();
                serialmain();
                initgraph(&gd,&gm,"");
                break;

        /* When ch is 5, it terminates the project by setting chek to 1 */
        case 5:
                chek=1;
                setcolor(2);
                outtextxy(150,400,"SUCCESS");
                break;
        }/* end of switch(ch) */
    } /* end of switch(kb) */

} /* end of while */
closegraph(); /* closes the graphics mode of the project */
} /* end of main menu module of the program */
```

2.B. ii) The LAN BUS module

/* This module deals with BUS topology in LAN network. The complete information about how the client signals are passed to the server and how server processes the request and gives back the response is shown with graphical demo. The number of nodes is limited to 10 and they are arranged on both the sides of the LAN cable that is represented by line. The clients and server are shown with the rectangles. The user has to enter the client number. Then the client is made to blink with the message to indicate 'the client in progress'. Then the signal passing from client to server is shown with colored pixels and respective message. The server is made to blink for a while to indicate its process and finally the response from server is shown again with coloured pixels */

/* This module is totally independent and to run it independently just change function name ' void busmain()' with 'void main()' and include all necessary header files. */

```
void busmain()
  {
  int gd=DETECT, gm;
  int i, k, j, n;
  char s[10],ch;

  /* Text mode user input of number of nodes and validity of input */
  do
  {
          printf("\n Enter no of nodes\n");
          scanf("%d",&n);
          if (n>10 || n<=0)
          printf("n must be <= 10 and n>0 \n re-enter...\n");

}while(n>10 || n<=0);

/* Graphics is initialized here */
initgraph(&gd,&gm,"");

/* LAN network construction starts from here */

/* displaying the rectangle and message for server */
rectangle(20,getmaxy()/2-40,80,getmaxy()/2+40);
outtextxy(25,getmaxy()/2-5,"Server");

/* drawing the line based on length required */
if(n%2==0)
          line(80,getmaxy()/2,100+(n/2)*80,getmaxy()/2);
 else
          line(80,getmaxy()/2,100+(n/2+1)*80,getmaxy()/2);

 k=1; /* Count for number of rectangles on top side of the line */

/* Draws the rectangles for clients and puts the client numbers within that rectangles. Also draws
a line connecting theses client nodes with LAN cable line */
  for(i=1;i<=n;i=i+2)
  {
          rectangle(160+(k-1)*80,getmaxy()/2-80,200+(k-1)*80,getmaxy()/2-40);
          line(180+(k-1)*80,getmaxy()/2,180+(k-1)*80,getmaxy()/2-40);
```

```
        sprintf(s,"%d",i);
        outtextxy(175+(k-1)*80,getmaxy()/2-65,s);
        k++;
  }

  k=1;/* Count for number of rectangles on bottom side of the line */

  /* Draws the rectangles for clients and puts the client numbers within that rectangles.
Also draws a line connecting theses client nodes with LAN cable line */
  for(i=2;i<=n;i=i+2)
  {
        rectangle(160+(k-1)*80,getmaxy()/2+80,200+(k-1)*80,getmaxy()/2+40);
        line(180+(k-1)*80,getmaxy()/2,180+(k-1)*80,getmaxy()/2+40);
        sprintf(s,"%d",i);
        outtextxy(175+(k-1)*80,getmaxy()/2+65,s);
        k++;
  }

/* LAN process demo starts from here */

do /* for processing as many times as user likes */
  {

        /* For inputting and validating the node number to process */
        do
        {
        outtextxy(10,10,"Enter terminal to process");
        moveto(10,20);
        scanf("%d",&j);
        if(j>n || j<=0) /* When the client number is not within the number of nodes */
         {
              outtextxy(20,30,"Terminal not existing");
              outtextxy(20,40,"re-enter...");
              delay(2000);
              setcolor(0);
              outtextxy(20,30,"Terminal not existing");
              outtextxy(20,40,"re-enter...");
              setcolor(15);
         }
        }while(j>n || j<=0);
```

```
/* When the client number is an odd number then that client is existing on top of the line. The following code implements it */
if(j%2==1)
{

/* making the client to blink 10 times and displaying the related message */
for(i=1;i<=10;++i)
{
        outtextxy(100,340,"Client in process");
        setcolor(i);
        rectangle(160+(j/2)*80,getmaxy()/2-80,200+(j/2)*80,getmaxy()/2-40);
        sprintf(s,"%d",j);
        outtextxy(175+(j/2)*80,getmaxy()/2-65,s);
        delay(200);/* waits for .2 seconds */
}
        /* Erases the message by rewriting with background color */
        setcolor(0);
        outtextxy(100,340,"Client in process");

/* Shows the clients request movement with respective message downwards */
for(i=getmaxy()/2-40;i<=getmaxy()/2;++i)
{
        putpixel(180+(j/2)*80,i,12);
        delay(20);
        setcolor(j);
        outtextxy(100,340,"Client signals to server");
}

/* Shows the clients request movement with respective message towards server */
for(i=180+(j/2)*80;i>=80;—i)
{
        putpixel(i,getmaxy()/2,12);
        delay(20);
}

/* Erases the message by rewriting with background color */
        setcolor(0);
        outtextxy(100,340,"Client signals to server");
```

```
/* Makes the server to blink 10 times and displays the related message */
for(i=1;i<=10;++i)
{
        setcolor(i);
        rectangle(20,getmaxy()/2-40,80,getmaxy()/2+40);
        outtextxy(25,getmaxy()/2-5,"Server");
        delay(200);
        setcolor(j);
        outtextxy(100,340,"server checking the request");
}

/* Erases the message by rewriting with background color */
        setcolor(0);
        outtextxy(100,340,"server checking the request");

/* Shows the server response movement with respective message horizontally towards client */
for(i=80;i<=180+(j/2)*80;++i)
{
        putpixel(i,getmaxy()/2,1);
        delay(20);
        setcolor(j+1);
        outtextxy(100,340,"server response to request");
}

/* Shows the server response movement with respective message up towards client */
for(i=getmaxy()/2;i>=getmaxy()/2-40;—i)
{
        putpixel(180+(j/2)*80,i,1);
        delay(20);
}
        setcolor(0);
        outtextxy(100,340,"server response to request");

} /* end of if and end of demo for upward clients */

else /* For the demo of clients present below the line */
{

/* making the client to blink 10 times and displaying the related message */
for(i=1;i<=10;++i)
{
```

```
        setcolor(i);
        rectangle(160+(j/2-1)*80,getmaxy()/2+40,200+(j/2-1)*80,getmaxy()/2+80);
        sprintf(s,"%d",j);
        outtextxy(175+(j/2-1)*80,getmaxy()/2+65,s);
        setcolor(j);
        outtextxy(100,340,"Client in process");
        delay(200);
}
        /* Erases the message by rewriting with background color */
        setcolor(0);
        outtextxy(100,340,"Client in process");

/* Shows the clients request movement with respective message upwards */
for(i=getmaxy()/2+40;i>=getmaxy()/2;--i)
{
        putpixel(180+(j/2-1)*80,i,12);
        setcolor(j);
        outtextxy(100,340,"Client signals to server");
        delay(20);
}

/* Shows the clients request movement with respective message towards server */
for(i=180+(j/2-1)*80;i>=80;--i)
{
        putpixel(i,getmaxy()/2,12);
        delay(20);
}

        setcolor(0);
        outtextxy(100,340,"Client signals to server");

/* Makes the server to blink 10 times and displays the related message */
for(i=1;i<=10;++i)
{
        setcolor(i);
        rectangle(20,getmaxy()/2-40,80,getmaxy()/2+40);
        outtextxy(25,getmaxy()/2-5,"Server");
        setcolor(j);
        outtextxy(100,340,"server checking the request");
```

```
            delay(200);
    }

    /* Erases the message by rewriting with background color */
            setcolor(0);
            outtextxy(100,340,"server checking the request");

    /* Shows the server response movement with respective message horizontally towards client */
    for(i=80;i<=180+(j/2-1)*80;++i)
    {
            putpixel(i,getmaxy()/2,1);
            setcolor(j+1);
            outtextxy(100,340,"server response to request");
            delay(20);
    }

    /* Shows the server response movement with respective message up towards client */
    for(i=getmaxy()/2;i<=getmaxy()/2+40;++i)
    {
            putpixel(180+(j/2-1)*80,i,1);
            delay(20);
    }

            setcolor(0);
            outtextxy(100,340,"server response to request");

    } /* end of else part */

    /* Checking user response for next node processing */
            setcolor(0);
            outtextxy(10,10,"Enter terminal to process");
            setcolor(15);
            outtextxy(10,10,"Any more operation (y/n)?");
            fflush(stdin); /* clears the buffer */
            ch=getch();
            setcolor(0);
            outtextxy(10,10,"Any more operation (y/n)?");
            setcolor(15);
            ch=toupper(ch);
    }while(ch=='Y');
```

```
delay(2000);/* waits for 2 seconds before going back to main menu */
} /* end BUS topology module */
```

2.B. iii) The LAN RING topology module

/* This module shows the demo of RING topology in LAN. The numbers of clients are restricted to 10. The first node itself is made as server and is also shown in the ring itself. The Bresneham's Circle drawing algorithm is used to draw the circle. The clients/nodes are shown with rectangles. Based on the number of nodes the circle is divided into parts. The movements of the signals from client to server and server to client are shown with putpixel and different colors are used to distinguish them. The proper delay is used to make the demo more effective. The signal movements from client to server make use of nearest path. The proper messages are displayed to make demo more effective. */

/* This module is totally independent and to run it independently just change function name 'void ringmain()' with 'void main()' and include all necessary header files. */

```
void ringmain()
{
int gd=DETECT,gm,i,j,k,n,x1,y1;
float x,y,ii;
int a,jj,b,c,d,l;
float e,e1,dx,dy;
char s[10],ch;

clrscr();

/* The user input for number of nodes and its validation */
do
{
        printf("\n enter no of nodes ");
        scanf("%d",&n);
        if(n>10 || n<=0)
        printf("\n n must be <=10 and n>0\n");
}while(n>10 || n<=0);

/* Graphical demo starts here */
initgraph(&gd,&gm,"");
```

```
/* movements of signals from client to server node and visa versa */
do
{
/* construction of LAN RING */
        x=125;
        y=125;
        k=360/n; /* The angle between each clients in degrees */
        j=1;
        setcolor(5);
        i=0;
/* The angle is converted to radian and a single pixel is drawn at the center of the server box */
        x1=x*cos(i*3.142/180)+y*sin(i*3.142/180);
        y1=-x*sin(i*3.142/180)+y*cos(i*3.142/180);
        putpixel(getmaxx()/2+x1,getmaxy()/2+y1,4);

/* To draw the server with rectangles */
        rectangle(getmaxx()/2+x1-20,getmaxy()/2+y1-20,getmaxx()/2+x1+20,getmaxy()/
        2+y1+20);
        rectangle(getmaxx()/2+x1-30,getmaxy()/2+y1-30,getmaxx()/2+x1+30,getmaxy()/
        2+y1+30);
        rectangle(getmaxx()/2+x1-25,getmaxy()/2+y1-25,getmaxx()/2+x1+25,getmaxy()/
        2+y1+25);
        delay(105);
/* To show the node a server and it is first node */
        sprintf(s,"%d",j);
        outtextxy(getmaxx()/2+x1-30,getmaxy()/2-30+y1,s);
        outtextxy(getmaxx()/2+x1-23,getmaxy()/2+3+y1,"server");

/* to draw the circle from server to node number 2 of the LAN Ring */
        for(ii=i;ii<=i+k;ii=ii+0.25)
        {
        x1=x*cos(ii*3.142/180)+y*sin(ii*3.142/180);
        y1=-x*sin(ii*3.142/180)+y*cos(ii*3.142/180);
        putpixel(getmaxx()/2+x1,getmaxy()/2+y1,2);
        }

/* to draw the remaining nodes and drawing the complete circle to make it as the ring */
        j=2;
        for(i=k;i<k*n;i=i+k)
        {
```

```
        setcolor(2);
    /* Circle segment drawing */
        for(ii=i;ii<=i+k;ii=ii+0.25)
        {
        x1=x*cos(ii*3.142/180)+y*sin(ii*3.142/180);
        y1=-x*sin(ii*3.142/180)+y*cos(ii*3.142/180);
        putpixel(getmaxx()/2+x1,getmaxy()/2+y1,2);
        }
        x1=x*cos(i*3.142/180)+y*sin(i*3.142/180);
        y1=-x*sin(i*3.142/180)+y*cos(i*3.142/180);
        putpixel(getmaxx()/2+x1,getmaxy()/2+y1,4);

    /* Draws the node rectangle */
        rectangle(getmaxx()/2+x1-20,getmaxy()/2+y1-
20,getmaxx()/2+x1+20,getmaxy()/2+y1+20);
        delay(105);

    /* Writes the node number inside the node */
        sprintf(s,"%d",j);
        outtextxy(getmaxx()/2+x1+3,getmaxy()/2+3+y1,s);
        j++;
    } /* LAN RING construction ends */

/* Inputs the client number for processing and checks for its validity */
    do
    {
    outtextxy(10,10,"Enter terminal to process");
    moveto(10,20);
    scanf("%d",&j);

    jj=j;
        if(j>n || j<=0)
        {
        outtextxy(20,30,"Terminal not existing");
        outtextxy(20,40,"re-enter...");
        delay(1200);
    /* erases the message */
        setcolor(0);
        outtextxy(20,30,"Terminal not existing");
        outtextxy(20,40,"re-enter...");
```

```
                setcolor(15);
                } /* end of if */
        }while(j>n || j<=0); /* end of inner do */

/* Checking for clockwise are anticlockwise movements. */
        if(j>(n+1)/2) /* when it is clockwise */
        {
        j—;
        for(ii=1;ii<=10;++ii)
        {
/* Displaying the message */
                setcolor(ii);
                outtextxy(200,240,"Client in Process");

/* sets the color and draws the client */
                setcolor(ii+1);
                x1=x*cos(j*k*3.142/180)+y*sin(j*k*3.142/180);
                y1=-x*sin(j*k*3.142/180)+y*cos(j*k*3.142/180);
                rectangle(getmaxx()/2+x1-20,getmaxy()/2+y1-
20,getmaxx()/2+x1+20,getmaxy()/2+y1+20);
                sprintf(s,"%d",j+1);
                outtextxy(getmaxx()/2+x1+3,getmaxy()/2+3+y1,s);
                delay(505);
        }

/* erasing the message */
                setcolor(0);
                outtextxy(200,240,"Client in Process");

/* Displaying the message */
                setcolor(ii);
                outtextxy(200,240,"Client request to server ");

/* Circular movement of client signals to server */
        for(ii=j*k;ii<=360;ii=ii+0.25)
        {
                setcolor(i);
                x1=x*cos(ii*3.142/180)+y*sin(ii*3.142/180);
                y1=-x*sin(ii*3.142/180)+y*cos(ii*3.142/180);
                putpixel(getmaxx()/2+x1,getmaxy()/2+y1,i);
```

```
                delay(20);
        }

/* Erasing the message */
                setcolor(0);
                outtextxy(200,240,"Client request to server ");

/* Displaying the message */
                setcolor(6);
                outtextxy(200,240,"Server is processing");
        /* Server redrawing */
        j=1;
        for(ii=1;ii<=10;++ii)
        {
        setcolor(ii);
        x1=x*cos(360*3.142/180)+y*sin(360*3.142/180);
        y1=-x*sin(360*3.142/180)+y*cos(360*3.142/180);
        putpixel(getmaxx()/2+x1,getmaxy()/2+y1,ii);

        rectangle(getmaxx()/2+x1-20,getmaxy()/2+y1-
20,getmaxx()/2+x1+20,getmaxy()/2+y1+20);
        rectangle(getmaxx()/2+x1-30,getmaxy()/2+y1-
30,getmaxx()/2+x1+30,getmaxy()/2+y1+30);
        rectangle(getmaxx()/2+x1-25,getmaxy()/2+y1-
25,getmaxx()/2+x1+25,getmaxy()/2+y1+25);
        sprintf(s,"%d",j);
        outtextxy(getmaxx()/2+x1+3,getmaxy()/2+3+y1,s);
        outtextxy(getmaxx()/2+x1-23,getmaxy()/2+3+y1,"server");
        delay(100);
        }
/* Erasing the message */
        setcolor(0);
        outtextxy(200,240,"Server is processing");

/* Displaying the message */
        setcolor(5);
        outtextxy(200,240,"Server response to client");

/* Circular movement of signals */
```

```
        for(ii=360;ii>=(jj-1)*k;ii=ii-0.25)
        {
              setcolor(ii);
              x1=x*cos(ii*3.142/180)+y*sin(ii*3.142/180);
              y1=-x*sin(ii*3.142/180)+y*cos(ii*3.142/180);
              putpixel(getmaxx()/2+x1,getmaxy()/2+y1,ii);
              delay(15);
        }
/* Erasing the message */
        setcolor(0);
        outtextxy(200,240,"Server response to client");
  }

  else /* when it is anticlockwise */
  {
        j—;
/* Displaying the message */
        setcolor(4);
        outtextxy(200,240,"Client in Process");

/* sets the color and draws the client */
        for(ii=1;ii<=10;++ii)
        {
              setcolor(ii);
              x1=x*cos(j*k*3.142/180)+y*sin(j*k*3.142/180);
              y1=-x*sin(j*k*3.142/180)+y*cos(j*k*3.142/180);
              rectangle(getmaxx()/2+x1-20,getmaxy()/2+y1-
20,getmaxx()/2+x1+20,getmaxy()/2+y1+20);
              sprintf(s,"%d",j+1);
              outtextxy(getmaxx()/2+x1+3,getmaxy()/2+3+y1,s);
              delay(105);
        }

 /* Erases the message */
        setcolor(0);
        outtextxy(200,240,"Client in Process");

 /* Displaying the message */
        setcolor(4);
```

```
        outtextxy(200,240,"Client request to server");

/* Circular movement of client request */
        for(ii=j*k;ii>=0;ii=ii-0.25)
        {
                setcolor(i);
                x1=x*cos(ii*3.142/180)+y*sin(ii*3.142/180);
                y1=-x*sin(ii*3.142/180)+y*cos(ii*3.142/180);
                putpixel(getmaxx()/2+x1,getmaxy()/2+y1,i);
                delay(10);
        }
/* Erasing the message */
        setcolor(0);
        outtextxy(200,240,"Client request to server");

/* Displaying the message */
        setcolor(5);
        outtextxy(200,240,"Server is processing");

/* Server blinking */
        j=1;
        for(ii=1;ii<=10;++ii)
        {
        setcolor(ii);
        rectangle(getmaxx()/2+x1-20,getmaxy()/2+y1-
20,getmaxx()/2+x1+20,getmaxy()/2+y1+20);
        rectangle(getmaxx()/2+x1-30,getmaxy()/2+y1-
30,getmaxx()/2+x1+30,getmaxy()/2+y1+30);
        rectangle(getmaxx()/2+x1-25,getmaxy()/2+y1-
25,getmaxx()/2+x1+25,getmaxy()/2+y1+25);
        delay(100);
        }

/* Erasing the message */
        setcolor(0);
        outtextxy(200,240,"Server is processing");

/* Displaying the message */
        setcolor(2);
```

```
        outtextxy(200,240,"Server response to client");

/* Movement of server signals to client */
        for(ii=0;ii<=(jj-1)*k;ii=ii+0.25)
        {
                setcolor(ii);
                x1=x*cos(ii*3.142/180)+y*sin(ii*3.142/180);
                y1=-x*sin(ii*3.142/180)+y*cos(ii*3.142/180);
                putpixel(getmaxx()/2+x1,getmaxy()/2+y1,ii);
                delay(15);
        }

/* Erasing the message */
        setcolor(0);
        outtextxy(200,240,"Server response to client");
} /* end of else */

/* Erasing the message */
        setcolor(0);
        outtextxy(10,10,"Enter terminal to process");
        setcolor(15);
        outtextxy(10,10,"Any more operation (y/n)?");
        fflush(stdin);
        ch=getch(); /* Gets the user response */
        setcolor(0);
        outtextxy(10,10,"Any more operation (y/n)?");
        setcolor(15);
        ch=toupper(ch);
}while(ch=='Y'); /* End of outer do */
delay(2000); /* waits for while before switching to main menu */
}
```

2.B. iv) The LAN Star topology module

/* This module shows the demo of STAR topology in LAN. The number of clients is restricted to 10. The center of the STAR is made as server. The Bresneham's Circle drawing algorithm is used to draw the clients in circular manner. The clients/nodes are shown with rectangles. Based on the number of nodes the 360-degree angle is divided into parts. The movements of the signals from client to server and server to client are shown with putpixel and different colors are used to distinguish them. The proper delay is used to make the demo more effective. */

```
/* This module is totally independent and to run it independently just change function name 'void
starmain()' with 'void main()' and include all necessary header files. */

#include<dos.h>
#include<conio.h>
#include<ctype.h>
#include<stdio.h>
#include<graphics.h>
#include<math.h>

void starmain()
 {
 int t,l1;
 int gd=DETECT,gm,i,j,k,n,x1,y1;
 float x,y;
 float a,b,c,d,l;
 float e,e1,dx,dy;
 char s[10],ch;

clrscr();

/* user inputs the number of nodes and its validation */
do
{
            printf("\n enter no of nodes ");
            scanf("%d",&n);
            if(n>10 || n<=0)
            printf("\n n must be <=10 and n must be > 0 \n");
}while(n>10 || n<=0);

initgraph(&gd,&gm,"");

/* construction of stars/clients and server */
            circle(getmaxx()/2, getmaxy()/2,30);
            outtextxy(getmaxx()/2-25, getmaxy()/2,"Server");
            x=125;
            y=125;
            k=360/n;
            j=1;
```

```
        for(i=0;i<k*n;i=i+k)
        {
                x1=x*cos(i*3.142/180)+y*sin(i*3.142/180);
                y1=-x*sin(i*3.142/180)+y*cos(i*3.142/180);
                putpixel(getmaxx()/2+x1,getmaxy()/2+y1,15);
                rectangle(getmaxx()/2+x1-20,getmaxy()/2+y1-
20,getmaxx()/2+x1+20,getmaxy()/2+y1+20);
                line(getmaxx()/2,getmaxy()/2,getmaxx()/2+x1,getmaxy()/2+y1);
                delay(105);
                sprintf(s,"%d",j);
                outtextxy(getmaxx()/2+x1+3,getmaxy()/2+3+y1,s);
                j++;
        }

/* Demo starts from here */
do
{

/* user input of node number to process and its validation */
        do
        {
        outtextxy(10,10,"Enter terminal to process");
        moveto(10,20);
        scanf("%d",&j);
        if(j>n || j<=0)
                {

        /* displays the message when wrong input is entered */
                outtextxy(20,30,"Terminal not existing");
                outtextxy(20,40,"re-enter...");
                delay(500);

        /* erases the message after .5 second */
                setcolor(0);
                outtextxy(20,30,"Terminal not existing");
                outtextxy(20,40,"re-enter...");
                setcolor(15);
                } /* end of if */
        }while(j>n || j<=0);
```

```
/* Makes the particular client node to blink with different colors */
            for(i=1;i<=10;++i)
            {
            setcolor(i);
            x1=x*cos((j-1)*k*3.142/180)+y*sin((j-1)*k*3.142/180);
            y1=-x*sin((j-1)*k*3.142/180)+y*cos((j-1)*k*3.142/180);
            putpixel(getmaxx()/2+x1,getmaxy()/2+y1,15);
            rectangle(getmaxx()/2+x1-20,getmaxy()/2+y1-
20,getmaxx()/2+x1+20,getmaxy()/2+y1+20);
            sprintf(s,"%d",j);
            outtextxy(getmaxx()/2+x1+3,getmaxy()/2+3+y1,s);
            delay(100);
            }

/* for sending the client request to server */

/* center of the star network */
            x1=x*cos((j-1)*k*3.142/180)+y*sin((j-1)*k*3.142/180);
            y1=-x*sin((j-1)*k*3.142/180)+y*cos((j-1)*k*3.142/180);

/* starting of the present processing node */
            c=getmaxx()/2+x1;
            d=getmaxy()/2+y1;
            putpixel((int)c,(int)d,12);
            a=getmaxx()/2;
            b=getmaxy()/2;
            c=getmaxx()/2+x1;
            d=getmaxy()/2+y1;

/* based on the quadrant of the present processing node we need to interchange the values for
x-axis */

            if(a>c)
                  l=a-c;
            else
                  l=c-a;

/* based on the quadrant of the present processing node we need to interchange the values for
y-axis */
            if(b>d)
```

```
            l1=b-d;
      else
            l1=d-b;

      if(l1>l)
            l=l1;

/* finds the slope of the line */
      if(a>c)
            dx=(a-c)/l;
      else
            dx=(c-a)/l;
      if(b>d)
            dy=(b-d)/l;
      else
            dy=(d-b)/l;

/* for the client that lies in first and fourth quadrant */
      if(c>a)
      {
      if(d>b) /* in forth quadrant */
      {

      /* signals from client to server */
       for(i=0;i<=l;++i)
            {
            putpixel((int)c,(int)d,4);
            c=c-dx;
            d=d-dy;
            delay(15);
            }

/* server will blink */
      for(i=1;i<=10;++i)
            {
            setcolor(i);
            circle(getmaxx()/2, getmaxy()/2,30);
            outtextxy(getmaxx()/2-25, getmaxy()/2,"Server");
            delay(100);
```

```
            }

/* signals from server to client */
        for(i=0;i<=l;++i)
            {
            putpixel((int)a,(int)b,1);
            a=a+dx;
            b=b+dy;
            delay(5);
            }
        }

        else /* in the first quadrant */
        {

/* client to server */
        for(i=0;i<=l;++i)
        {
            putpixel((int)c,(int)d,4);
            c=c-dx;
            d=d+dy;
            delay(10);
        }

/* server processes with blinking effect */
        for(i=1;i<=10;++i)
        {
            setcolor(i);
            circle(getmaxx()/2, getmaxy()/2,30);
            outtextxy(getmaxx()/2-25, getmaxy()/2,"Server");
            delay(100);
        }

/* server to client */
        for(i=0;i<=l;++i)
        {
            putpixel((int)a,(int)b,1);
            a=a+dx;
            b=b-dy;
            delay(5);
```

```
            }
        }
    }

else /* when in second or third quadrant */
    {
        if(d>b) /* third quadrant */
        {

        /* client to server */
        for(i=0;i<=l;++i)
        {
            putpixel((int)c,(int)d,4);
            c=c+dx;
            d=d-dy;
            delay(15);
        }

        /* server process */
        for(i=1;i<=10;++i)
        {
            setcolor(i);
            circle(getmaxx()/2, getmaxy()/2,30);
            outtextxy(getmaxx()/2-25, getmaxy()/2,"Server");
            delay(100);
        }

            /* server to client */
            for(i=0;i<=l;++i)
        {
            putpixel((int)a,(int)b,1);
            a=a-dx;
            b=b+dy;
            delay(5);
        }
    }
else /* for second quadrant nodes */
        {

        /* client to server signal movements */
```

```
        for(i=0;i<=l;++i)
        {
                putpixel((int)c,(int)d,4);
                c=c+dx;
                d=d+dy;
                delay(15);
        }

        /* server processing effect */
        for(i=1;i<=10;++i)
        {
                setcolor(i);
                circle(getmaxx()/2, getmaxy()/2,30);
                outtextxy(getmaxx()/2-25, getmaxy()/2,"Server");
                delay(100);
        }

        /* server to client response movement */
        for(i=0;i<=l;++i)
        {
                putpixel((int)a,(int)b,1);
                a=a-dx;
                b=b-dy;
                delay(5);
        }
    }
    }

/* Erasing the message */
        setcolor(0);
        outtextxy(10,10,"Enter terminal to process");

/* Displaying the message */
        setcolor(15);
        outtextxy(10,10,"Any more operation (y/n)?");

        fflush(stdin);
        ch=getch();

/* Erasing the message */
```

```
        setcolor(0);
        outtextxy(10,10,"Any more operation (y/n)?");
        setcolor(15);

        ch=toupper(ch);
   }while(ch=='Y'); /* end of outer do..while loop */

   delay(2000);
} /* End of STAR topology module */
```

2.B. v) The Serial Topology Module

/* This module deals with Serial topology in LAN network. The complete information about how the client signals are passed to the server and how server process the request and gives back the response is shown graphically. The number of nodes is limited to 10 and are arranged on one side of the LAN cable that is represented by line. The clients and server are shown with the rectangles. The user has to enter the client number. Then the client will be made to blink with the message to indicate 'the client in progress'. Then the signal passing from client to server is shown with coloured pixels and respected message. The server is made to blink for a while to indicate its process and finally the response from server is shown again with pixels with colors */

/* This module is totally independent and to run it independently just change function name ' void serialmain()' with 'void main()' and include all necessary header files. */

```
void serialmain()
        {
        int gd=DETECT,gm;
        int i,k,j,n;
        char s[10],ch;
        do
        {
        printf("\n Enter no of nodes\n");
        scanf("%d",&n);
        if (n>10)
        printf("n must be <= 10\n re-enter...\n");
        }while(n>10);

        initgraph(&gd,&gm," ");

        rectangle(20,getmaxy()/2-40,70,getmaxy()/2+40);
```

```
outtextxy(22,getmaxy()/2-5,"Server");
line(70,getmaxy()/2,100+n*50,getmaxy()/2);

for(i=1;i<=n;i=i+1)
{
rectangle(120+(i-1)*50,getmaxy()/2-30,150+(i-1)*50,getmaxy()/2);
sprintf(s,"%d",i);
outtextxy(128+(i-1)*50,getmaxy()/2-23,s);
}
do
{
do
{
outtextxy(10,10,"Enter terminal to process");
moveto(10,20);
scanf("%d",&j);
if(j>n)
{
outtextxy(20,30,"Terminal not existing");
outtextxy(20,40,"re-enter...");
delay(2000);
setcolor(0);
outtextxy(20,30,"Terminal not existing");
outtextxy(20,40,"re-enter...");
setcolor(15);
}
}while(j>n);

outtextxy(100,340,"Client in process");
for(i=1;i<=10;++i)
{
setcolor(i);
        rectangle(120+(j-1)*50,getmaxy()/2-30,150+(j-1)*50,getmaxy()/2);
        sprintf(s,"%d",j);
        outtextxy(128+(j-1)*50,getmaxy()/2-23,s);
                delay(400);
}
setcolor(j);
        rectangle(120+(j-1)*50,getmaxy()/2-30,150+(j-1)*50,getmaxy()/2);
        sprintf(s,"%d",j);
```

```
        outtextxy(128+(j-1)*50,getmaxy()/2-23,s);
                delay(800);
                setcolor(0);
                outtextxy(100,340,"Client in process");
                setcolor(j);
                outtextxy(100,340,"Client signals to server");

for(i=120+(j-1)*50;i>=70;—i)
{
putpixel(i,getmaxy()/2,j);
delay(20);
}
                setcolor(0);
                outtextxy(100,340,"Client signals to server");
                setcolor(j);
                outtextxy(100,340,"server checking the request");

for(i=1;i<=10;++i)
{
setcolor(i);
rectangle(20,getmaxy()/2-40,70,getmaxy()/2+40);
        outtextxy(22,getmaxy()/2-5,"Server");
        delay(400);
}

setcolor(j);
rectangle(20,getmaxy()/2-40,70,getmaxy()/2+40);
        outtextxy(22,getmaxy()/2-5,"Server");
        delay(800);

                setcolor(0);
                outtextxy(100,340,"server checking the request");
                setcolor(j);
                outtextxy(100,340,"server response to request");

setcolor(15);
rectangle(20,getmaxy()/2-40,70,getmaxy()/2+40);
        outtextxy(22,getmaxy()/2-5,"Server");
        delay(800);
```

```
for(i=70;i<=120+(j-1)*50;++i)
{
putpixel(i,getmaxy()/2,15);
delay(20);
}
        rectangle(120+(j-1)*50,getmaxy()/2-30,150+(j-1)*50,getmaxy()/2);
        sprintf(s,"%d",j);
        outtextxy(128+(j-1)*50,getmaxy()/2-23,s);
            delay(800);

            setcolor(0);
            outtextxy(100,340,"server response to request");

setcolor(0);
outtextxy(10,10,"Enter terminal to process");
setcolor(15);
outtextxy(10,10,"Any more operation (y/n)?");
ch=getch();
setcolor(0);
outtextxy(10,10,"Any more operation (y/n)?");
setcolor(15);

ch=toupper(ch);
}while(ch=='Y');
getch();
}
```

PROJECT 3

CPU SCHEDULING ALGORITHMS

3.A) SYNOPSIS

This project simulates different CPU Scheduling algorithms. In any of the multiprogramming environment it is essential for the operating system to assign the schedules for each and every task. Mainly there are two types of scheduling namely, Non Preemptive and Preemptive. In case of non-preemptive once any process enters into the processor it continues to execute until it gets completed or its time slice expires. In case of preemptive scheduling if a process is executing and still has its allotted time it needs to leave the processor for the high priority process which enters by interrupting the existing process.

This project deals with both non-preemptive and preemptive algorithms, which are explained below.

3.A. i) FIRST IN FIRST OUT

First come, first serve is by far the simple scheduling discipline. The workload is simply processed in the order of arrival, with no preemption, implementation of the FCFS scheduler is quite straightforward, and its execution result in little overhead.

In this method all the processes will make a queue on their entry and take the processor one by one according to their arrival. Once a process enters into the processor it remains in the processor until its completion. This is shown in the following diagram.

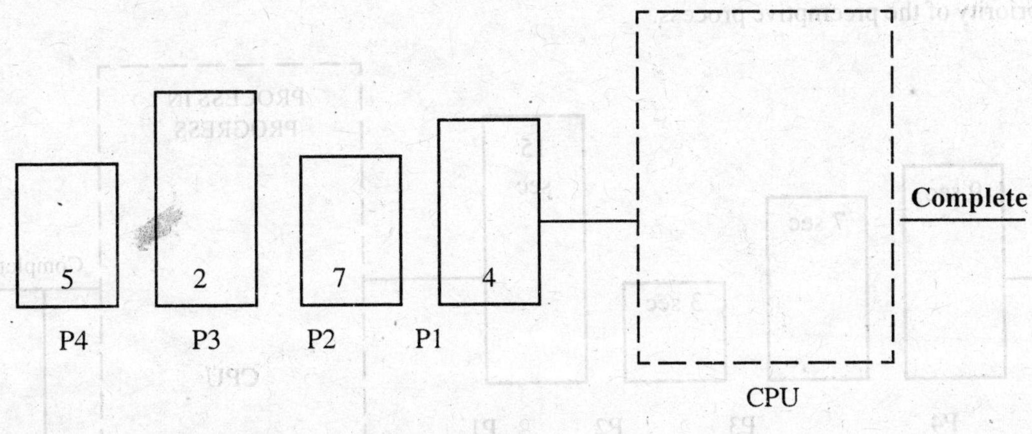

3.A. ii) SMALLEST JOB FIRST PROCESS SCHEDULER

In this scheduling algorithm each and every process enter the queue according to their arrival. While scheduling the processor for different processes does not follow the queue instead the process with smallest process time will be considered and allotted the CPU and it continues its processing until its completion. The following diagram illustrates this.

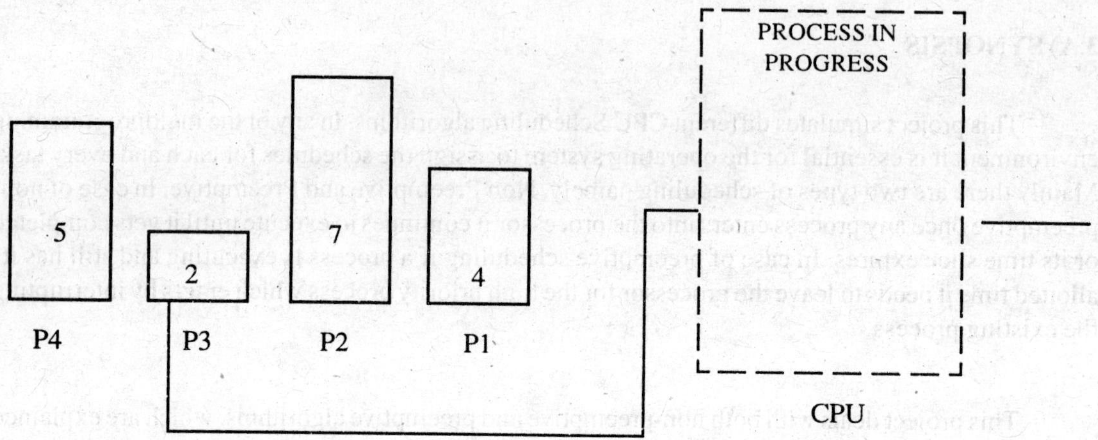

3.A. *iii) ROUND ROBIN*

In interactive environments, such as time-sharing systems, the primary requirement is to provide reasonably good response time and in general, to share system recourses equally among all users in an efficient manner. Obviously, only primitive disciplines may be considered in such environment, and one of the most popular is time-sharing, also know as Round Robin (RR). Basically the processor time is divided into slices, which are allocated to processes. No process can run for more than one time slice when there are others waiting in the ready queue. If a process needs more time to complete after exhausting its time slice, it is placed at the end of the ready queue to await the next allocation. This rearrangement of the ready list effectively lowers the scheduling priority of the preemptive process.

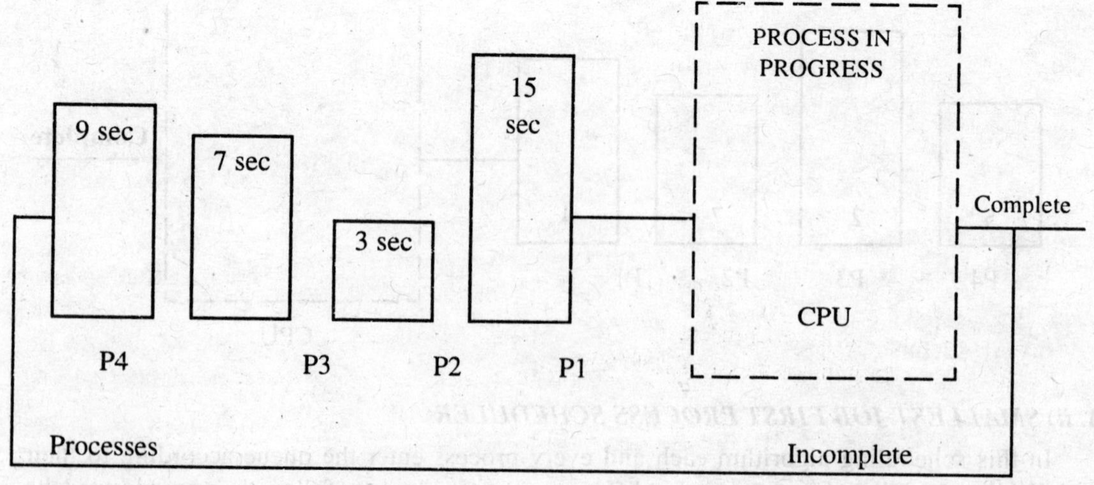

Round Robin scheduling achieves equal sharing of system resources. Short process may be executed within a single time quantum and thus exhibit good response times. Long processes may require several quanta and thus be forced to cycle through the ready queue a few times before completion.

3.A. iv) SHORTEST REMAINING TIME NEXT

Shortest Remaining time next is a scheduling discipline in which the next scheduling entity, a job or a process, is selected on the basis of the shortest remaining execution time. In this technique all the processes arrive and make the queue. For each process time slice is fixed. Each and every process is allotted the processor according to the queue in FIFO order. Process will remain in the processor for its execution until its time expires or its execution completes whichever is earlier. In case time expires and still process is not completed its task then how much remaining time is essential for its completion has to be calculated and it will be compared with time necessary for any of the other processes in the queue. In case the additional time necessary is smaller than time of any of the other processes in the queue then it will be allowed to continue until its completion. Otherwise the process has to leave the processor for the next process and come back in the queue for its remaining processing and wait for its next turn.

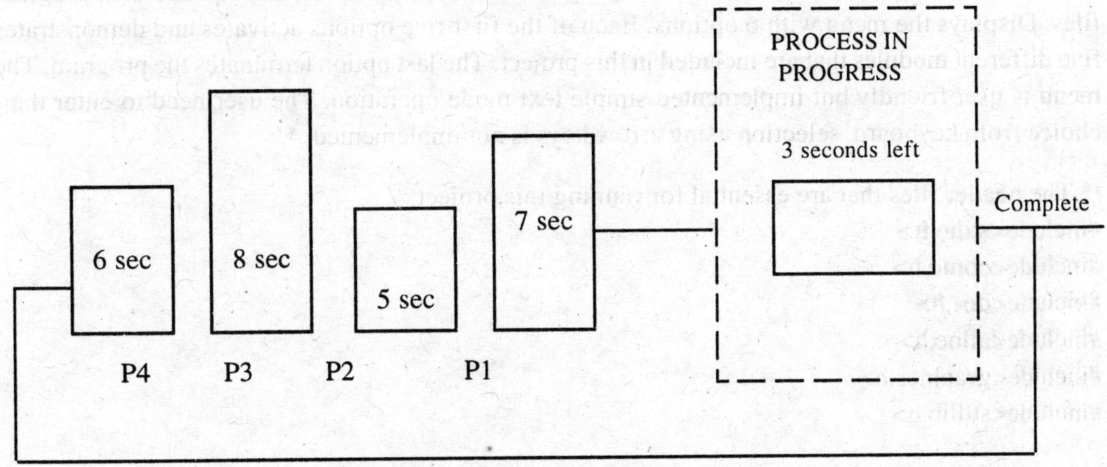

3.A. v) PRIORITY BASED CPU SCHEDULING

In this technique number of processes, which request for the processor make a queue. Each process is assigned a priority. Based on this priority the process is assigned a CPU for execution. The process with the highest priority gets the processor first than the process with the lower priority. Once the process gets the CPU it continues to execute until it completes and next highest priority process follows. This is shown as follows.

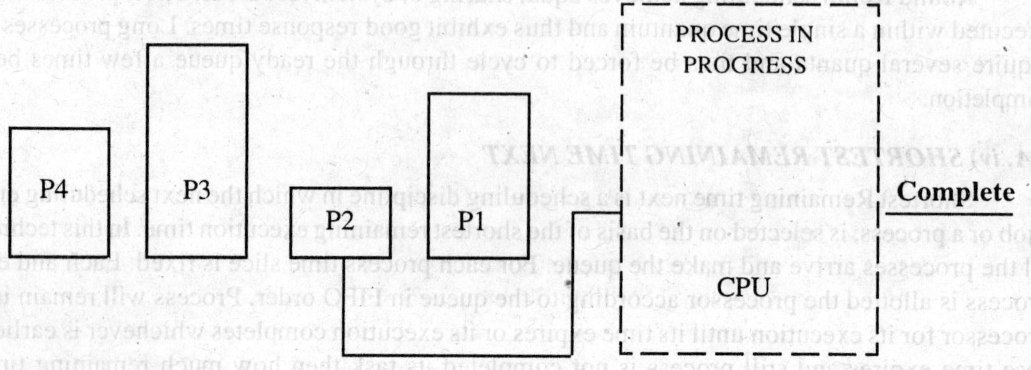

3.B) SOURCE CODE

3.B. i) MAIN MENU MODULE

/* This is the main module of the CPU scheduling project. It includes all the necessary header files that are essential for the project and other program modules, which are kept in different program files. Displays the menu with 6 options. Each of the first five options activates and demonstrates five different modules that are included in this project. The last option terminates the program. The menu is user friendly but implemented simple text mode operation. The user need to enter their choice from keyboard, selection using arrow keys is not implemented. */

```
/* The header files that are essential for running this project */
#include<stdio.h>
#include<conio.h>
#include<dos.h>
#include<alloc.h>
#include<graphics.h>
#include<stdlib.h>
```

/* The program files that are developed for demonstrating five different modules present in this project.*/

```
#include "cpufifo.c"
#include "cpusjf.c"
#include "cpurr.c"
#include "cpusrtn.c"
#include "cpuprio.c"
```

/* The function declarations for the functions of different modules */

```
void fifomain();
void sjfmain();
void rrmain();
void srtnmain();
void priomain();

/* CPU scheduling project execution starts from here */
void main()
{
int ch;
/* menu design */
do
{
clrscr();
        printf("\n\n\t\t         ********************************************\n\t\t\t
        MAIN - MENU \n\t\t ********************************************\n\n\t\t l\t 1
        FIRST IN FIRST OUT l\n\n\t\t l\t 2 SMALLEST JOB FIRST l\n\n\t\t l\t 3 ROUND
        ROBIN SCHEDULING l\n\n\t\t l\t 4 SMALLEST REMAINING TIME NEXT l\n\n\t\t
        l\t 5 SCHEDULING BASED ON PRIORITY l\n\n\t\t l\t 6 EXIT FROM THE PROGRAM
        l\n\n\n\t\t l\t ENTER YOUR C H O I C E : ");
        scanf("%d",&ch);
 switch(ch) /* switches to different modules according to the users options */
 {
        case 1: fifomain();
                break;
        case 2: sjfmain();
                break;
        case 3: rrmain();
                break;
        case 4: srtnmain();
                break;
        case 5: priomain();
                break;
        case 6:
                break;
  }
  }while(ch!=6);
  } /* End of main program */
```

3.B. ii) FIFO MODULE

/* This module demonstrates first in first out CPU scheduling algorithm. The number of processes and their sizes are taken from keyboard. Because of the resolution restrictions the maximum size of any of the process is restricted to ten and also the number of processes is also restricted to ten. Each process is placed in a rectangular box with size according to the size of the process and the corresponding label for indicating the process number is displayed. A big rectangular box for CPU is also included. Each and every process will enter CPU one by one and stay there according to their individual execution times (sizes). After finishing execution they leave the processor and exit out of screen. */

/* This is an independent module that individually runs for FIFO algorithm. To run it individually just remove the function "fifomain()" and replace it with "main()" and include all necessary header files */

```
void fifomain()
{
        int gd=DETECT,gm;
        int n,p[11],p2[20],i,j;
        char s[20];
        void *z;
/* The labels for indicating process numbers */
        char p1[10][4]={"p1","p2","p3","p4","p5","p6","p7","p8","p9","p10"};
        /* getting the number of processes from user and checking its validity and limit before
        accepting it */
do
{
clrscr();
printf("\t ******************************************************");
printf("\n\t\t FIRST IN FIRST OUT CPU SCHEDULING");
printf("\n\t ******************************************************\n\n");
printf("\t\t ENTER N : ");
scanf("%d",&n);
if(n<=0||n>10)
printf("\n\n\t\t NUMBER OF PROCESSES SHOULD BE <= 10 \n");
}while(n>10||n<=0);

/* inputting individual process sizes */
printf("\n\n\t\t ENTER PROCESS SIZES :\n");

for(i=1;i<=n;++i)
```

```
{
        do /* validity for individual process sizes*/
        {
        printf("\n\t\t PROCESS %d : ",i);
        scanf("%d",&p[i]);
        if(p[i]>10||p[i]<=0)
        printf("\n\n\t\t PROCESS SIZE SHOULD BE <=10 ");
        } while(p[i]>10||p[i]<=0);
}

/* reversing the given list */
for(i=1;i<=n;++i)
        p2[n-i+1]=p[i];

for(i=1;i<=n;++i)
        p[i]=p2[i];

/* initializing the graphics mode which starts the graphical demo */
initgraph(&gd,&gm,"");
/* with the values accepted from the above code we start constructing FIFO model */
        setcolor(1);
        rectangle(480,200,560,350); /* for CPU */
        setcolor(5);
        settextstyle(3,0,2);
        outtextxy(500,360,"CPU");
/* setting the font color and styles and displaying heading of the algorithm*/
        setcolor(8);
        settextstyle(3,0,4);
        outtextxy(20,5,"FIRST IN FIRST OUT CPU SCHEDULING");
        graphdefaults();/* resets all graphical settings to default*/
/* drawing the process boxes with proper labeling including process name like p1,p2 etc. and their
        sizes */
        setcolor(15);
        setbkcolor(0);
        for(i=1;i<=n;++i)
        {
                rectangle(5+(i-1)*40,310-p[i]*10,5+i*40-2,310);
                sprintf(s,"%d",p[i]);
                outtextxy(15+(i-1)*40,302,s);
                outtextxy(13+(i-1)*40,320,p1[n-i]);
```

```
        }

/* we start with FIFO process demonstration from here through animation with the above constructed
model */


for(i=n;i>=1;—i)
{
        z=malloc(imagesize(5+(i-1)*40,310-p[i]*10,5+i*40-2,340)); /* allocating the image
        size memory to a variable z for storing an image of the process*/
        getimage(5+(i-1)*40,310-p[i]*10,5+i*40-2,340,z);
/* movement of process from its position in the queue to the CPU */
for(j=5+(i-1)*40;j<=500;++j)
        {
        if(j==481) /* to redraw the CPU rectangle when the process passes into the CPU */
        rectangle(480,200,560,350);
        putimage(j,310-p[i]*10,z,2);
        delay(10);
        putimage(j,310-p[i]*10,z,1);
        }
putimage(j,310-p[i]*10,z,2);

/* display the message while the process in progress for any process according to their sizes */


for(j=1;j<=p[i]*1000;j=j+500)
{
        setcolor(j);/* writing the message in different colors.*/
        settextstyle(2,0,5);
        outtextxy(480,170," PROGRESS");
        outtextxy(480,150,"PROCESS IN");
        delay(500);
        setcolor(0); /* erasing the message that makes it to appear like blinking */
        settextstyle(2,0,5);
        outtextxy(480,170," PROGRESS");
        outtextxy(480,150,"PROCESS IN");
        delay(200);
        }
graphdefaults();

/* movement of process box from CPU to out of screen */
```

```
setbkcolor(0);
        for(j=500;j<=640;++j)
              {
              if(j==561) /* rewriting the rectangle when the image crosses the CPU
              rectangle box */
              rectangle(480,200,560,350);
              putimage(j,310-p[i]*10,z,2);
              delay(10);
              putimage(j,310-p[i]*10,z,1);
              }
              putimage(j,310-p[i]*10,z,2);
        }
sleep(2); /* waits for 2 seconds before switching automatically to the main menu */
closegraph();
} /* end of FIFO algorithm module */
```

3.B. iii) THE SHORTEST JOB FIRST MODULE

/* This module demonstrates shortest job first CPU scheduling algorithm. The number of processes and their sizes are taken from keyboard. Because of the resolution restrictions the maximum size of any of the process is restricted to ten and also the number of processes is also restricted to ten. Each process is placed in a rectangular box with size according to the size of the process and the corresponding label for indicating the process number is displayed. A big rectangular box for CPU is also included. Each and every process will enter CPU one by one and stay there according to their individual execution times (sizes). After finishing execution they leave the processor and exit out of screen. Processes are chosen for execution on the CPU based on the shortest execution time (size) of the process */

/* This is an independent module that individually runs for SJF algorithm. To run it individually just remove the function "sjfmain()" and replace it with "main()" and include all necessary header files */

```
void sjfmain()
{
        int gd=DETECT,gm;
        int n,p[11],p2[11],i,j,s11,l=0,k;
        char s[20];
        void *z;
        char p1[10][4]={"p1","p2","p3","p4","p5","p6","p7","p8","p9","p10"};

/* inputting the size with validation*/
```

```
do
{
        clrscr();
        printf("\t ************************************************");
        printf("\n\t\t SMALLEST JOB FIRST CPU SCHEDULING");
        printf("\n\t ************************************************\n\n");
        printf("\t\t ENTER N : ");
        scanf("%d",&n);
        if(n>10||n<=0)
        printf("\n\n\t\t NUMBER OF PROCESSES SHOULD BE <=10 \n");
}while(n>10||n<=0);

printf("\n\n\t\t ENTER PROCESS SIZES\n");

/* individual process sizes with validations from keyboard */
for(i=1;i<=n;++i)
{
        do
        {
            printf("\n\t\t PROCESS %d : ",i);
            scanf("%d",&p[i]);
            if(p[i]>10||p[i]<=0)
            printf("\n\n\t\t PROCESS SIZE SHOULD BE <=10 ");
        }while(p[i]>10||p[i]<=0);

/* to avoid the process size duplication for more than one processes */
        j=1;
        do
        {
            if(i!=j)
            if(p[i]==p[j])
            {
             i—;
            printf("\n\t\t SAME PROCESS SIZE IS NOT ALLOWED\n ");
             break;
            }
            j++;
        }while(j<i);
}
/* finds the largest process */
```

```
for(i=1;i<=n;++i)
        if(l<p[i])
        l=p[i];

/* swapping to print the process queue in the order */
for(i=1;i<=n;++i)
        p2[n-i+1]=p[i];

for(i=1;i<=n;++i)
        p[i]=p2[i];

initgraph(&gd,&gm,"");
        rectangle(480,165,560,315);
        setcolor(6);
        settextstyle(8,0,3);
        outtextxy(500,325,"CPU");
        setcolor(2);
        settextstyle(3,0,4);
        outtextxy(20,440,"SMALLEST JOB FIRST CPU SCHEDULING");
        outtextxy(21,441,"SMALLEST JOB FIRST CPU SCHEDULING");
        graphdefaults();
        setcolor(15);

for(i=1;i<=n;++i)
{
        rectangle(5+(i-1)*40,260-p[i]*10,5+i*40-2,260);
        sprintf(s,"%d",p[i]);
        outtextxy(15+(i-1)*40,262,s);
        outtextxy(13+(i-1)*40,270,p1[n-i]);
}

for(i=1;i<=n;++i)
{
        s11=p[1];
        /* finding the smallest process in the list */
        for(j=1;j<=n;++j)
        if(p[j]<s11)
        {
        s11=p[j];
        }
```

```
        for(j=1;j<=n;++j)
        {
        if(s11==p[j]) /* position of the smallest process in the list */
        {
        /* movement of process from its position to the CPU and then to disappear from
        screen */

        z=malloc(imagesize(5+(j-1)*40,260-p[j]*10,5+j*40-2,280));
        getimage(5+(j-1)*40,260-p[j]*10,5+j*40-2,280,z);
        for(k=260-p[j]*10;k<=280;++k)
        {
        putimage(5+(j-1)*40,k,z,2);
        delay(10);
        putimage(5+(j-1)*40,k,z,1);
        }
        putimage(5+(j-1)*40,280,z,2);

for(k=5+(j-1)*40;k<=420;++k)
{
        putimage(k,280,z,2);
        delay(10);
        putimage(k,280,z,1);
}
        putimage(k-1,280,z,2);

for(k=280;k>=280-p[j]*10;—k)
{
        putimage(420,k,z,2);
        delay(10);
        putimage(420,k,z,1);
        }
        putimage(420,280-p[j]*10,z,2);

for(k=420;k<=500;++k)
        {
        if(k==481)
        rectangle(480,165,560,315);

        putimage(k,280-p[j]*10,z,2);
        delay(10);
```

```
        putimage(k,280-p[j]*10,z,1);
        }
        putimage(500,280-p[j]*10,z,2);

for(k=1;k<=p[j]*1000;k=k+500)
{
        setcolor(k);
        settextstyle(2,0,5);
        outtextxy(480,135," PROGRESS");
        outtextxy(480,115,"PROCESS IN");

        delay(500);
        setcolor(0);
        settextstyle(2,0,5);
        outtextxy(480,135," PROGRESS");
        outtextxy(480,115,"PROCESS IN");
        delay(200);
}
graphdefaults();

for(k=500;k<=640;++k)
{
        if(k==561)
        rectangle(480,165,560,315);
        putimage(k,280-p[j]*10,z,2);
        delay(10);
        putimage(k,280-p[j]*10,z,1);
}
        putimage(k-1,280-p[j]*10,z,2);


        p[j]=l+1;
    }
  }
}
sleep(2);

closegraph();
}
```

3.B. iv) THE ROUND ROBIN MODULE

/* This module demonstrates round robin or time slice CPU scheduling algorithm. The number of processes and their sizes are taken from keyboard. Because of the resolution restrictions the maximum size of any of the process is restricted to ten and also the number of processes is also restricted to ten. Each process is placed in a rectangular box with size according to the size of the process and the corresponding label for indicating the process number is displayed. A big rectangular box for CPU is also included. Each and every process will enter CPU one by one and stay there until their time slice expires or their execution completes. After finishing execution they leave the processor and exit out of screen. In case their time slice expires before completing the execution then they will go back in the queue and wait for their next chance of execution */

/* This is an independent module, which individually runs for round robin or time slice algorithm. to run it individually just remove the function "rrmain()" and replace it with "main()" and include all necessary header files */

```
void rrmain()
{
        int gd=DETECT,gm,qt,k,kk,ll=0;
        int n,p[11],p22[11],p2[11],i,j,n1=0,n2;
        char s[20];
        char tp1[10][4];
        void *z;
        char p1[10][4]={"p1","p2","p3","p4","p5","p6","p7","p8","p9","p10"};

do
{
        clrscr();
        printf("\t ****************************************************\n\t\t ROUND
        ROBIN                    CPU                    SCHEDULING\n\t
        ****************************************************\n\n");
        printf("\t\t ENTER N : ");
        scanf("%d",&n);
        if(n>10||n<=0)
        printf("\n\t NUMBER OF PROCESSES SHOULD BE <=10 \n");
}while(n>10||n<=0);

printf("\n\n\t\t ENTER PROCESS SIZES\n");
for(i=1;i<=n;++i)
{
        do
        {
```

```
                printf("\n\t\t PROCESS %d : ",i);
                scanf("%d",&p[i]);
                if(p[i]>10||p[i]<=0)
                printf("\n\n\t PROCESS SIZE SHOULD BE <=10 ");
        }while(p[i]>10||p[i]<=0);
}

/* to take input for time slice */
        printf("\n\t\t ENTER THE QUANTAM TIME : ");
        scanf("%d",&qt);

for(i=1;i<=n;++i)
        p2[n-i+1]=p[i];

for(i=1;i<=n;++i)
        p[i]=p2[i];

/* graphical mode initialization */
initgraph(&gd,&gm,"");
xyz:
        cleardevice();
        n1=0;
        ll=0;
        n2=0;
        rectangle(460,100,560,270);
        setcolor(5);
        settextstyle(3,0,2);
        outtextxy(485,280,"CPU");
        setcolor(2);
        settextstyle(3,0,3);
        outtextxy(20,5,"ROUND ROBIN/ TIME SLICE CPU SCHEDULING");
        graphdefaults();
        setcolor(15);
for(i=1;i<=n;++i)
        {
        rectangle(5+(i-1)*40,240-p[i]*10,5+i*40-2,240);
        sprintf(s,"%d",p[i]);
        outtextxy(15+(i-1)*40,242,s);
        outtextxy(13+(i-1)*40,250,p1[n-i]);
        }
```

```
for(i=n;i>=1;—i)
{
        kk=i;
        for(k=n;k>=(n-i+1);—k)
        {
                z=malloc(imagesize(5+(k-1)*40,240-p[kk]*10,5+(k)*40-2,260));
                getimage(5+(k-1)*40,240-p[kk]*10,5+(k)*40-2,260,z);
                for(j=5+(k-1)*40;j<=(k)*40+5;++j)
                {
                        if(j==461)
                        rectangle(460,100,560,270);
                        putimage(j,240-p[kk]*10,z,2);
                        delay(1);
                        putimage(j,240-p[kk]*10,z,1);
                }
                putimage((k)*40+5,240-p[kk]*10,z,2);
                free(z);
                kk—;
        }

        z=malloc(imagesize(5+(n)*40,240-p[i]*10,5+(n+1)*40-2,260));
        getimage(5+n*40,240-p[i]*10,5+(n+1)*40-2,260,z);
for(j=5+n*40;j<=490;++j)
{
        if(j==461)
        rectangle(460,100,560,270);
        putimage(j,240-p[i]*10,z,2);
        delay(10);
        putimage(j,240-p[i]*10,z,1);
}
        putimage(490,240-p[i]*10,z,2);

/*when the process size is within the quantum time it completes its execution and goes out of
screen */

if(p[i]<=qt)
{
        for(j=1;j<=p[i]*1000;j=j+500)
        {
```

```
        setcolor(j);
        settextstyle(2,0,5);
        outtextxy(460,70," PROGRESS");
        outtextxy(460,50,"PROCESS IN");
        delay(500);
        setcolor(0);
        settextstyle(2,0,5);
        outtextxy(460,70," PROGRESS");
        outtextxy(460,50,"PROCESS IN");
        delay(200);
    }

    graphdefaults();

    for(j=490;j<=640;++j)
    {
        if(j==561)
        rectangle(460,100,560,270);
        putimage(j,240-p[i]*10,z,2);
        delay(10);
        putimage(j,240-p[i]*10,z,1);
    }
    putimage(640,240-p[i]*10,z,2);

}
```

else /*when quantum time is less than the process size the partially executed process will get back to the queue */

```
{
    for(j=1;j<=qt*1000;j=j+500)
    {
        setcolor(j);
        settextstyle(2,0,5);
        outtextxy(460,70," PROGRESS");
        outtextxy(460,50,"PROCESS IN");

        delay(500);
        setcolor(0);
        settextstyle(2,0,5);
        outtextxy(460,70," PROGRESS");
```

```
        outtextxy(460,50,"PROCESS IN");
        delay(200);
  }
  ll++;

  graphdefaults();
  putimage(490,240-p[i]*10,z,1);
  p[i]=p[i]-qt;
  n1++;
  p22[n1]=p[i];
  rectangle(490,240-p[i]*10,528,240);
  sprintf(s,"%d",p[i]);
  outtextxy(505,242,s);
  outtextxy(503,250,p1[i-1]);
  free(z);
  strcpy(tp1[n2],p1[i-1]);
  n2++;

  z=malloc(imagesize(490,240-p[i]*10,528,260));
  getimage(490,240-p[i]*10,528,260,z);

  for(j=490;j<=580;++j)
  {
  if(j==561)
  rectangle(460,100,560,270);
  putimage(j,240-p[i]*10,z,2);
  delay(10);
  putimage(j,240-p[i]*10,z,1);
  }
  putimage(580,240-p[i]*10,z,2);

  for(j=240-p[i]*10;j<=310;j++)
  {
        putimage(580,j,z,2);
        delay(10);
        putimage(580,j,z,1);
  }
  putimage(580,310,z,2);

  for(j=580;j>=5+(ll-1)*40;j—)
```

```
            {
                putimage(j,310,z,2);
                delay(10);
                putimage(j,310,z,1);
            }
            putimage(5+(ll-1)*40,310,z,2);

        }
    }
if(n1>0) /* when any process is left in the queue they will be considered */
        {
            for(i=n1;i>=1;—i)
                    p[n1-i+1]=p22[i];
            for(i=0;i<n2;++i)
                    strcpy(p1[i],tp1[n2-i-1]);
            n=n1;
            goto xyz;
        }
        sleep(2);
        closegraph();
}
```

3.B. v) THE SHORTEST REMAINING TIME NEXT MODULE

/* This module demonstrates shortest remaining time next CPU scheduling algorithm. The number of processes and their sizes are taken from keyboard. Because of the resolution restrictions the maximum size of any of the process is restricted to ten and also the number of processes is also restricted to ten. Each process is placed in a rectangular box with size according to the size of the process and the corresponding label for indicating the process number is displayed. A big rectangular box for CPU is also included. Each and every process will enter CPU one by one in FIFO order and stay there according to their individual execution times (sizes). After finishing execution they leave the processor and exit out of screen. If before completing the execution, the time slice expires for a currently executing process then how much additional time necessary will be calculated and checked with the remaining process's execution time in the queue. If the remaining processing time is found to be smaller than any process's size in the queue then it is allowed to continue its execution towards its completion and the extra time execution is indicated with the proper message/

/* This is an independent module, which individually runs for SRTN algorithm. To run it individually just remove the function "srtnmain()" and replace it with "main()" and include all necessary header files */

```
void srtnmain()
{
	int gd=DETECT,gm,qt,k,kk,ll=0,sm=0,k1;
	int n,p[11],p22[11],p2[11],i,j,n1=0,n2;
	char s[20];
	char tp1[10][4];
	void *z;
	char p1[10][4]={"p1","p2","p3","p4","p5","p6","p7","p8","p9","p10"};
do
{
	clrscr();
	printf("\t ***************************************************");
	printf("\n\t\t SMALLEST REMAINING TIME NEXT CPU SCHEDULING");
	printf("\n\t ****************************************************\n\n");
	printf("\t\t ENTER N : ");
	scanf("%d",&n);
	if(n>10||n<=0)
	printf("\n\n\t NUMBER OF PROCESSES SHOULD BE <=10 \n");
}while(n>10||n<=0);

printf("\n\n\t\t ENTER PROCESS SIZES\n");
for(i=1;i<=n;++i)
{
	do
	{
	printf("\n\t\t PROCESS %d : ",i);
	scanf("%d",&p[i]);
	if(p[i]>10||p[i]<=0)
	printf("\n\n\t PROCESS SIZE SHOULD BE <=10 ");
	}while(p[i]>10||p[i]<=0);
}
printf("\n\n\t\t ENTER QUANTUM TIME : ");
scanf("%d",&qt);

/* swapping*/
for(i=1;i<=n;++i)
	p2[n-i+1]=p[i];
```

```
for(i=1;i<=n;++i)
        p[i]=p2[i];

/* graphical mode initialization */
initgraph(&gd,&gm,"");
        xyz:
        cleardevice();
        n1=0;
        ll=0;
        n2=0;
        rectangle(460,100,560,270);
        setcolor(5);
        settextstyle(3,0,2);
        outtextxy(4    85,280,"CPU");
        setcolor(2);
        settextstyle(3,0,3);
        outtextxy(20,445,"SMALLEST REMAINING TIME NEXT CPU SCHEDULING");
        graphdefaults();
        setcolor(15);
        for(i=1;i<=n;++i)
        {
                rectangle(5+(i-1)*40,240-p[i]*10,5+i*40-2,240);
                sprintf(s,"%d",p[i]);
                outtextxy(15+(i-1)*40,242,s);
                outtextxy(13+(i-1)*40,250,p1[n-i]);

        }

 for(i=n;i>=1;—i)
        {
        kk=i;
        sm=11;
        for(k1=n-1;k1>=1;—k1)
                if(p[k1]<sm)
                sm=p[k1];
        for(k=n;k>=(n-i+1);—k)
        {
                z=malloc(imagesize(5+(k-1)*40,240-p[kk]*10,5+(k)*40-2,260));
                getimage(5+(k-1)*40,240-p[kk]*10,5+(k)*40-2,260,z);
                for(j=5+(k-1)*40;j<=(k)*40+5;++j)
```

```
            {
                    if(j==461)
                    rectangle(460,100,560,270);
                    putimage(j,240-p[kk]*10,z,2);
                    delay(1);
                    putimage(j,240-p[kk]*10,z,1);
            }
            putimage((k)*40+5,240-p[kk]*10,z,2);
            free(z);
            kk—;
        }
z=malloc(imagesize(5+(n)*40,240-p[i]*10,5+(n+1)*40-2,260));
getimage(5+n*40,240-p[i]*10,5+(n+1)*40-2,260,z);
for(j=5+n*40;j<=490;++j)
{
        if(j==461)
        rectangle(460,100,560,270);
        putimage(j,240-p[i]*10,z,2);
        delay(10);
        putimage(j,240-p[i]*10,z,1);
}
        putimage(490,240-p[i]*10,z,2);

/* when the quantum time plus the allowable additional time are within the limit process takes CPU
till it executes completely and goes out of screen */

if(p[i]<=(qt+sm))
{
        /* actual allotted processing time with related message */
        if(p[i]>qt)
        {
        for(j=1;j<=qt*1000;j=j+500)
        {
            setcolor(j);
            settextstyle(2,0,5);
            outtextxy(460,70," PROGRESS");
            outtextxy(460,50,"PROCESS IN");

            delay(500);
            setcolor(0);
```

```
            settextstyle(2,0,5);
            outtextxy(460,70," PROGRESS");
            outtextxy(460,50,"PROCESS IN");
            delay(200);
        }
/* whenever the additional time is utilized by any of the process then that will be indicated with the
proper message */
for(j=1;j<=(p[i]-qt)*1000;j=j+500)
{
        setcolor(j);
        settextstyle(2,0,5);
        outtextxy(460,20," EXTRA TIME");
        outtextxy(460,70," PROGRESS");
        outtextxy(460,50,"PROCESS IN");

        delay(500);
        setcolor(0);
        settextstyle(2,0,5);
        outtextxy(460,20," EXTRA TIME");
        outtextxy(460,70," PROGRESS");
        outtextxy(460,50,"PROCESS IN");
        delay(200);
        }
}
else /* when processing completely within the allotted time */
{
        for(j=1;j<=p[i]*1000;j=j+500)
        {
            setcolor(j);
            settextstyle(2,0,5);
            outtextxy(460,70," PROGRESS");
            outtextxy(460,50,"PROCESS IN");

            delay(500);
            setcolor(0);
            settextstyle(2,0,5);
            outtextxy(460,70," PROGRESS");
            outtextxy(460,50,"PROCESS IN");
            delay(200);
```

```
        }
}

graphdefaults();

for(j=490;j<=640;++j)
        {
                if(j==561)
                rectangle(460,100,560,270);
                putimage(j,240-p[i]*10,z,2);
                delay(10);
                putimage(j,240-p[i]*10,z,1);
        }
        putimage(640,240-p[i]*10,z,2);

}

else /* when additional time is not allowable process executes only for the allotted time */
{
        for(j=1;j<=qt*1000;j=j+500)
        {
                setcolor(j);
                settextstyle(2,0,5);
                outtextxy(460,70," PROGRESS");
                outtextxy(460,50,"PROCESS IN");

                delay(500);
                setcolor(0);
                settextstyle(2,0,5);
                outtextxy(460,70," PROGRESS");
                outtextxy(460,50,"PROCESS IN");
                delay(200);
        }
        ll++;

        graphdefaults();
        putimage(490,240-p[i]*10,z,1);
        p[i]=p[i]-qt;
        n1++;
```

```
        p22[n1]=p[i];
        rectangle(490,240-p[i]*10,528,240);
        sprintf(s,"%d",p[i]);
        outtextxy(505,242,s);
        outtextxy(503,250,p1[i-1]);
        free(z);
        strcpy(tp1[n2],p1[i-1]);
        n2++;

        z=malloc(imagesize(490,240-p[i]*10,528,260));
        getimage(490,240-p[i]*10,528,260,z);

        for(j=490;j<=580;++j)
        {
              if(j==561)
              rectangle(460,100,560,270);
              putimage(j,240-p[i]*10,z,2);
              delay(10);
              putimage(j,240-p[i]*10,z,1);
              }
              putimage(580,240-p[i]*10,z,2);

        for(j=240-p[i]*10;j<=310;j++)
        {
              putimage(580,j,z,2);
              delay(10);
              putimage(580,j,z,1);
              }
              putimage(580,310,z,2);

              for(j=580;j>=5+(ll-1)*40;j--)
              {
                    putimage(j,310,z,2);
                    delay(10);
                    putimage(j,310,z,1);
              }
              putimage(5+(ll-1)*40,310,z,2);

              }
}
```

```
if(n1>0)
{
        for(i=n1;i>=1;—i)
        p[n1-i+1]=p22[i];
        for(i=0;i<n2;++i)
                strcpy(p1[i],tp1[n2-i-1]);
        n=n1;
        goto xyz;
}
sleep(2);
closegraph();
}
```

3.B. vi) THE PRIORITY BASED MODULE

/* This module demonstrates priority based CPU scheduling algorithm. The number of processes, their sizes and their priorities are taken from keyboard. Because of the resolution restrictions the maximum size of any of the process is restricted to ten and also the number of processes is also restricted to ten. Each process is placed in a rectangular box with size according to the size of the process and the corresponding label for indicating the process number and their size are displayed just below the rectangle and their priority is displayed within the rectangle. A big rectangular box for CPU is also included. Each and every process will enter CPU one by one according to their priority and stay there according to their individual execution times (sizes). After finishing execution they leave the processor and exit out of screen. */

/* This is an independent module which individually runs for priority based algorithm. to run it individually just remove the function "priomain()" and replace it with "main()" and include all necessary header files */

```
void priomain()
{
        int gd=DETECT,gm;
        int n,p[11],p2[11],i,j,s11,l=0,k;
        int pp[11],tt;
        char s[20];
        void *z;
        char p1[10][4]={"p1","p2","p3","p4","p5","p6","p7","p8","p9","p10"};
do
{
        clrscr();
        printf("\t ************************************************************");
```

```
        printf("\n\t\t SCHEDULING BASED ON PRIORITY");
        printf("\n\t ****************************************************\n\n");
        printf("\t\t ENTER N : ");
        scanf("%d",&n);
        if(n>10||n<=0)
                printf("\n\t NUMBER OF PROCESSES SHOULD BE <=10 \n");
}while(n>10||n<=0);

printf("\n\n\t\t ENTER PROCESS SIZES AND THEIR PRIORITY :- \n");
for(i=1;i<=n;++i)
{
        do
        {
        tt=0;
        printf("\n\t\t PROCESS %d : ",i);
        scanf("%d",&p[i]);

        if(p[i]>10||p[i]<=0)
        printf("\n\n\t\t PROCESS SIZE SHOULD BE <=10 ");
        else
        {
                do
                {
                tt=0;
                printf("\n\t\t PRIORITY %d : ",i);
                scanf("%d",&pp[i]);
                if(pp[i]>n||pp[i]<=0)
                {
                tt=1;
                printf("\n\n\t PRIORITY SHOULD BE <= %d",n) ;
                }
                else
                for(j=1;j<i;++j)
                if(pp[j]==pp[i])
                {
                printf("\n\n\t THIS PRIORITY IS ALREADY ENTERED ... ENTER 
ANOTHER ...\n");
                tt=1;
                }
                } while(tt==1);
```

```
        }
      }while((p[i]>10||p[i]<=0));
}

/* swapping priority */
for(i=1;i<=n;++i)
p2[n-i+1]=pp[i];

for(i=1;i<=n;++i)
pp[i]=p2[i];

for(i=1;i<=n;++i)
if(l<pp[i])
l=pp[i];

/* swapping process sizes */
for(i=1;i<=n;++i)
p2[n-i+1]=p[i];

for(i=1;i<=n;++i)
p[i]=p2[i];

/* initializing graphics mode */
initgraph(&gd,&gm,"");
        rectangle(480,165,560,315);
        setcolor(5);
        settextstyle(3,0,2);
        outtextxy(500,325,"CPU");
        setcolor(2);
        settextstyle(3,0,4);
        outtextxy(20,440,"PRIORITY QUEUE CPU SCHEDULING");
        outtextxy(21,441,"PRIORITY QUEUE CPU SCHEDULING");
        graphdefaults();
        setcolor(15);

for(i=1;i<=n;++i)
{
        rectangle(5+(i-1)*40,260-p[i]*10,5+i*40-2,260);
        sprintf(s,"%d",p[i]);
        outtextxy(15+(i-1)*40,262,s);
```

```
        sprintf(s,"%d",pp[i]);
        outtextxy(15+(i-1)*40,268-p[i]*10,s);
        outtextxy(13+(i-1)*40,270,p1[n-i]);
}

/* finds the process with highest priority */
for(i=1;i<=n;++i)
{
        s11=pp[1];
        for(j=1;j<=n;++j)
        if(pp[j]<s11)
        {
                s11=pp[j];
        }
        for(j=1;j<=n;++j)
        {
        if(s11==pp[j])
        { /* highest priority process is considered for execution */
                z=malloc(imagesize(5+(j-1)*40,260-p[j]*10,5+j*40-2,280));
                getimage(5+(j-1)*40,260-p[j]*10,5+j*40-2,280,z);
        for(k=260-p[j]*10;k<=280;++k)
        {
        putimage(5+(j-1)*40,k,z,2);
        delay(10);
        putimage(5+(j-1)*40,k,z,1);
        }
        putimage(5+(j-1)*40,280,z,2);

        for(k=5+(j-1)*40;k<=420;++k)
        {
        putimage(k,280,z,2);
        delay(10);
        putimage(k,280,z,1);
        }
        putimage(k-1,280,z,2);

        for(k=280;k>=280-p[j]*10;—k)
        {
        putimage(420,k,z,2);
        delay(10);
```

```
putimage(420,k,z,1);
}
putimage(420,280-p[j]*10,z,2);

for(k=420;k<=500;++k)
{
        if(k==481)
        rectangle(480,165,560,315);

        putimage(k,280-p[j]*10,z,2);
        delay(10);
        putimage(k,280-p[j]*10,z,1);
}
putimage(500,280-p[j]*10,z,2);

for(k=1;k<=p[j]*1000;k=k+500)
{
        setcolor(k);
        settextstyle(2,0,5);
        outtextxy(480,135," PROGRESS");
        outtextxy(480,115,"PROCESS IN");
        delay(500);

        setcolor(0);
        settextstyle(2,0,5);
        outtextxy(480,135," PROGRESS");
        outtextxy(480,115,"PROCESS IN");
        delay(200);
}
graphdefaults();

for(k=500;k<=640;++k)
{
        if(k==561)
                rectangle(480,165,560,315);
        putimage(k,280-p[j]*10,z,2);
        delay(10);
        putimage(k,280-p[j]*10,z,1);
```

```
            }
            putimage(k-1,280-p[j]*10,z,2);

            pp[j]=l+1;
            }
      }
   }
   sleep(2);
   closegraph();
}
```

PROJECT 4

SIMULATION OF SEARCHING, SORTING AND MERGING ALGORITHMS

4.A) SYNOPSIS:

This project demonstrates the working of searching, sorting and merging methods. The working of actual algorithms are not changed, but simulated effectively so that each and every operations or steps will be shown visually through computer graphics. The main modules in this project are divided into three categories as follows.

4.A. i) SEARCHING METHODS

In this section we are discussing two popular searching techniques namely linear and binary searching.

Linear Search

The simplest technique for searching an unordered table for a particular record is to scan each entry in the table in a sequential manner until the desired record is found. In case of duplicate elements in the table it is essential to search the entire table for the desired element.

Binary Search

Binary searching method requires the elements of a list to be in some specific order. The middle element of a list is compared with the search element and if the search is successful the program terminates. Otherwise there are two possibilities. The search element is present in the first half of the list or in the second half of the list depending on the middle element and a search element comparison. In either of the case the respective half of the list will be considered as the new list and search process is continued until the search element is found or list gets exhausted.

4.A ii) SORTING METHODS

Here we are discussing three popular sorting techniques and arranging the list in ascending order. The methods are explained below.

Selection Sort

One of the easiest ways to sort a table is by Selection. Beginning with the first record in the table, a search is performed to locate the element, which has the smallest key. When this element is found, it is interchanged with the first record in the table. The interchange places the record with the smallest key in the first position of the table. A search for the second smallest key is then carried out. This is accomplished by examining the keys of the records from the second. Then second smallest key is interchanged with the second record that is to be located in the second position of the table. This process continues until all the records are in ascending order of the table.

Sequential Sort

In this method, the first element is compared with all other elements of the list and exchanged whenever they are not in order. Then leaving the first element, the second element is compared with remaining elements of the list and exchanged whenever necessary. This continues until getting the ordered list.

Bubble Sort

In this technique two consecutive elements are compared and interchanged whenever necessary throughout the list. Then this process has to be repeated (n-1) times for a list of n elements.

4.A. iii) MERGING OF LISTS

Sorted Merge

In this sub module the two ordered lists will be merged by maintaining same order in the target list. For this purpose the first element of both the lists will be compared and the smallest element among them will be transferred to the target list. At the same time the counter of the list whose element is transferred has to be incremented by one. Now the top two elements are compared and smallest element is transferred to the target list. This process continues until one of the two lists or both the lists get exhausted. When one list gets exhausted the elements of the other list will be simply transferred to the target list.

Unsorted Merge

In this method the two lists given will be in unsorted form. The smallest element in both the list will be searched and it will be placed in the first place of target list then next smallest in both the list will be searched and placed in the second place of target list and this process gets continued until all elements of both the list are transferred to target list.

4.B) CODE DETAILS

This project consists of total eight modules. Each of these modules are explained below.

1. The first module generates the menu which is user friendly and depending on menu selection it activates other modules of the project. The program file "ssmmain.c" implements this. It is having all header files and other program modules included in it. The necessary function declarations are also included.
2. **Linear search module**: This module demonstrates linear search algorithm with the help of animations. The rectangular box containing the search element is moved throughout the list and whenever the element is present related message will be displayed. In case the element is not present throughout the list then un successful search message will be displayed. The program file "ssmlin.c" contains the related code of this module.
3. **Binary search module**: For demonstrating the binary search the function "binarymain()" is implemented. In this the ordered list is shown in the list of consecutive rectangle boxes. And the rectangular box containing search element is animated by moving it to

the middle of the list. Depending on the situation the search element may either be searched in the first half or second half of the list. If the middle element compared itself is the search element then the search is ended .This module is defined in the program file "ssmbin.c".

4. **Bubble sort**: This module "bubblemain()" is defined in the program file "ssmbub.c". The elements of the list are shown using rectangular boxes and sorting of these elements is shown by the movement of these rectangles.
5. **Selection sort**: The function "selectiomain()" present in the program file "ssmsel.c" demonstrates the working logic of the selection sort algorithm. The elements are placed in the rectangles and during sorting the elements along with their rectangle boxes are moved through animation.
6. **Sequential sort**: This module "sequentialmain()" is defined in the program file "ssmseq.c".
7. **Sorted lists merge**: In this module two user lists and sorted lists are displayed as a lists of rectangles. The sorted lists are also displayed in the rectangles. The merged target list is shown in the middle of the screen. The module "sortedmergemain()" present in the program file "ssmsm.c" implements this demo.
8. **Unsorted lists merge**: This module moves the rectangle choosing from both the lists which has smallest element. It is implemented in "ssmusm.c" program file using "unsortedmergemain()" function.

4.C) Searching, sorting and merging project source code

4.C. i) Main Menu Module

```
/* The main module for generating menu and calling other program modules that are related */

#include<conio.h>
#include<graphics.h>
#include<stdio.h>
#include<alloc.h>
#include<dos.h>

/* The other program modules in this project */

#include "ssmlin.c" /* Linear search module */
#include "ssmbin.c" /* Binary search module */
#include "ssmbub.c" /* Bubble sort module */
#include "ssmsel.c" /* Selection sort module */
#include "ssmseq.c" /* Sequential sort module */
#include "ssmsm.c" /* Merging of sorted lists module */
#include "ssmusm.c" /* Merging of unsorted lists module */
```

```
/* function declarations */

void linearmain(); /* for linear search */
void binarymain(); /* binary search */
void bubblemain(); /* bubble sort */
void selectionmain(); /* selection sort */
void sequentialmain(); /* sequential sort */
void sortedmergemain(); /* Merging of sorted lists */
void unsortedmergemain(); /* Merging of unsorted lists */

void main()
{

int gd,gm,i,j,n,m,kb,chek=0;
int ch=1;
gd=DETECT; /* detects the graph driver during run time */
initgraph(&gd,&gm,""); /* Initializes the graph, by
        specifying graph driver, graph mode and path. The empty
        path is specified means the compiler automatically chooses
        the path */
setcolor(15); /* sets the writing color as white color */
for(i=1;i<=8;++i) /* for 8 menu items draws 8 rectangles */
        {
        rectangle(180,i*42+10,407,i*42+52);
        /* each rectangle size is 227 pixels along x-axis
        and 40 pixels along y-axis starting at (180, 52) */
        }

setcolor(2); /* sets the writing color as green */
settextstyle(0,0,3); /* sets the text style */
outtextxy(25,15,"SIMULATION OF SEARCHING"); /* heading displayed
                                        at (25,15) */
setcolor(3);/* sets the writing color to CYAN */
outtextxy(25,410," AND SORTING METHODS"); /* heading displayed
                                        at (25,410) */
settextstyle(3,0,4);
setcolor(12); /* sets writing color to light red */

/* display of menu item names in the rectangles */
outtextxy(185,56," LINEAR");
```

```
outtextxy(185,98," BINARY");
outtextxy(185,140," BUBBLE");
outtextxy(185,182,"SELECTION");
outtextxy(185,220."SEQUENTIAL");
outtextxy(185,262,"SORTED MERGE");
outtextxy(185,304,"UNSORT MERGE");
outtextxy(185,346," EXIT ");

floodfill(184,ch*42+12,15); /* fills the first menu item box
                              with default fill effects */

/* menu selections and filling different menu item boxes when selected using arrow keys. We need
to re-draw the rectangles, unfill and refill the menu item boxes and re-write the menu items to get
the complete effects */

chek=0;
while(chek==0)
        {
        chek=0;
        setcolor(15);
        for(i=1;i<=8;++i)
        {
                rectangle(180,i*42+10,407,i*42+52);
        }
        setcolor(2);
        settextstyle(0,0,3);
        outtextxy(25,15,"SIMULATION OF SEARCHING");
        setcolor(3);
        outtextxy(25,410," AND SORTING METHODS");
        settextstyle(3,0,4);
        setcolor(12);
        outtextxy(185,56," LINEAR");
        outtextxy(185,98," BINARY");
        outtextxy(185,140," BUBBLE");
        outtextxy(185,182,"SELECTION");
        outtextxy(185,220,"SEQUENTIAL");
        outtextxy(185,262,"SORTED MERGE");
        outtextxy(185,304,"UNSORT MERGE");
        outtextxy(185,346," EXIT ");
```

```
setcolor(15);
floodfill(184,ch*42+12,15);
setcolor(12);

if(ch==1)
{
        settextstyle(3,0,4);
        setcolor(12);
        outtextxy(185,56," LINEAR");
}

if(ch==2)
{
        settextstyle(3,0,4);
        setcolor(12);
        outtextxy(185,98," BINARY ");
}

if(ch==3)
{
        settextstyle(3,0,4);
        setcolor(12);
        outtextxy(185,140," BUBBLE");
}

if(ch==4)
{
        settextstyle(3,0,4);
        setcolor(12);
        outtextxy(185,182,"SELECTION");
}

if(ch==5)
{       settextstyle(3,0,4);
        setcolor(12);
        outtextxy(185,220,"SEQUENTIAL");
}
```

```
        if(ch==6)
        {
            settextstyle(3,0,4);
            setcolor(12);
            outtextxy(185,262,"SORTED MERGE");
        }
        if(ch==7)
        {
            settextstyle(3,0,4);
            setcolor(12);
            outtextxy(185,304,"UNSORT MERGE");
        }

        if(ch==8)
        {
            settextstyle(3,0,4);
            setcolor(12);
            outtextxy(185,346," EXIT ");
        }

/* choosing the menu item by arrow keys and
selection by enter keys the key pressed will
be identified by their ASCII values */

if(ch==1)
{
        settextstyle(3,0,4);
        setcolor(12);
        outtextxy(185,56," LINEAR");
}
        kb=getche(); /* gets the key pressed into variable kb */

switch(kb)
        {
    case 72: /* 72 is the ASCII value for up arrow so that counter will be decreased
by one */
                ch--;
                if(ch<1) /* when the control is on first item then we need to send it to last item on
pressing up arrow again */
```

```
            ch=8;
            cleardevice(); /* clears the graphical screen */
            break;
        case 80: /* 80 is the ASCII value for down arrow so that counter will be incremented
by one */
            ch++;
            if(ch>8)/* when the control is on last item then we need to send it to first item on
pressing down arrow again */
            ch=1;
            cleardevice(); /* clears the graphical screen */
            break;
        case 13: /* 13 is the ASCII value for entry key and it shows selection of menu item that
is highlighted. The highlighted item is indicated by the value of variable ch */
            switch(ch)
            {
            case 1: /* When the first menu item is selected we are calling the linear search
module. The linear search module needs certain text mode inputs from user, so the graphics mode
must be closed before calling the module and re-initialized after program control comes back */
                    closegraph();
                    linearmain();
                    initgraph(&gd,&gm,"");
                    break;

            case 2: /* When the second menu item is selected we are calling the binary search
module. The binary module needs certain text mode inputs from user, so the graphics mode must be
closed before calling the module and re-initialized after program control comes back */
                    closegraph();
                    binarymain();
                    initgraph(&gd,&gm,"");
                    break;

            case 3: /* When the third menu item is selected we are calling the bubble sort
module. */
                    closegraph();
                    bubblemain();
                    initgraph(&gd,&gm,"");
            break;

            case 4: /* When the fourth menu item is selected we are calling the selection sort
module. */
```

```
                closegraph();
                selectionmain();
                initgraph(&gd,&gm,"");
                break;

        case 5: /* When the fifth menu item is selected we are calling the sequential sort
module. */
                closegraph();
                sequentialmain();
                initgraph(&gd,&gm,"");
                break;

        case 6: /* When the sixth menu item is selected we are calling the sorted list
merging module. */
                closegraph();
                sortedmergemain();
                initgraph(&gd,&gm,"");
                break;

        case 7: /* When the seventh menu item is selected we are calling the unsorted list
merging module. */
                closegraph();
                unsortedmergemain();
                initgraph(&gd,&gm,"");
                break;
        case 8: /* this case closes the program */
                chek=1;
                cleardevice();
                setcolor(2);
                outtextxy(120,200,"THANKS FOR USING");
                break;
        } /* end of inner switch statement switch(ch) */

    } /* end of outer switch statement switch(kb) */

  } /* end of while statement while(chek==0) */
  delay(3000); /* makes the processor idle for 3000 milli seconds */
  closegraph(); /* closes the graph mode */
} /* end of main program of this project */
```

4.C. ii) The linear search module

/* This module shows the demo of linear search algorithm. The elements considered are simple integer array placed in rectangular boxes. The search element is also placed in a rectangular box with an arrow pointing towards the given list. This search element box starts its movements from first element in the given list box. It keeps on moving from one element to other element and waits for a while in each element. When the search element is present then it displays a message indicating its position. In case the search element is not present in the list at all then it displays the message that " the element not present in the list". After completing the execution the program control automatically goes back to the main menu module of the project */

/* This module also works independently. For this just the function name "void linearmain()" has to be changed to "void main()" and necessary header files has to be included */

```
void linearmain() /* This name has to be changed to void main() to make it independent */
{
  int gd=DETECT,gm,i,n,a[100],x,t=0,j;
  char s[10];
  char *z; /* for storing the image needed for movement */

  clrscr(); /* clears the screen in text mode */

/* For inputting the size of the list with checking for limits */
do
        {
        t=0;
        printf("enter n\n");
        scanf("%d",&n);
        if(n>18 && n<=0) /* The size of list must be +ve integer <= 18 */
        {
                t=1;
                printf("\n size of list must be <=18 and > 0 \n re-enter...\n");
        }

        }while(t==1);

/* For inputting the elements of the list */
printf("\n enter elements\n");
        for(i=1;i<=n;++i)
                scanf("%d",&a[i]);
```

```
/* For inputting the element to search */
printf("enter number to search\n");
scanf("%d",&x);

initgraph(&gd,&gm,""); /* Initialization of graph */

/* Drawing n rectangles and putting the n elements in the rectangular boxes. The 'n' is the size of
the list */

for(i=1;i<=n;++i)
{
rectangle(50,i*20+30,100,i*20+48); /* Draws the rectangles and in between each rectangle 2
pixels gap is maintained for effective demonstration */
  sprintf(s,"%d",a[i]); /* converts the array elements ( integer ) into string and stores in the pointer
variable s */

  outtextxy(55,i*20+36,s); /* Displays the string value contained in 's' (array element) in the
respective rectangular box */

}

/* For the search element */

rectangle(130,50,180,68); /* Draw the rectangle for search element */
sprintf(s,"%d",x); /* Search element converted into string */
outtextxy(135,56,s); /* Displays the search element in the respective box */

/* For making an arrow towards the list from search element */
line(130,56,124,56);
line(124,56,124,50);
line(124,50,108,60);
line(108,60,124,68);
line(124,68,124,62);
line(124,62,130,62);

z=malloc(imagesize(108,50,180,68)); /* allocates the memory for storing the search element
along with arrow to the char * variable 'z' */

getimage(108,50,180,68,z); /* Stores the search element into the variable 'z' */

/* For displaying the Heading of the algorithm */
```

```
settextstyle(3,0,5);
outtextxy(20,420,"LINEAR SEARCH ALGORITHM");

graphdefaults(); /* All graphics settings get reset to default values */

/* Searching process. Shows the movement of search element rectangular box across the elements
of the list and in case of successful search displays the message along with position and sets the
flag variable 't' */

for(i=1;i<=n-1;++i)
     {
     if (x==a[i])
          {
          sprintf(s,"%d",i); /* Converting the position value into string */
          outtextxy(190,i*20+36,"number present at position ");
          outtextxy(410,i*20+36,s);/* Displaying the position */
          t=1; /* Flag is set to 1 on success */
          }
     delay(2000); /* Waits for 2 seconds */

     /* Movement of search element rectangular box to the next successive elements */
     for(j=i*20+30;j<=i*20+50;++j)
     {
     putimage(108,j,z,2); /* Writes the image on the screen */
     delay(30);
     putimage(108,j,z,1); /* Erases the image */
     }
     putimage(108,i*20+50,z,2);/* Writes the image at the next element position */
     }

     if (x==a[i]) /* Checks whether the last element of the list is matching */
     {
          sprintf(s,"%d",i);
          outtextxy(190,i*20+36,"number present at position");
          outtextxy(410,i*20+36,s);
          t=1;
     }
     delay(1000);

     if(t==0) /* When the flag 't' remains unset it displays unsuccessful message */
```

```
        outtextxy(190,i*20+50," number not present in list");
        delay(2000);
}
```

4.C. iii) The Binary Search Module

/* The Binary search module. This module shows the complete demo of Binary search algorithm. The elements of the list are taken from the keyboard dynamically. They will be arranged into ascending order. The search element is placed in a rectangular box with an arrows headed towards list. The given list and the arranged list are also placed in the rectangular boxes. */

/* This module also works independently, for this we need to change the name of the function 'binarymain ()' to just 'main()' and include all necessary header files to the program */

```
void arrange(int [], int); /* function for arranging the given list */

void main() /* The main module for binary search */
{
int gd=DETECT,gm,i,n,a[100],x,t=0,j,l,m,h;
char s[10];
char *z;
clrscr(); /* Clears the screen in text mode */

/* For inputting the size of the list with validation for limits */
do
{
        t=0; /* flag set to zero */
        printf("enter n\n");
        scanf("%d",&n);
        if(n>18 || n<=0 ) /* Size is limited to a maximum of 18 elements */
        {
                t=1; /* flag is set to 1 */
                printf("\n size of list must be <=18 \n re-enter...\n");
                }
}while(t==1); /* end of do.. while loop */

/* For inputting the elements of the list */
   printf("\n enter elements\n");
   for(i=1;i<=n;++i)
      scanf("%d",&a[i]);
/* inputting the search element */
```

```
  printf("enter number to search\n");
    scanf("%d",&x);

initgraph(&gd,&gm,""); /* Initialization of graph */

  /* Drawing 'n' rectangles and placing the given elements in the rectangular boxes. This list is
unordered */
  for(i=1;i<=n;++i)
  {
  rectangle(580,i*20+30,630,i*20+48); /* Draws the rectangles with 50 pixels width and 18
pixels height, maintains 2 pixels gap in between rectangles */
  sprintf(s,"%d",a[i]); /* Gets the array element into the string variable */
  outtextxy(585,i*20+36,s); /* Displays the array element in the rectangular box */
  delay(200);
}

/* For displaying the message indicating 'given list' just below the rectangular boxes containing
the given list. Its position along y-axis depends on the size of list and along x-axis remains constant
*/
      outtextxy(550,i*20+36,"given list");

  arrange(a,n); /* Calls the function by array and its size for arranging the given list in ascending
order. The list must be in ascending or descending order for using Binary search algorithm. The
program logic in this module is using the list in ascending order only */

  /* Drawing 'n' rectangles and placing the arranged elements in the rectangular boxes. This list
is ordered */

  for(i=1;i<=n;++i)
  {
  rectangle(50,i*20+30,100,i*20+48);
  sprintf(s,"%d",a[i]);
  outtextxy(55,i*20+36,s);
  delay(200);
  }

/* For displaying the message indicating 'arranged list' just below the rectangular boxes containing
the arranged list. Its position along y-axis depends on the size of list and along x-axis remains
constant */
  outtextxy(20,i*20+36,"Arrnged list");
```

```
/* Rectangle for the search element and an arrow pointing towards the arranged list. */
        rectangle(130,50,180,68);
        sprintf(s,"%d",x);
        outtextxy(135,56,s);
        line(130,56,124,56);
        line(124,56,124,50);
        line(124,50,108,60);
        line(108,60,124,68);
        line(124,68,124,62);
        line(124,62,130,62);

/* Following statements allocate the memory for the pointer variable to store the rectangular image and stores the image into the variable by using getimage and finally erases the image from the screen using putimage function with option 1 */

z=malloc(imagesize(108,50,180,68));
getimage(108,50,180,68,z);
putimage(108,50,z,1);

/* Following statements set the color and text style and displays the text related to algorithm heading on the screen in appropriate position. */
settextstyle(3,0,5);
outtextxy(20,420,"BINARY SEARCH ALGORITHM");
graphdefaults(); /* All graphic settings are resetted to default settings */

/* The main algorithm follows */
l=1; /* Low is set to 1 */
h=n; /* high is set to size of list */
t=0; /* flag variable is set to 0 */

while((l<=h) &&(t==0)) /* Loop continues until l<=h or flag variable t is set */
{
        m=(l+h)/2; /* finds the middle position */
        putimage(108,m*20+30,z,2); /* Places the search element box against the middle element
        */

        if (x==a[m]) /* Checks for element in the list */
        {
                /* if present puts the successful message along with position and sets the flag
variable */
```

```
            sprintf(s,"%d",m);
            outtextxy(190,m*20+36,"number present at position ");
            outtextxy(410,m*20+36,s);
            t=1;
        }
        else
        if (x>a[m]) /* When not present checks the search element is larger than the middle
        element if so sets low as mid+1 */
            l=m+1;
        else
        h=m-1; /* Otherwise sets High as mid-1 */

        delay(5000); /* Waits for 5 seconds */

        if (t==0) /* On unsuccessful search the search element box is erased */
            putimage(108,m*20+30,z,1);
}

if(t==0) /* When the search fails it displays the necessary message */
        outtextxy(190,i*20+50," number not present in list");

delay(2000); closegraph(); /* closes the graph */
}

/* Function for arranging the given list in ascending order */
void arrange(int a[],int n)
{
        int i,j,t;

        for(i=1;i<n;++i)
        for(j=1;j<n;++j)
        if(a[j]>a[j+1])
            {
            t=a[j];
            a[j]=a[j+1];
            a[j+1]=t;
            }
}
```

4.C. iv) The Bubble sort module

/* This module shows the demo of bubble sort algorithm. Here we are displaying the given elements in a list of rectangles. For simplicity we considered the integer elements. All the elements are placed in the rectangles. The element first and second will be compared and the rectangle boxes along with elements are exchanged when they are not in order. For this purpose the first rectangle is shifted to left side of the list through animation. Then the second element is shifted to right side of the list. The first element is then moved down for the pixels equivalent to width of the rectangle and similarly the second element is shifted up. Finally the first element is shifted in the second position and second element in the first position. Then we continue with second and third elements and so on. */

/* This is again an independent module. To run this independently just change the name of the function 'void bubblemain()' with 'void main' and include all necessary header files. */

```
void bubblemain()
{
 int gd=DETECT,gm,i,k,n,a[100],t,j;
 char s[10],ch;
 void *z,*z1; /* for storing two rectangles at the time of exchange of elements */
 clrscr(); /* clears the screen */

/* Text mode input for inputting the size of list and its boundary validation */
do
{
 t=0; /* flag variable reseted to 0 */
 printf("enter n\n");
 scanf("%d",&n);
 if(n>16 && n<1) /* maximum number of elements in the list is limited to 16 */
  {
  t=1; /* Flag is set when the size is beyond the limit */
  printf("\n size of list must be <=16\n re-enter...\n");
  }
}while(t==1);
```

/* Here user is having the option to enter the numbers from keyboard or make the system to take random numbers directly by using rand() function. */

```
 printf("are you entering the numbers (y/n)?\n");
 fflush(stdin);
 ch=getche();
```

```
if(ch=='y' || ch=='Y')
        {
        printf("\n enter elements\n");
        for(i=0;i<n;++i) /* When user wishes then he has to enter the integer list */
        scanf("%d",&a[i]);
        }
else
        {
        for(i=0;i<n;++i) /* The program will take random numbers directly into the list as input
        */
        a[i]=rand();
        }

/* Graphical demo starts here */

initgraph(&gd,&gm,""); /* Graphics mode initialized */
setbkcolor(1); /* Background color is set to 1 */
/* For drawing 'n' rectangles and placing the elements in the rectangle */
for(i=0;i<n;++i)
{
        rectangle(180,i*20+10,230,i*20+28);
        sprintf(s,"%d",a[i]); /* convert the number into string format and stores it in s */
        outtextxy(185,i*20+16,s);
        delay(200);
}
/* for displaying the heading of the algorithm with color and style settings */
settextstyle(3,0,5);
setcolor(14);
outtextxy(60,410,"BUBBLE SORT ALGORITHM");

/* Memory allocated to z,z1 for storing two equal sized rectangular blocks */
z=malloc(imagesize(0,0,50,28));
z1=malloc(imagesize(0,0,50,28));

/* bubble sort algorithm starts here */
for(i=0;i<n-1;++i)
{
        /* for displaying the size and text styles for each pass */
        settextstyle(3,0,3);
        setcolor(12);
```

```
        outtextxy(50,(n+3)*20,"PASS IN PROGRESS");
        sprintf(s,"%d",i+1);
        setcolor(15);
        outtextxy(108,(n+3)*20,s);

/* for comparing and exchanging of elements when they are not in order */
for(j=0;j<n-1;++j)
        {
         if (a[j]>a[j+1]) /* checks for ascending order */
         {
          t= a[j];
          a[j]=a[j+1]; /* exchange of elements in the original list */
          a[j+1]=t;

        /* gets the images of corresponding rectangles into z and z1 */
        getimage(180,j*20+10,230,j*20+28,z);
        getimage(180,(j+1)*20+10,230,(j+1)*20+28,z1);

/* movement of first rectangle from its original position to 70 pixels left side of the list */
for (k=180;k>=110;—k)
        {
                putimage(k,j*20+10,z,2);/* writing the image */
                delay(5); /* Based on delay the movements will be slow or fast */
                putimage(k,j*20+10,z,1);/* erasing the image after delay, that makes the image to
look like moving */
        }
        putimage(110,j*20+10,z,2); /* writing the image in the final position after movement */

/* movement of second rectangle from its original position to 70 pixels right side of the list */
 for (k=180;k<=250;++k)
        {
        putimage(k,(j+1)*20+10,z1,2); /* writing the image */
        delay(5); /*    Based on delay the movements will be slow or fast */
        putimage(k,(j+1)*20+10,z1,1); /* erasing the image after delay, that makes the image to
        look like moving */
        }
        putimage(250,(j+1)*20+10,z1,2); /* writing the image in the final position after
movement */

/* movement of first rectangle from its shifted position to 20 pixels (the width of rectangle) down
```

```
side of the list */
for (k=j*20+10;k<=(j+1)*20+10;++k)
        {
        putimage(110,k,z,2); /* writing the image */
        delay(5);
        putimage(110,k,z,1); /* erasing the image after delay */
        }
        putimage(110,(j+1)*20+10,z,2); /* writing the image in the final position after movement
        */

/* movement of second rectangle from its shifted position to 20 pixels (the width of rectangle) up
side of the list */
 for (k=(j+1)*20+10;k>=j*20+10;—k)
        {
        putimage(250,k,z1,2);
        delay(5);
        putimage(250,k,z1,1);
        }
        putimage(250,j*20+10,z1,2);

/* Movement of first shifted element 70 pixels towards right to place it in the second elements
position */
 for (k=110;k<=180;++k)
        {
        putimage(k,(j+1)*20+10,z,2);
        delay(5);
        putimage(k,(j+1)*20+10,z,1);
        }
        putimage(180,(j+1)*20+10,z,2);

/* Movement of second shifted element 70 pixels towards left to place it in the first elements
position */
 for (k=250;k>=180;—k)
        {
        putimage(k,j*20+10,z1,2);
        delay(5);
        putimage(k,j*20+10,z1,1);
        }
        putimage(180,j*20+10,z1,2);
```

```
} /* The end of if statement */

} /* end of inner for loop */

/* Following statements erase the pass number after completion of each pass. This is done by
writing the pass number by background color on the same position */
setcolor(1);
outtextxy(108,(n+3)*20,s);
} /* end of outer for loop and the algorithm itself */

/* Following statements erase the pass information after completion of algorithm. This is done by
writing the same information with background color on the same position */
setcolor(0);
outtextxy(50,(n+3)*20,"PASS IN PROGRESS");

delay(2000); /* waits for 2 seconds before going back to the main menu automatically */

} /* end of bubblemain() */
```

4.C. v) The selection sort module

/* This module shows the demo of selection sort algorithm. Here we are displaying the given elements in a list of rectangles. For simplicity we considered the integer elements. All the elements are placed in rectangles. The first smallest element is found and the first element is exchanged with first smallest. For this the rectangle boxes along with elements are exchanged. For this purpose the first rectangle is shifted to left side of the list through animation. Then the rectangle box containing smallest element is shifted to right side of the list. The first element is then moved down for the pixels equivalent to position of the rectangle containing smallest element and similarly the smallest element box is shifted up. Finally the first element is shifted in the smallest element position and smallest element in the first position. Then we are continuing with second smallest and so on. */

/* This is again an independent module. To run this independently just change the name of the function 'void selectionmain()' with 'void main' and include all necessary header files. */

```
void selectionmain()
{
int gd=DETECT,gm,a[100],i,k,n,sm,j,t;
void *z,*z1; /* for storing two rectangles at the time of exchange of elements */
char s[10],ch;
clrscr();
```

```
/* Text mode input for inputting the size of list and its boundary validation */
do
{
        t=0;
        printf("enter n\n");
        scanf("%d",&n);
        if(n>16 && n<=0) /* The size is limited to maximum 16 elements because of resolution
of the screen and effective demo */
         {
          t=1;
          printf("\n size of list must be <=16\n re-enter...\n");
         }
}while(t==1);

/* Here user is having the option to enter the numbers from keyboard or make the system to take
random numbers directly by using rand() function. */
 printf("are you entering the numbers (y/n)?\n");
 fflush(stdin);
 ch=getche();
 if(ch=='y' || ch=='Y')
        {
        printf("\n enter elements\n");
        for(i=1;i<=n;++i) /* Taking the elements from keyboard */
        scanf("%d",&a[i]);
        }
 else
        {
        for(i=1;i<=n;++i)
        a[i]=rand(); /* taking the elements from system randomly */
        }
 /* Simulation of algorithm starts here */
 initgraph(&gd,&gm,""); /* graphics mode is initialized */
 /* For drawing 'n' rectangles and placing the elements in them */
 for(i=1;i<=n;++i)
 {
        rectangle(180,(i-1)*20+10,230,i*20+8);
        sprintf(s,"%d",a[i]); /* Converts the integer element to string */
        outtextxy(185,(i-1)*20+15,s); /* writes the element in the rectangle box */

 }
```

```
/* Memory is allocated dynamically for storing two rectangle boxes in the variables z and z1 */
z=malloc(imagesize(180,10,230,30));
z1=malloc(imagesize(180,10,230,30));

/* Sets the text styles, sizes and displays the algorithm heading on the screen */

settextstyle(3,0,3);
outtextxy(220,410,"Selection Sort Algorithm");
settextstyle(1,0,1);

/* Algorithm main logic starts from here */
for(i=1;i<n;++i)
{
        sm=a[i]; /* Assumes the ith element is small */
        /* For pass information text styles, sizes and colors */
        setcolor(3);
        outtextxy(10,n*20+10,"Pass In process");
        setcolor(5);
        sprintf(s,"%d",i);
        outtextxy(55,n*20+10,s);

        /* for finding the smallest element in the list from ith position */
        for(j=i+1;j<=n;++j)
        if(sm>a[j]) /* if any element is smaller than small then */
        sm=a[j]; /* assigns that element to sm variable */
        /* now variable sm contains the smallest element */

                /* finding the smallest elements position. Actual movement of elements starts from
        here */
                for(j=i;j<=n;++j)
                if (sm==a[j]) /* when ith smallest elements is found then */
                {
                t=a[j];
                a[j]=a[i]; /* exchanging that element with ith element in the list */
                a[i]=t;
                /* getting the images of the rectangles containing ith element and ith smallest
element in z and z1 respectively */
```

```
getimage(180,(i-1)*20+10,230,i*20+8,z);
getimage(180,(j-1)*20+10,230,j*20+8,z1);

/* Moving the ith element 60 pixels left of the list */
for(k=180;k>=120;—k)
{
putimage(k,(i-1)*20+10,z,2);/* writing the image */
delay(5); /* delay to make animation effect*/
putimage(k,(i-1)*20+10,z,1); /* erasing the image */
}
putimage(120,(i-1)*20+10,z,2); /* writing the image in the final position */

/* Moving the ith smallest element 60 pixels right of the list */
for(k=180;k<=240;++k)
{
putimage(k,(j-1)*20+10,z1,2); /* writing the image */
delay(5); /* delay to make animation effect*/
putimage(k,(j-1)*20+10,z1,1); /* erasing the image */
}
putimage(240,(j-1)*20+10,z1,2); /* writing the image in the final position */

/* Moving the ith element downwards the number of pixels equivalent to position
of ith smallest element in the list */
for(k=(i-1)*20+10;k<=(j-1)*20+10;++k)
{
putimage(120,k,z,2);
delay(5);
putimage(120,k,z,1);
}
putimage(120,(j-1)*20+10,z,2);

/* Moving the ith smallest element upwards the number of pixels equivalent to
position of ith element in the list */
for(k=(j-1)*20+10;k>=(i-1)*20+10;—k)
{
putimage(240,k,z1,2);
delay(5);
putimage(240,k,z1,1);
}
putimage(240,(i-1)*20+10,z1,2);
```

/* Moving the ith element 60 pixels right to place it in ith smallest elements position */

```
for(k=120;k<=180;++k)
{
putimage(k,(j-1)*20+10,z,2);
delay(5);
putimage(k,(j-1)*20+10,z,1);
}
putimage(180,(j-1)*20+10,z,2);
```

/* Moving the ith smallest element 60 pixels left to place it in ith elements position */

```
for(k=240;k>=180;—k)
{
putimage(k,(i-1)*20+10,z1,2);
delay(5);
putimage(k,(i-1)*20+10,z1,1);
}
putimage(180,(i-1)*20+10,z1,2);

} /* movements end here with inner loop */
/* To erase the pass information before starting the next pass */
setcolor(0);
outtextxy(10,n*20+10,"Pass In process");
setcolor(0);
sprintf(s,"%d",i);
outtextxy(55,n*20+10,s);

} /* end of algorithms main loop */

delay(2000); /* waits for 2 seconds before automatically switching back to the main module of the project */
} /* End of module selectionmain() */
```

4.C. vi) The sequential sort module

/* This module shows the demo of sequential sort algorithm. Here we are displaying the given elements in a list of rectangles. For simplicity we have considered only the integer elements. All the elements are placed in rectangles. The element first and second will be compared and the rectangle boxes along with elements are exchanged when they are not in order. For this purpose the first rectangle is shifted to left side of the list through animation. Then the second element is shifted to right side of the list. The first element is then moved down for the pixels equivalent to width of the rectangle and similarly the second element is shifted up. Finally the first element is shifted in the second position and second element in the first position. Then we are continuing with first and third elements and so on until the first smallest is placed in the first position. Then in the same way we are continuing with second element and comparing it with third element onwards and so on.*/

```
/* This is an independent module. To run this independently just change the name of the function
'void sequentialmain()' with 'void main' and include all necessary header files. */

void sequentialmain()
{
int gd=DETECT,gm,i,k,n,a[100],t,j;
ch          ar s[10],ch;
void *z,*z1; /* for storing two rectangles at the time of exchange of elements */
clrscr(); /* clears the screen */

/* Text mode input for inputting the size of list and its boundary validation */
do
{
        t=0; /* flag variable is reseted to 0 */
        printf("enter n\n");
        scanf("%d",&n); /* inputs the size of the list */
        if(n>16 && n<=0) /* Size is limited to maximum 16 */
                {
                t=1; /* flag is set when the size is beyond limits */
                printf("\n size of list must be <=16\n re-enter...\n");
                } /* end of if */
}while(t==1); /* end of do... while loop */

/* Here user is having the option to enter the numbers from keyboard or make the system to take
        random numbers directly by using rand() function. */
printf("are you entering the data (y/n)?\n");
fflush(stdin); /* clears the input buffer */
ch=getch();
if (toupper(ch)=='Y') /* enter the elements from keyboard when the choice is Y */
{
printf("\n enter elements\n");
for(i=0;i<n;++i)
        scanf("%d",&a[i]);
}
else /* takes the random numbers automatically when the choice is other than Y */
```

```
{
for(i=0;i<n;++i)
        a[i]=rand();
}

/* Graphical demo of the module starts here */
initgraph(&gd,&gm,""); /* Graphics mode is initialized */
setbkcolor(1); /* Sets the background color of the screen to blue */

/* Drawing the rectangles and placing the elements in rectangles. Delay is maintained to give the
animation effect */
for(i=0;i<n;++i)
{
rectangle(180,i*20+10,230,i*20+28);
sprintf(s,"%d",a[i]);
outtextxy(185,i*20+16,s);
delay(200);
}

/* Setting the size, font and colors for displaying the algorithm heading during process */
settextstyle(3,0,5);
setcolor(14);
outtextxy(20,410,"SEQUENTIAL SORT ALGORITHM");

/* allocation of memory to z and z1 for storing rectangles needed for movements during exchange
of elements */
z=malloc(imagesize(0,0,50,28));
z1=malloc(imagesize(0,0,50,28));

/* Algorithms main logic starts here */
for(i=0;i<n-1;++i)
{
/* Setting and displaying the pass information */
settextstyle(3,0,3);
setcolor(12);
outtextxy(50,(n+3)*20,"PASS IN PROGRESS");
sprintf(s,"%d",i+1);
setcolor(15);
outtextxy(108,(n+3)*20,s);
```

```
/* Comparing the ith element with next successive elements and exchanging them whenever
necessary */
for(j=i+1;j<n;++j)
{
        if (a[i]>a[j])
        {
        t= a[j];
        a[j]=a[i]; /* exchange of elements in the list */
        a[i]=t;

/* getting images of the rectangles that need to exchange with each other */
        getimage(180,i*20+10,230,i*20+28,z);
        getimage(180,(j)*20+10,230,(j)*20+28,z1);

/* movement of ith rectangle 70 pixels left to its original position */
        for (k=180;k>=110;—k)
        {
        putimage(k,i*20+10,z,2);/* writing the image */
        delay(5); /* delay for effectiveness */
        putimage(k,i*20+10,z,1); /* erasing the image to make it to look like moving */
        }
        putimage(110,i*20+10,z,2); /* writing the image */

/* movement of jth rectangle 70 pixels right to its original position */
        for (k=180;k<=250;++k)
        {
        putimage(k,(j)*20+10,z1,2);/* writing the image */
        delay(5);        /* delay for effectiveness of animation */
        putimage(k,(j)*20+10,z1,1); /* erasing the image to make it to look like moving */
        }
        putimage(250,(j)*20+10,z1,2); /* writing the image */

/* movement of ith rectangle down to the number of pixels until getting the original position of jth
element */
        for (k=i*20+10;k<=(j)*20+10;++k)
        {
        putimage(110,k,z,2);
        delay(5);
        putimage(110,k,z,1);
```

```
            }
            putimage(110,(j)*20+10,z,2);

/* movement of jth rectangle up to the original position of ith element */
            for (k=(j)*20+10;k>=i*20+10;—k)
            {
            putimage(250,k,z1,2);
            delay(5);
            putimage(250,k,z1,1);
            }
            putimage(250,i*20+10,z1,2);

/* movement of ith rectangle right 70 pixels to place it in the original position of jth element */
            for (k=110;k<=180;++k)
            {
            putimage(k,(j)*20+10,z,2);
            delay(5);
            putimage(k,(j)*20+10,z,1);
            }
            putimage(180,(j)*20+10,z,2);

/* movement of jth rectangle left 70 pixels to place it in the original position of ith element */
            for (k=250;k>=180;—k)
            {
            putimage(k,i*20+10,z1,2);
            delay(5);
            putimage(k,i*20+10,z1,1);
            }
            putimage(180,i*20+10,z1,2);

      } /* end of if statement */

    } /* end of inner for loop */

/* for erasing the pass information before going to the next pass */
setcolor(0);
outtextxy(108,(n+3)*20,s);
} /* end of outer loop and the algorithm itself */

/* erasing the pass information after completion of sorting */
```

```
setcolor(0);
outtextxy(50,(n+3)*20,"PASS IN PROGRESS");

delay(2000); /* waits for 2 seconds before switching to the main menu module automatically */
} /* End of sequential sort module */
```

4.C. vii) The merging of sorted lists module

/* This module shows the demo of merging of two sorted lists. They are taken from the keyboard in any order, the lists are then arranged and finally merged in ascending order. For this the given lists are displayed first with required labels. Then the arranged lists are displayed with labels. The merging is done by choosing the smallest element from both the lists and placing in the target list. For simplicity only integer arrays are considered and rectangle boxes with elements are used for effective demonstration through animation */

/* This is an independent module. To run it independently just change the function name 'void sortedmergemain() ' with 'void main()' and include all necessary header files */

```
/* Function declaration for sorting the given list in ascending order */
void sort(int [],int);

void sortedmergemain()
{
int gd=DETECT,gm,a[20],b[20],c[40],i,k,n,m,j,t,p,ii,l;
void *z,*z1;
char s[10],ch;

clrscr();

/* Text mode input of necessary data*/

/* size of first list with limits validation */
 do
 {
        t=0;
        printf("enter size of first list n\n");
        scanf("%d",&n);
        if (n>=20 && n<=0) /* maximum number of elements limited to 19 */
        {
        t=1; /* flag variable is set when the limit is not within the range */
        printf("\n size of both lists together must be <=20\n");
```

```
            }
}while(t==1);

/* elements of first list */
/* here user is having the option to enter the elements manually from keyboard or making the
system to choose the elements randomly */
 printf("\n are you entering numbers( y/n?)\n");
 fflush(stdin);/* Clears the buffer */
 ch=getche();

/* Enter the elements of the first list when the chosen option is 'Y' */
if(ch=='y' || ch== 'Y')
{
            printf("Enter Number of first list\n");
            for(i=1;i<=n;++i)
            scanf("%d",&a[i]);
}
else
{
            for(i=1; i<=n;++i)
            a[i]=rand(); /* Random numbers are chosen by the system as elements of the list */
}

/* size of first list with limits validation */
do
{
t=0;
printf("enter size of second list m\n");
scanf("%d",&m);
if ((n+m)>20 && m<0) /* size of both the lists together is limited to a maximum of 20 elements */
            {
            t=1;
            printf("\n size of both lists together must be <=20\n");
            }
}while(t==1); /* end of do.. while */

/* elements of second list */
/* here user is having the option to enter the elements manually from keyboard or making the
system to choose the elements randomly */
```

```
printf("\n are you entering numbers( y/n?)\n");
fflush(stdin);
ch=getche();
if(ch=='y' || ch== 'Y')
        {
        printf("Enter Number of first list\n");
        for(i=1;i<=m;++i)
        scanf("%d",&b[i]); /* Manual entry of elements from keyboard */
        }
else
        {
        for(i=1; i<=m;++i)
        b[i]=rand(); /* Random elements from system */
        }

/* finding the largest element from both the lists. This element is necessary to replace the smallest
element from the lists for avoiding the finding of same smallest element again during the process */
l=a[1];
for(i=1;i<=n;++i)
        if (l<a[i])
        l=a[i]; /* largest element from first list is in l */

for(i=1;i<=m;++i)
        if (l<b[i])
        l=b[i]; /* largest element from both the lists is in l */

/* Graphical demo starts from here */

initgraph(&gd,&gm,""); /* graphics is initialized */

setcolor(3); /* sets the drawing color to CYAN */

/* drawing the rectangles and placing the given elements in that rectangles for the first list */
for(i=1;i<=n;++i)
        {
        rectangle(10,(i-1)*20+10,60,i*20+8);
        sprintf(s,"%d",a[i]);
        outtextxy(15,(i-1)*20+15,s);
        }
```

```
/* drawing the rectangles and placing the given elements in that rectangles for the second list */
for(i=1;i<=m;++i)
        {
        rectangle(getmaxx()-60,(i-1)*20+10,getmaxx()-10,i*20+8);
        sprintf(s,"%d",b[i]);
        outtextxy(getmaxx()-55,(i-1)*20+15,s);
        }

/* Messages for both given lists just below the respective rectangular blocks */
        setcolor(2);
        outtextxy(10,n*20+15,"Given");
        outtextxy(10,n*20+28,"List A");
        outtextxy(getmaxx()-60,m*20+15,"Given");
        outtextxy(getmaxx()-60,m*20+28,"List B");

sort(a,n); /* Function call to sort the first list in ascending order */
sort(b,m); /* Function call to sort the second list in ascending order */

/* drawing the rectangles and placing the arranged elements in that rectangles for the first list */
setcolor(4);
for(i=1;i<=n;++i)
        {
        rectangle(70,(i-1)*20+10,120,i*20+8);
        sprintf(s,"%d",a[i]);
        outtextxy(75,(i-1)*20+15,s);
        }

/* drawing the rectangles and placing the arranged elements in that rectangles for the second list */
for(i=1;i<=m;++i)
        {
        rectangle(getmaxx()-120,(i-1)*20+10,getmaxx()-70,i*20+8);
        sprintf(s,"%d",b[i]);
        outtextxy(getmaxx()-115,(i-1)*20+15,s);
        }

/* Messages for both of the sorted lists just below the respective rectangular blocks */
        setcolor(5);
        outtextxy(70,n*20+15,"Sorted");
        outtextxy(70,n*20+28,"List A");
```

```
            outtextxy(getmaxx()-120,m*20+15,"Sorted");
            outtextxy(getmaxx()-120,m*20+28,"List B");

/* Message for algorithm process */
            setcolor(3);
            settextstyle(3,0,3);
            outtextxy(165,getmaxy()-40,"MERGING OF SORTED LISTS");

/* allocation of memory to the variables to store rectangular boxes during process of merging */
z=malloc(imagesize(180,10,230,30));
z1=malloc(imagesize(180,10,230,30));

i=1; /* loop counter for first list */
j=1; /* loop counter for second list */
k=1; /* loop counter for target list */

p=m+n; /* total number of elements in both the lists */

/* main logic for merging starts from here */
while(i<=n && j<=m) /* continues until any one list or both the lists get exhausted */
  {
  if (a[i]<b[j]) /* when the element from first list is smaller then */
    {
    c[k]=a[i]; /* that element is transferred to target list */

/* gets the image of top element of first list into variable z */
getimage(70,(i-1)*20+10,120,i*20+8,z);

/* Moves the top rectangle from first list 60 pixels horizontally right */
            for(ii=70;ii<=130;++ii)
            {
            putimage(ii,(i-1)*20+10,z,2);
            delay(5);
            putimage(ii,(i-1)*20+10,z,1);
            }
            putimage(130,(i-1)*20+10,z,2);

/* Moves the top rectangle from first list (from new position) k*20 pixels down */
            for(ii=(i-1)*20+10;ii<=(k-1)*20+10;++ii)
```

```
        {
        putimage(130,ii,z,2);
        delay(5);
        putimage(130,ii,z,1);
        }
        putimage(130,(k-1)*20+10,z,2);

/* Moves the top rectangle from first list (from new position) 150 pixels right and places it in the
        target list */
        for(ii=130;ii<=280;++ii)
        {
        putimage(ii,(k-1)*20+10,z,2);
        delay(5);
        putimage(ii,(k-1)*20+10,z,1);
        }
        putimage(280,(k-1)*20+10,z,2);

i++; /* loop counter for first list and target list has got increased by 1 so as to point to the next
        locations */
k++;
}
else /* when the element from second list is smaller then */
if (a[i]>b[j])
{
c[k]=b[j]; /* that element is transferred to target list */

/* gets the image of top element of second list into variable z1 */
        getimage(getmaxx()-120,(j-1)*20+10,getmaxx()-70,j*20+8,z1);

/* Moves the top rectangle from second list 60 pixels horizontally left */
        for(ii=getmaxx()-120;ii>=getmaxx()-180;—ii)
        {
        putimage(ii,(j-1)*20+10,z1,2);
        delay(5);
        putimage(ii,(j-1)*20+10,z1,1);
        }
        putimage(getmaxx()-180,(j-1)*20+10,z1,2);

/* Moves the top rectangle from second list (from new position) k*20 pixels down */
        for(ii=(j-1)*20+10;ii<=(k-1)*20+10;++ii)
```

```
{
putimage(getmaxx()-180,ii,z1,2);
delay(5);
putimage(getmaxx()-180,ii,z1,1);
}
putimage(getmaxx()-180,(k-1)*20+10,z1,2);

/* Moves the top rectangle from second list (from new position) 150 pixels left and places it in the
target list */
for(ii=getmaxx()-180;ii>=280;—ii)
{
putimage(ii,(k-1)*20+10,z1,2);
delay(5);
putimage(ii,(k-1)*20+10,z1,1);
}
putimage(280,(k-1)*20+10,z1,2);

j++; /* loop counters for second list and target list is increased by 1 so as to point to the next
locations */
k++;
}
else /* when the top elements of both the lists are same then */
{
c[k]=a[i]; /* first list top element is transferred to target list */

/* gets the image of top element of first list into variable z */
getimage(70,(i-1)*20+10,120,i*20+8,z);

/* Moves the top rectangle from first list (from new position) k*20 pixels down */
for(ii=70;ii<=130;++ii)
{
putimage(ii,(i-1)*20+10,z,2);
delay(5);
putimage(ii,(i-1)*20+10,z,1);
}
putimage(130,(i-1)*20+10,z,2);

/* Moves the top rectangle from first list (from new position) k*20 pixels down */
for(ii=(i-1)*20+10;ii<=(k-1)*20+10;++ii)
{
```

```
putimage(130,ii,z,2);
delay(5);
putimage(130,ii,z,1);
}
putimage(130,(k-1)*20+10,z,2);

/* Moves the top rectangle from first list (from new position) 150 pixels right and places it in the
target list */
for(ii=130;ii<=280;++ii)
{
putimage(ii,(k-1)*20+10,z,2);
delay(5);
putimage(ii,(k-1)*20+10,z,1);
}
putimage(280,(k-1)*20+10,z,2);

/* gets the top element of second list and erases it */
getimage(getmaxx()-120,(j-1)*20+10,getmaxx()-70,j*20+8,z1);
putimage(getmaxx()-120,(j-1)*20+10,z1,1);

/* loop counters for all three lists are increased by 1 so as to point to the next locations */
i++;
j++;
k++;
p—; /* total number of elements are reduced by one as duplicate is removed */
}
}/* end of while */

/* Handling the remaining elements from the first list if any */
while(i<=n)
{
c[k]=a[i];
getimage(70,(i-1)*20+10,120,i*20+8,z);

for(ii=70;ii<=130;++ii)
{
putimage(ii,(i-1)*20+10,z,2);
delay(5);
putimage(ii,(i-1)*20+10,z,1);
```

```
        }
        putimage(130,(i-1)*20+10,z,2);

for(ii=(i-1)*20+10;ii<=(k-1)*20+10;++ii)
        {
        putimage(130,ii,z,2);
        delay(5);
        putimage(130,ii,z,1);
        }
        putimage(130,(k-1)*20+10,z,2);

for(ii=130;ii<=280;++ii)
        {
        putimage(ii,(k-1)*20+10,z,2);
        delay(5);
        putimage(ii,(k-1)*20+10,z,1);
        }
        putimage(280,(k-1)*20+10,z,2);


  i++;
  k++;
  } /* end of while */

 /* Handling the remaining elements from the second list if any */
  while(j<=m)
  {
  c[k]=b[j];

  getimage(getmaxx()-120,(j-1)*20+10,getmaxx()-70,j*20+8,z1);

 for(ii=getmaxx()-120;ii>=getmaxx()-180;—ii)
         {
         putimage(ii,(j-1)*20+10,z1,2);
         delay(5);
         putimage(ii,(j-1)*20+10,z1,1);
         }
         putimage(getmaxx()-180,(j-1)*20+10,z1,2);

 for(ii=(j-1)*20+10;ii<=(k-1)*20+10;++ii)
```

```
        {
        putimage(getmaxx()-180,ii,z1,2);
        delay(5);
        putimage(getmaxx()-180,ii,z1,1);
        }
        putimage(getmaxx()-180,(k-1)*20+10,z1,2);

for(ii=getmaxx()-180;ii>=280;—ii)
        {
        putimage(ii,(k-1)*20+10,z1,2);
        delay(5);
        putimage(ii,(k-1)*20+10,z1,1);
        }
        putimage(280,(k-1)*20+10,z1,2);
 j++;
 k++;
 } /* end of while loop */

 graphdefaults();

/* labeling of target list */
        setcolor(14);
        outtextxy(280,k*20+15,"merged");
        outtextxy(280,k*20+38," List ");

/* erasing the labels from both sorted lists that are merged */
        setcolor(0);
        outtextxy(70,n*20+15,"Sorted");
        outtextxy(70,n*20+28,"List A");
        outtextxy(getmaxx()-120,m*20+15,"Sorted");
        outtextxy(getmaxx()-120,m*20+28,"List B");

/* Labeling the merged list*/
setcolor(3);
settextstyle(3,0,3);
outtextxy(165,getmaxy()-40,"MERGING OF SORTED LISTS");

delay(2000); /* Waits for 2 seconds before program control transfers to main module of the project
*/
```

```
} /* End of this module */

/* function for arranging the given lists in ascending order */
void sort(int x[],int y)
 {
        int i,j,t;
        for(i=1;i<y;++i)
               for(j=1;j<y;++j)
                      if(x[j]>x[j+1])
                      {
                      t=x[j];
                      x[j]=x[j+1];
                      x[j+1]=t;
                      }
} /* End of sort function */
```

4.C. viii) The merging of unsorted lists module

/* This module shows the demo of merging of two unsorted lists. They are taken from the keyboard in any order and merged in ascending order. For this the given lists are displayed first with required labels. The merging is done by choosing the smallest element from both the lists and placing it in the target list and then choosing the next smallest among the remaining elements of both the lists. This process will continue until both the lists get exhausted. For simplicity only integer arrays are considered and rectangle boxes with elements are used for effective demonstration through animation */

/* This is an independent module. To run it independently just change the function name 'void unsortedmergemain() ' with 'void main()' and include all necessary header files */

```
void unsortedmergemain()
{
 int gd=DETECT,gm,a[20],b[20],c[40],i,k,n,m,j,t,p,ii,l,sm,pp;
 void *z,*z1;
 char s[10],ch;

/* Text mode input of data */

/* size of first list with limits validation */

clrscr(); /* Clears the screen */
 do
```

```
{
        t=0;
        printf("enter size of first list n\n");
        scanf("%d",&n);
        if (n>=20 && n<=0) /* number of elements limited to 19 */
        {
         t=1; /* flag variable is set when the limit is not within the range */
         printf("\n size of both lists together must be <=20\n");
        }
 }while(t==1);

/* elements of first list */
/* here user is having the option to enter the elements manually from keyboard or making the
system to choose the elements randomly */
 printf("\n are you entering numbers( y/n?)\n");
 fflush(stdin);/* Clears the buffer */
 ch=getche();

/* Enter the elements of the first list when the chosen option is 'Y' */
 if(ch=='y' || ch== 'Y')
 {
        printf("Enter Number of first list\n");
        for(i=1;i<=n;++i)
        scanf("%d",&a[i]);

 }
 else
 {
        for(i=1; i<=n;++i)
        a[i]=rand(); /* Random numbers are choosen by the system as elements of the list */
}

/* size of first list with limits validation */
do
{
t=0;
printf("enter size of second list m\n");
scanf("%d",&m);
if ((n+m)>20 && m<0) /* size of both the lists is limited to 20 elements */
        {
```

```
            t=1;
            printf("\n size of both lists together must be <=20\n");
            }
}while(t==1); /* end of do.. while */

/* elements of second list */
/* here user is having the option to enter the elements manually from keyboard or making the
system to choose the elements randomly */
 printf("\n are you entering numbers( y/n?)\n");
 fflush(stdin);
 ch=getche();
 if(ch=='y' || ch== 'Y')
            {
            printf("Enter Number of first list\n");
            for(i=1;i<=m;++i)
            scanf("%d",&b[i]); /* Manual entry of elements from keyboard */
            }
 else
            {
            for(i=1; i<=m;++i)
            b[i]=rand(); /* Random elements from system */
            }

/* finding the largest element from both the lists. This element is necessary to replace the smallest
element from the lists for avoiding the finding of same smallest again during the process */
 l=a[1];
 for(i=1;i<=n;++i)
            if (l<a[i])
            l=a[i]; /* largest element from first list is in l */

 for(i=1;i<=m;++i)
            if (l<b[i])
            l=b[i]; /* largest element from both the lists is in l */


/* Graphical demo starts from here */

initgraph(&gd,&gm,""); /* graphics is initialized */
setcolor(4); /* sets the drawing color to red */
```

```
/* drawing the rectangles and placing the given elements in those rectangles for the first list */
 for(i=1;i<=n;++i)
 {
         rectangle(70,(i-1)*20+10,120,i*20+8);
         sprintf(s,"%d",a[i]);
         outtextxy(75,(i-1)*20+15,s);
 }

/* drawing the rectangles and placing the given elements in that rectangles for the second list */
 for(i=1;i<=m;++i)
 {
         rectangle(getmaxx()-120,(i-1)*20+10,getmaxx()-70,i*20+8);
         sprintf(s,"%d",b[i]);
         outtextxy(getmaxx()-115,(i-1)*20+15,s);
 }

/* Messages for both of the given lists just below the respective rectangular blocks */
         setcolor(5);
         outtextxy(70,n*20+15,"Given");
         outtextxy(70,n*20+28,"List A");
         outtextxy(getmaxx()-120,m*20+15,"Given");
         outtextxy(getmaxx()-120,m*20+28,"List B");

/* Message for the module process */
         setcolor(3);
         settextstyle(3,0,3);
         outtextxy(165,getmaxy()-40,"MERGING OF UNSORTED LISTS");
         graphdefaults();

/* allocation of memory to the variables that store rectangular boxes during process of merging */
         z=malloc(imagesize(180,10,230,30));
         z1=malloc(imagesize(180,10,230,30));

i=1; /* loop counter for first list */
j=1; /* loop counter for second list */
k=1; /* loop counter for target list */

p=m+n; /* total number of elements in both the lists */

/* main logic for merging starts from here */
```

```
while(k<=p) /* while target list contains all the elements of both the lists */
{

/* finding smallest from both the lists */
  t=0; /* sets the flag variable to 0 */
  sm=a[1]; /* first element of the first list is assumed as small */

for(i=2;i<=n;++i)
        if(a[i]<sm) /* if any element is smaller than the sm in first list then */
        sm=a[i]; /* then that element is assigned to sm */

for(j=1;j<=m;++j)
        if(b[j]<sm) /* if any element is smaller than the sm in second list then */
        sm=b[j]; /* then that element is assigned to sm */

/* finding smallest element position and replacing with large */
for(i=1;i<=n;++i)
 {

/* background processing */
        if(a[i]==sm) /* compare the smallest element in the first list */
        {
        t=1; /* flag is set */
        c[k]=sm;/* smallest element is taken into target list */
        a[i]=l+1; /* smallest element in the first list is replaced with largest element +1, so that
        this same element should not be selected again as smallest */

/* foreground demo of merging */
        getimage(70,(i-1)*20+10,120,i*20+8,z); /* gets the image of the smallest element from
 first list into z */

/* Movement of image 60 pixels right horizontally */
for(ii=70;ii<=130;++ii)
{
         putimage(ii,(i-1)*20+10,z,2);   /* writes the image*/
         delay(5); /* waits for 5 milli seconds */
         putimage(ii,(i-1)*20+10,z,1);   /* erases the image */

}
         putimage(130,(i-1)*20+10,z,2);/* writes the image in final position */
```

```
/* movement of rectangle box with element into the target list position */

/* if the target list contains more elements than i? then move the rectangle with ith element
downwards */
if(k>=i)
{
/* moves the ith element rectangle box k*20 pixels downwards */
for(ii=(i-1)*20+10;ii<=(k-1)*20+10;++ii)
{
        putimage(130,ii,z,2);
        delay(5);
        putimage(130,ii,z,1);
}
        putimage(130,(k-1)*20+10,z,2);
}
else /* when the target list position is less than ith position*/
{
/* move the ith element rectangle box upwards k * 20 pixels */
for(ii=(i-1)*20+10;ii>=(k-1)*20+10;—ii)
{
        putimage(130,ii,z,2);
        delay(5);
        putimage(130,ii,z,1);
}
        putimage(130,(k-1)*20+10,z,2);
}

/* move the ith element rectangle box horizontally right 150 pixels */
for(ii=130;ii<=280;++ii)
{
        putimage(ii,(k-1)*20+10,z,2);
        delay(5);
        putimage(ii,(k-1)*20+10,z,1);
}
        putimage(280,(k-1)*20+10,z,2);

/* searching for same duplicate element in the second list */
for(ii=1;ii<=m;++ii)
        if(b[ii]==sm) /* if present then */
        {
```

```
            p—; /* reduce the size of target list by one */
            b[ii]=l+1; /* replace that element in second list with large + 1, so that it should not be
            selected again */

        getimage(getmaxx()-120,(ii-1)*20+10,getmaxx()-70,ii*20+8,z1); /* get the image of that
corresponding rectangle */
            putimage(getmaxx()-120,(ii-1)*20+10,z1,1); /* erase the rectangle */
            }
            k++; /* position in the target list is increased by one */
}
}

/* movement of element from second list to target list after searching */
/* checking for flag which remains to be zero when the element is not present in the first list */
if(t==0)
{

/* background process */
for(i=1;i<=m;++i) /* searching for the element in second list */
if(b[i]==sm) /* when the element is present then */
{
            t=1; /* flag is set */
            c[k]=sm; /* smallest element transferred to target list */
            b[i]=l+1; /* second list element is replaced with large + 1 so that it should not be selected
            again */

/* foreground demo */
/* getting the image into the variable z1 */
            getimage(getmaxx()-120,(i-1)*20+10,getmaxx()-70,i*20+8,z1);

/* movement of rectangle box with element from second list 60 pixels horizontally left */
  for(ii=getmaxx()-120;ii>=getmaxx()-180;—ii)
  {
            putimage(ii,(i-1)*20+10,z1,2); /* writes the image */
            delay(5); /* waits for 5 milliseconds */
            putimage(ii,(i-1)*20+10,z1,1); /* erases the image */

  }
            putimage(getmaxx()-180,(i-1)*20+10,z1,2);
```

```
/* when k the target list counter is greater than position of smallest element in second list then the
        rectangular image is moved downwards */
if (k>=i)
{
 for(ii=(i-1)*20+10;ii<=(k-1)*20+10;++ii)
  {
        putimage(getmaxx()-180,ii,z1,2);
        delay(5);
        putimage(getmaxx()-180,ii,z1,1);
 }
        putimage(getmaxx()-180,(k-1)*20+10,z1,2);
}
else
{
/* when k the target list counter is less than position of smallest element in second list then the
        rectangular image is moved upwards */
for(ii=(i-1)*20+10;ii>=(k-1)*20+10;—ii)
{
        putimage(getmaxx()-180,ii,z1,2);
        delay(5);
        putimage(getmaxx()-180,ii,z1,1);
}
        putimage(getmaxx()-180,(k-1)*20+10,z1,2);
}

/* movement of rectangle image 150 pixels left, so as to fit in the target list position */
for(ii=getmaxx()-180;ii>=280;—ii)
{
        putimage(ii,(k-1)*20+10,z1,2);
        delay(5);
        putimage(ii,(k-1)*20+10,z1,1);
}
        putimage(280,(k-1)*20+10,z1,2);

k++; /* increase the target list size by 1 */
}
}
}

/* Labeling the target list */
```

```
setcolor(14);
outtextxy(280,k*20,"merged");
outtextxy(280,k*20+13," List ");

/* Erasing the labels of given lists */
setcolor(0);
outtextxy(70,n*20+15,"Given");
outtextxy(70,n*20+28,"List A");
outtextxy(getmaxx()-120,m*20+15,"Given");
outtextxy(getmaxx()-120,m*20+28,"List B");

delay(2000); /* waits for 2 seconds before transferring the program control to the main module */
} /* end of unsorted merge module */
/* end of search, sort and merge project */
```

PROJECT 5

DATA STRUCTURES DEMO

5.A) SYNOPSIS:

The study of data and its storage in the computer memory is called data structure. Data structures are all about how the data is represented in computer's memory internally. For storing data and information effectively in the computer utilization of data structures is essential. Basically there are two types of data structures namely primitive and non primitive.

Primitive data structures or data types are those that are available along with the language compiler and they cannot be subdivided again. The non primitive data structures are those data structures that are defined explicitly by user according to his requirements with the help of primitive data types. Non primitive data types are again divided into two types namely linear and non linear data structures.

Linear data structures are those whose elements are of same type and size. Their location in the memory may be continuous or non continuous. In case of arrays and strings it is continuous and in case of other data structures like linked lists, stacks, queues it need not be continuous.

Non linear data structures are those whose elements need not be of same type and size. The data structures like trees, graphs, structures, unions etc. Come under this category.

In this project we are implementing linear data structures like stacks, queues, singly linked lists and doubly linked lists. Each of these are explained below.

5.A. i) STACKS.

STACK is a special type of data structure where insertion is done from one end called 'top' of stack and deletion will be done from the same end.

Here, the last element inserted will be on the top of the stack. Since deletion is done from the same end, last element inserted is the first element to be deleted. So, stack is also called Last In First Out (LIFO) data structure.

In stacks we perform two operations namely, Push and Pop. Push is the operation of inserting an element into the stack. Before inserting the element into the stack we need to check whether the stack is full or it can accommodate some more elements. The situation where stack is full and we are trying to insert the element is called overflow. Stack maintains a counter which represents 'top' of stack which will be incremented by one whenever an element is inserted. Before inserting the element we need to check the stack's 'top' counter with the maximum allowed limit. If the counter value is already reached the maximum limit of the stack then insertion operation leads to overflow situation.

Pop is the process of deleting an element from the stack. On each and every pop operation the top counter is decremented by one. Before deleting an element from the stack it is essential to check whether any element is there are not. Because whenever we try to delete an element from an empty stack it leads to underflow situation.

The stacks can be implemented using arrays or linked lists. The stack can be used in several applications like recursion, keeping track of function calls, evaluation of expression etc.

Pictorial representation of stack

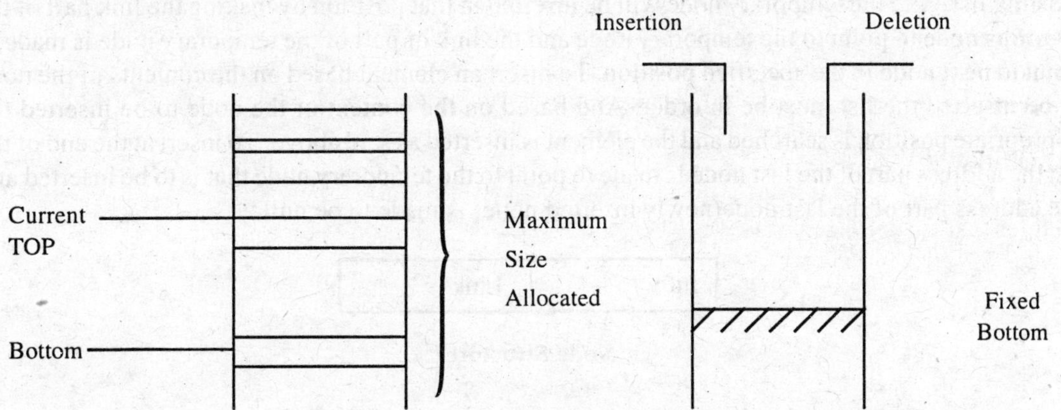

5.A. ii) Queues

Queue is a data structure in which an element can be inserted from one end and deleted from an other end. The end at which we are inserting the element is called 'rear' end and the end at which we are deleting the element is called 'front' end. The first element inserted in the queue is the first element to be deleted from the queue. So it can also be called as FIFO(first in first out) list.

Similar to stacks in queues also we need to check overflow and underflow conditions. Unlike in stacks we maintain two pointers in queues one to keep track of front end and the other to keep track of rear end. When an element is inserted into the queue the rear pointer must be incremented by one. It will be checked with maximum allowed limit in the queue to check overflow. When the queue is empty both rear and front pointers remain zero.

Queues like stacks, also arise quite naturally in the computer solutions of many problems. Perhaps the most common occurrence of a queue in computer applications is for the scheduling of the jobs. In batch processing the jobs are "queued-up" as they are read-in and executed, one after another in the order they were received.

5.A. iii) Linked Lists

Linked list is a data structure which contains number of nodes each of which in turn contain data part and link part. Based on the number of link parts the linked lists may be singly linked lists or doubly linked lists.

The linked list in which there is a data part and an address part is called singly linked list. Each node point to its next node through its link or address part. And the last node's address part will be null. The main operations we can do on any linked list are insertion, deletion and display the contents of a list. Insertion can be done in the beginning of the list or at the end of the list or in any position of the list. Similarly deletion of a list can be done in the same manner. For inserting the element in the beginning of the list a temporary node will be created and its address part is made to point to first element of an existing list. Inserting in the middle of the list can be done on the basis of a specified position or on the basis of contents of the node to be inserted. In case of insertion based on position a temporary node is created and the specified position will be searched in the existing list. And the temporary node will be inserted in that position by making the link part of the previous node to point to the temporary node and the link of part of the temporary node is made to point to next node in the specified position. To insert an element based on the contents of the node to be inserted the list must be in order. And based on the content of the node to be inserted the appropriate position is searched and the element is inserted as said above. To insert at the end of the list the address part of the last node is made to point to the temporary node that is to be inserted and the address part of the last node(newly inserted node) is made to be null.

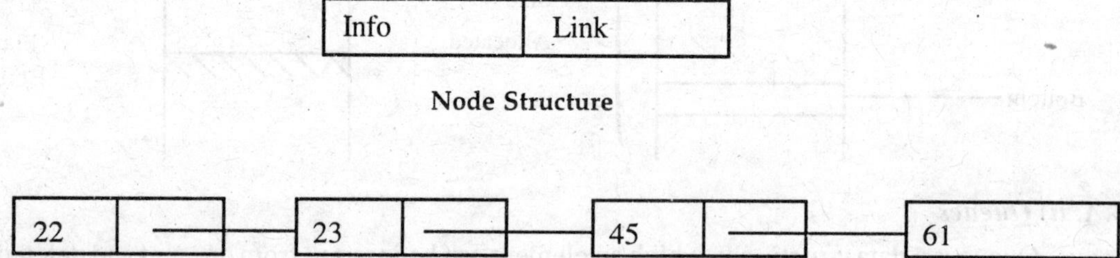

Node Structure

Deleting an element from a singly list is possible at the beginning of a list or at the end of the list or from any specified position in the list. To delete at the beginning the present node at the beginning is copied into the temporary node. The list pointer will be made to point to the next node. And the temporary node is removed by freeing the memory allocated to it. Deleting at the specified position is done by copying the element to be deleted into the temporary node and the previous node pointer is made to point to the next node after the specified element and the temporary node is deleted by freeing the memory. To delete at the end of a list the last node of the list is transferred to temporary node and the previous node's address is made as null. The temporary node is deleted or freed from memory.

Doubly linked lists:

The linked list in which there is a data part and two address parts is called doubly linked list. The two address parts are for one to point to the next node in the list and the other to point to the

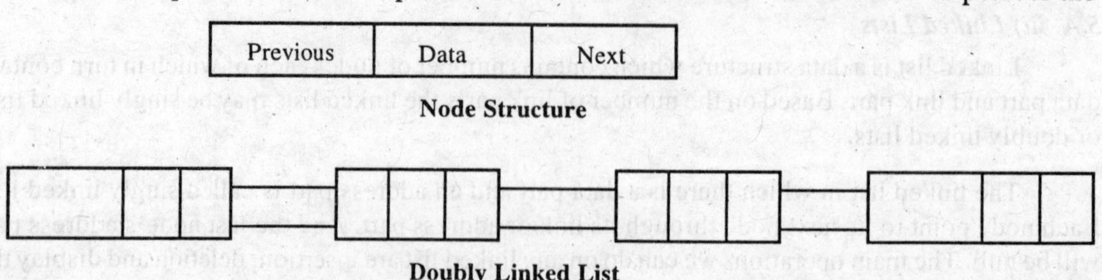

Node Structure

Doubly Linked List

previous node of the list. The previous address part of the first node will be null and the next address part of the last node is also null. All the operations that can be performed on a singly linked list can also be performed on a doubly linked list as well. While implementing these operations in doubly linked list we manipulate both the address parts of nodes involved instead of one address part as compared to the singly linked lists.

5.B) Implementation details:

This project is completely menu driven whose menu items can be selected through arrow and entry keys. It consists of number of sub menus for each of the items in the main menu. The four modules namely

1. Stack,
2. Queue,
3. Singly linked lists and
4. Doubly linked lists

are four options in the main menu. These options are explained in the following sections.

1. Stack

The stack menu item implements push and pop operations on the stacks. Whenever the user chooses this menu item another sub menu which is text oriented gets displayed on the screen with three options. They are,

1. Push,
2. Pop and
3. Return.

Whenever the push option is selected it will ask for the element to push if stack is not full and inserts that element into a rectangular one side open box which we consider as a stack. The stack top will be incremented by one. When the user chooses Pop operation it checks for underflow condition and if elements are there it throws out the from top of the stack at the same time the stack top is decremented by one. The third option takes the program control back to the main menu.

2. Queues

This option implements the complete queue operations. A rectangular box with both the sides open will be used for representing the queue. Each element is represented by making the partitions within the given box. The empty positions are represented with the help of crossed lines. Initially both front and rear counters are set to zero. The main queue operations are,

1. Insert
2. Delete
3. Display and
4. Return

By selecting the first menu item the program checks for the overflow condition of a queue if it is not then it asks for the element to insert. A rectangle with the element is animated for inserting the element into the queue. The rear pointer is incremented by one. And according to the necessity the front pointer is set to one. By selecting second option the program checks for the underflow condition. If the queue is not empty it adjusts the front and the rear pointers and throws the front element of the queue out of the screen. The third option displays the present status of the queue and the last option returns the program control back to the main menu.

3. Singly linked list

This sub option in the main menu demonstrates complete operations on the singly linked lists. The operations can be insertion, deletion or display. These operations are carried out with sub menu that consists of eight menu items. They are,

1. Insertion at beginning.
2. Insertion at the specified position.
3. Insertion at the end.
4. Deletion from beginning.
5. Deletion from the specified position.
6. Deletion from the end.
7. Displaying the contents of the list.
8. Return.

Each of these menu items are self explanatory and each one will check necessary conditions before carrying out its assigned tasks.

4. Doubly linked lists.

This sub option in the main menu demonstrates complete operations on the doubly linked lists. The operations can be insertion, deletion or display. These operations are carried out with sub menu that consists of eight menu items. They are,

1. Insertion at beginning.
2. Insertion at the specified position.
3. Insertion at the end.
4. Deletion from beginning.
5. Deletion from the specified position.
6. Deletion from the end.
7. Displaying the contents of the list.
8. Return.

Each of these menu items are self explanatory and each one will check necessary conditions before carrying out its assigned tasks.

5.C) Source Code

5.C. i) The main module

/* This program demonstrates working of popular data structures namely stacks, queues, single linked lists and double linked list. This is completely menu driven and function oriented. User can use the arrow and entry keys for selecting the menu options. Each menu option is implemented in the different program file. Each sub module in turn contains number of functions according to requirements. */

```
/* header files used*/
#include<conio.h>
#include<graphics.h>
#include<stdio.h>
#include<alloc.h>
#include<dos.h>
#include<process.h>

/* sub modules */
#include"dssll.c"
#include "dsstack.c"
#include "dsqueue.c"
#include "dsdll.c"

/* function declarations */
void stmain();
void quemain();
void sllmain();
void dllmain();

/* the project execution starts from here */
void main()
{
int gd=DETECT,gm,i,j,n,m,kb,chek=0;
int ch=1;

initgraph(&gd,&gm,"");
/* menu design */
setcolor(15);
for(i=2;i<=6;++i)
{
rectangle(150,i*50,405,i*50+50);
}
setcolor(2);
```

```
settextstyle(3,0,5);
outtextxy(25,15," GRAPHICAL REPRESENTATION");
setcolor(3);
outtextxy(25,375," OF DATA STRUCTURES");
settextstyle(3,0,3);
setcolor(12);
outtextxy(155,105," STACKS ");
outtextxy(155,155," QUEUE ");
outtextxy(155,205,"SINGLE LINKED LIST");
outtextxy(155,255,"DOUBLE LINKED LIST");
outtextxy(155,305," EXIT ");
floodfill(154,ch*50+52,15);
chek=0;
while(chek==0)
{
rectangle(1,1,getmaxx()-1,getmaxy()-1);
setcolor(5);
rectangle(0,0,getmaxx(),getmaxy());

chek=0;
setcolor(15);
for(i=2;i<=6;++i)
{
rectangle(150,i*50,405,i*50+50);
}
setcolor(2);
settextstyle(3,0,5);
outtextxy(25,15," GRAPHICAL REPRESENTATION");
setcolor(3);
outtextxy(25,375," OF DATA STRUCTURES");
settextstyle(3,0,3);
setcolor(12);
outtextxy(155,105," STACKS ");
outtextxy(155,155," QUEUE ");
outtextxy(155,205,"SINGLE LINKED LIST");
outtextxy(155,255,"DOUBLE LINKED LIST");
outtextxy(155,305," EXIT ");
floodfill(154,ch*50+52,15);
setcolor(15);
```

```
floodfill(154,ch*50+55,15);
setcolor(12);
if(ch==1)
{
settextstyle(3,0,3);
setcolor(12);
outtextxy(155,105," STACKS ");
settextstyle(3,0,3);
setcolor(12);
}
if(ch==2)
{settextstyle(3,0,3);
setcolor(12);
outtextxy(155,155,"QUEUE");
settextstyle(3,0,3);
setcolor(12);
}
if(ch==3)
{
settextstyle(3,0,3);
setcolor(12);
outtextxy(155,205,"SINGLE LINKED LIST");
}
if(ch==4)
{
settextstyle(3,0,3);
setcolor(12);
outtextxy(155,255,"DOUBLE LINKED LIST");
}
if(ch==5)
{
settextstyle(3,0,3);
setcolor(12);
outtextxy(155,305," EXIT ");
}
if(ch==1)
{
settextstyle(3,0,3);
setcolor(12);
```

```
outtextxy(155,105," STACKS ");
}
kb=getche(); /* menu item selection */
switch(kb)
{
        case 72:
                ch—;
                if(ch<1)
                ch=5;
                cleardevice();
                break;
        case 80:
                ch++;
                if(ch>5)
                ch=1;
                cleardevice();
                break;
        case 13:
                switch(ch)
                {
                case 1: closegraph();
                        stmain();
                        initgraph(&gd,&gm,"");
                        break;
                case 2: closegraph();
                        quemain();
                        initgraph(&gd,&gm,"");
                        break;
                case 3: closegraph();
                        sllmain();
                        initgraph(&gd,&gm,"");
                        break;

                case 4: closegraph();
                        dllmain();
                        initgraph(&gd,&gm,"");
```

```
                    break;
          case 5:
                    chek=1;
                    setcolor(2);
                    outtextxy(150,400,"SUCCESS");
                    break;
          }
}
}
closegraph();
}
```

5.C. ii) The Stack Module

/* This module describes the stack operations. We can push the elements into the stack or we can pop the elements from the stack or we can list the elements of the stack. The boundary value checking that leads to over flow during insertion and underflow during deletion is checked. For avoiding the graphical resolution problem the number of elements is restricted. The different functions are used for each of the operations.*/

/* it is completely independent module. to run it independently replace the function name "stmain()" with "main()" and include the necessary header files */

int max=5;/* the maximum stack size is five elements. it can be extended up to 15 elements.*/

/* FUNCTION DECLARATIONS */

```
void pop(int);
void push(int,int);
int t=0,aaa33[20];
void stmain()
{
          int ch=0;
          int t1;
while(ch!=3)
{
          clrscr();
          printf("1 PUSH \n2 POP \n3 EXIT\n ENTER CHOICE\n");
          scanf("%d",&ch);
switch(ch)
{
```

```
case 1:
            if(t<max)
                  {
                  printf("enter no to push : ");
               scanf("%d",&t1);
                  t++;
                  aaa33[t]=t1;
                  push(t1,t);
                  }
           else
                  printf(" STACK IS FULL \n");

           break;
 case 2:
           if(t==0)
                  printf("STACK IS EMPTY \n");
           else
                  {
                  pop(t);
                  t—;
                  }
                  delay(1000);
           break;
case 3:
           break;
default :
           printf("INVALID OPTION\n");
           break;
} /* end of switch()*/
           sleep(2);
           closegraph();

}          /* end of while*/
}          /* end of stmain()*/


/*************************************************************************
                    FUNCTION FOR PUSHING THE ELEMENT INTO STACK
*************************************************************************/
```

```
void push(int x,int t)
{
 int gd=DETECT,gm,i;
 char *e;
 void *z;
 initgraph(&gd,&gm,"");
            line(289,100,289,400);
            line(289,400,341,400);
            line(341,100,341,400);

            /* FOR WRITING PREVIOUS NOS */

            for(i=1;i<t;++i)
            {
            sprintf(e,"%d",aaa33[i]);
            rectangle(290,400-i*20,340,400-(i-1)*20);
            outtextxy(300,400-i*20+5,e);
            }
            sprintf(e,"%d",t-1);
            outtextxy(235,400-(t-1)*20+5,"TOP=");
            outtextxy(270,400-(t-1)*20+5,e);

            rectangle(50,75,100,95);
            sprintf(e,"%d",x);
            outtextxy(60,80,e);

            z=malloc(imagesize(50,75,100,95));
            getimage(50,75,100,95,z);
            putimage(50,75,z,1);

            for(i=50;i<=290;++i)
            {
                    putimage(i,75,z,2);
                    delay(1);
                    sound(rand()/100);
                    putimage(i,75,z,1);
            }

            for(i=75;i<=400-t*20;++i)
```

```
        {
                putimage(290,i,z,2);
                delay(1);
                sound(i*8);
                putimage(290,i,z,1);
        }

                nosound();
                putimage(290,400-t*20,z,2);
                setcolor(0);
                sprintf(e,"%d",t-1);
                outtextxy(235,400-(t-1)*20+5,"TOP=");
                outtextxy(270,400-(t-1)*20+5,e);
                setcolor(15);
                sprintf(e,"%d",t);
                outtextxy(235,400-t*20+5,"TOP=");
                outtextxy(270,400-t*20+5,e);
        sleep(1);
}

/*****************************************************************************
                FUNCTION FOR POPING THE ELEMENT FROM THE STACK
*****************************************************************************/

void pop(int t)
{
int gd=DETECT,gm,i;
char *e;
void *z;
initgraph(&gd,&gm,"");
        line(289,100,289,400);
        line(289,400,341,400);
        line(341,100,341,400);

        /* FOR WRITING PREVIOUS NOS */

        for(i=1;i<=t;++i)
        {
        sprintf(e,"%d",aaa33[i]);
```

```
	rectangle(290,400-i*20,340,400-(i-1)*20);
	outtextxy(300,400-i*20+5,e);
	}
	sprintf(e,"%d",t);
	outtextxy(235,400-(t)*20+5,"TOP=");
	outtextxy(270,400-(t)*20+5,e);

	z=malloc(imagesize(50,75,100,95));
	rectangle(290,400-t*20,340,400-(t-1)*20);

	getimage(290,400-t*20,340,400-(t-1)*20,z);
	putimage(290,400-t*20,z,1);

	for(i=400-t*20;i>=50;—i)
	{
		if(t>1)
		rectangle(290,400-(t-1)*20,340,400-(t-2)*20);
		putimage(290,i,z,2);
		delay(10);
		putimage(290,i,z,1);
		line(290,400,340,400);
	}

	for(i=290;i<=getmaxx();++i)
	{
		putimage(i,50,z,2);
		delay(1);
		putimage(i,50,z,1);
	}
		nosound();
		setcolor(0);
		sprintf(e,"%d",t);
		outtextxy(235,400-(t)*20+5,"TOP=");
		outtextxy(270,400-(t)*20+5,e);
		setcolor(15);
		sprintf(e,"%d",t-1);
		outtextxy(235,400-(t-1)*20+5,"TOP=");
		outtextxy(270,400-(t-1)*20+5,e);
```

```
}
```

5.C. iii) The Queue Module

/* This module describes the queue operations. We can insert the elements into the queue or we can delete the elements from the queue or we can list the elements of the queue. The boundary value checking that leads to over flow during insertion and underflow during deletion are checked. For avoiding the graphical resolution problem the numbers of elements are restricted. The different functions are used for each of the operations.*/

/* it is completely independent module. To run it independently replace the function name "quemain()" with "main()" and include the necessary header files */

```
int aaa55[100];
int f=0;

void qinsert(int,int);
void qdisplay(int);
void qdelete(int);

void quemain()
{
        int n,r=0;
        int chq=0;
        while(chq!=4)
        {
        clrscr();
        printf("\n QUEUE OPERATION\n");
        printf("\n 1 insertion\n 2 deletion\n 3 display\n 4 exit\n enter choice\n");
        scanf("%d",&chq);
        switch(chq)
        {
             case 1:
                        printf("enter no to insert \n");
                        scanf("%d",&n);
                        r++;
                        aaa55[r]=n;
                        qinsert(r,n);
                        break;
```

```
        case 2:
                if(r<=0)
                printf("QUEUE IS EMPTY\n");
                 else
                qdelete(r);
                r=r-1;
                if(r==0)
                f=0;
                break;

        case 3:
                qdisplay(r);
                break;

        case 4: break;

        default : printf("\ninvalid option\n");
        }
    sleep(2);
    }
    }


/**************************************************************************
                FUNCTION FOR DISPLAYING THE QUEUE
**************************************************************************/

void qdisplay(int r)
{
        int gd=DETECT,gm,i,k,l,j,f=0;
        void *zq;
        char *eq;
        if(r>1)
        f=1;
        initgraph(&gd,&gm,"");
        for(i=0;i<12;++i)
        rectangle(150+i*30,199,180+i*30,251);
```

```
        for(i=1;i<=r;++i)
        {
        sprintf(eq,"%d",aaa55[i]);
        outtextxy(512-i*30,220,eq);
        }

        sprintf(eq,"%d",f);
        outtextxy(500,260,"F=");
        outtextxy(520,260,eq);

        sprintf(eq,"%d",r);
        outtextxy(500-r*30,290,"R=");
        outtextxy(520-r*30,290,eq);

        for(i=0;i<12-r;++i)
        {
        line(150+i*30,199,180+i*30,251);
        line(150+i*30,251,180+i*30,199);
        }
        sleep(1);
        closegraph();

}

/***************************************************************************
                FUNCTION FOR DELETION FROM THE QUEUE
***************************************************************************/

void qdelete(int r)
{
        int gd=DETECT,gm,i,k,l,j,f=0;
        void *zq;
        char *eq;
        if(r>1)
        f=1;
        initgraph(&gd,&gm,"");
        for(i=0;i<12;++i)
        rectangle(150+i*30,199,180+i*30,251);
```

```
for(i=1;i<=r;++i)
{
sprintf(eq,"%d",aaa55[i]);
outtextxy(512-i*30,220,eq);
}

sprintf(eq,"%d",f);
outtextxy(500,260,"F=");
outtextxy(520,260,eq);

sprintf(eq,"%d",r);
outtextxy(500-r*30,290,"R=");
outtextxy(520-r*30,290,eq);

for(i=0;i<12-r;++i)
{
line(150+i*30,199,180+i*30,251);
line(150+i*30,251,180+i*30,199);
}

zq=malloc(imagesize(150,200,500,250));
getimage(150,200,500,250,zq);
putimage(150,200,zq,1);

for(i=150;i<=180;++i)
{
putimage(i,200,zq,2);
delay(10);
putimage(i,200,zq,1);
}
putimage(180,200,zq,2);

setcolor(0);
sprintf(eq,"%d",f);
outtextxy(500,260,"F=");
outtextxy(520,260,eq);

sprintf(eq,"%d",(r-1));
outtextxy(500-(r-1)*30,290,"R=");
```

```
        outtextxy(520-(r-1)*30,290,eq);

        setcolor(15);
        f=1;
        sprintf(eq,"%d",f);
        outtextxy(500,260,"F=");
        outtextxy(520,260,eq);

        sprintf(eq,"%d",(r-1));
        outtextxy(500-r*30,290,"R=");
        outtextxy(520-r*30,290,eq);

        for(i=0;i<12-r+1;++i)
        {
        rectangle(150+i*30,199,180+i*30,251);
        line(150+i*30,199,180+i*30,251);
        line(150+i*30,251,180+i*30,199);
        }
        zq=malloc(imagesize(500,200,530,250));
        rectangle(511,200,540,250);
        getimage(511,200,540,250,zq);
        putimage(511,200,zq,1);
        for(i=511;i<=getmaxx();++i)
        {
        putimage(i,200,zq,2);
        delay(10);
        putimage(i,200,zq,1);
        }

        sleep(1);
        closegraph();

}

/**************************************************************************
                    FUNCTION FOR INSERTION INTO THE QUEUE
**************************************************************************/

void qinsert(int r, int n)
```

```
{
        int gd=DETECT,gm,i,k,l,j,f=0;
        void *zq;
        char *eq;
        if(r>1)
        f=1;
        initgraph(&gd,&gm,"");
        for(i=0;i<12;++i)
        rectangle(150+i*30,199,180+i*30,251);

        for(i=1;i<=(r-1);++i)
        {
        sprintf(eq,"%d",aaa55[i]);
        outtextxy(512-i*30,220,eq);
        }

        sprintf(eq,"%d",f);
        outtextxy(500,260,"F=");
        outtextxy(520,260,eq);

        sprintf(eq,"%d",(r-1));
        outtextxy(500-(r-1)*30,290,"R=");
        outtextxy(520-(r-1)*30,290,eq);

        for(i=0;i<12-(r-1);++i)
        {
        line(150+i*30,199,180+i*30,251);
        line(150+i*30,251,180+i*30,199);
        }
        sprintf(eq,"%d",n);
        rectangle(10,200,40,250);
        outtextxy(12,220,eq);
        zq=malloc(imagesize(10,200,40,250));
        getimage(10,200,40,250,zq);
        putimage(10,200,zq,1);
        for(i=10;i<=480-(r-1)*30;++i)
        {
        putimage(i,200,zq,2);
        delay(10);
```

```
        putimage(i,200,zq,1);
        }
        putimage(480-(r-1)*30,200,zq,2);

        setcolor(0);
        sprintf(eq,"%d",f);
        outtextxy(500,260,"F=");
        outtextxy(520,260,eq);

        sprintf(eq,"%d",(r-1));
        outtextxy(500-(r-1)*30,290,"R=");
        outtextxy(520-(r-1)*30,290,eq);

        setcolor(15);
        f=1;
        sprintf(eq,"%d",f);
        outtextxy(500,260,"F=");
        outtextxy(520,260,eq);

        sprintf(eq,"%d",r);
        outtextxy(500-r*30,290,"R=");
        outtextxy(520-r*30,290,eq);

        for(i=0;i<12-r;++i)
        {
        rectangle(150+i*30,199,180+i*30,251);
        line(150+i*30,199,180+i*30,251);
        line(150+i*30,251,180+i*30,199);
        }

        sleep(1);
        closegraph();
}
```

5.C. iv) The Single Linked List Module

/* This module demonstrates single linked list and its operations. The main operations we can do are insertion, deletion and display of elements. In the insertion the elements can be inserted in the beginning of the list or at the end of the list or in the middle of the list. Similarly the elements can be deleted from beginning or end or by position. This is achieved with the help of a sub menu with eight menu options in which six for insertion and deletion one for displaying and last for taking back the program control to the main menu. */

/* This is completely independent module. to run it independently we can change the name "sllmain()" with "main()" and include all header files. */

/* The function declarations for each of the operations in this module */

```
void insatbeg();
void insatend();
void insatpos();
void display();
void display1();
void delatpos(int);

int ch=0;
int c=0;
int p,a[100],i,b[100],j,n;
int lp;
int gd=DETECT, gm;

void sllmain()
{

while(ch!=8)
{
clrscr();
printf("\t\t LINKED LIST\n\n 1 INSERTION AT BEGINNING\n");
printf("2 INSERTION AT POSITION\n 3 INSERTION AT END\n");
printf("4 DELETION FROM BEGINNING\n 5 DELETION FROM POSITION\n");
printf("6 DELETION FROM END\n 7 DISPLAY LIST\n8 EXIT\n");
printf("\nENTER YOUR CHOICE :");
scanf("%d",&ch);
switch(ch)
{
case 1:    insatbeg();
           break;
case 2:
           insatpos();
           break;
```

```
case 3:     insatend();
            break;
case 4:     if(c>=1)
            {
            p=1;
            delatpos(p);
            }
            else
            printf(" no elements in the list\n");
            break;

case 5:
            printf("\nenter position\n");
            scanf("%d",&lp);
            if((lp<=0)||(lp>c))
            printf("no valid position\n");
            else
            delatpos(lp);
            break;
case 6:
            if(c!=0)
            {
            p=c;
            delatpos(p);
            }
            else
            printf(" no elements in the list\n");
            break;
case 7:     display();
            break;
case 8:     break;

}
getch();
}
}
```

```
/***************************************************************/
/* function for insertion at specified position the list */
/***************************************************************/

void insatpos()
{
char *inz;
clrscr();
//c++;
printf("enter position \n");
scanf("%d",&p);
if(p==1)
insatbeg();
else
if(p==(c+1))
insatend();
else
{
printf("enter number to insert :");
scanf("%d",&n);

initgraph(&gd,&gm,"");
for(i=1;i<=c;++i)
{
rectangle(10+(i-1)*80+20,200,10+(i-1)*80+80,230);
line(10+(i-1)*80+60,200,10+(i-1)*80+60,230);
sprintf(inz,"%d",a[i]);
outtextxy(10+(i-1)*80+25,205,inz);
}
for(i=1;i<c;++i)
{
line(10+(i-1)*80+70,215,10+(i-1)*80+100,215);
}
line(10+(c-1)*80+60,200,10+(c-1)*80+80,230);
sound(300);
delay(500);

rectangle(10+(p-1)*80+20,300,10+(p-1)*80+80,330);
```

```
sound(350);
delay(500);
sprintf(inz,"%d",n);
outtextxy(10+(p-1)*80+25,305,inz);
sound(100);
delay(500);
line(10+(p-1)*80+5,315,10+(p-1)*80+20,315);
sound(300);
delay(500);
line(10+(p-1)*80+70,315,10+(p-1)*80+90,315);
sound(200);
delay(500);
line(10+(p-1)*80+60,300,10+(p-1)*80+60,330);
sound(400);
delay(500);
setcolor(0);
line(10+(p-1)*80,215,10+(p-1)*80+20,215);
sound(300);
delay(500);
setcolor(15);
line(10+(p-1)*80,215,10+(p-1)*80+5,215);
sound(100);
delay(500);
line(10+(p-1)*80+15,215,10+(p-1)*80+20,215);
sound(300);
delay(500);
line(10+(p-1)*80+5,215,10+(p-1)*80+5,315);
sound(500);
delay(500);
line(10+(p-1)*80+15,215,10+(p-1)*80+15,250);
sound(100);
delay(500);
line(10+(p-1)*80+90,315,10+(p-1)*80+90,250);
sound(400);
delay(500);
line(10+(p-1)*80+90,250,10+(p-1)*80+15,250);

for(i=1;i<p;++i)
b[i]=a[i];
```

```
b[p]=n;
for(i=p;i<=c;i++)
b[i+1]=a[i];
c++;
nosound();

for(i=1;i<=c;++i)
a[i]=b[i];


getch();
closegraph();
}
}

/*********************************************************************/
/* function for deletion at position of the list */
/*********************************************************************/

void delatpos(int p)
{
char *inz;
void *z;
display1();
        z=malloc(imagesize(p*80+20,200,p*80+80,230));
        getimage(p*80+20,200,p*80+80,230,z);
        putimage(p*80+20,200,z,1);
        if(p==1)
        {
        setcolor(0);
        line(p*80+70,215,p*80+100,215);
        for(i=2;i<=c;++i)
        b[i-1]=a[i];
        c--;
        for(i=1;i<=c;++i)
        a[i]=b[i];
        setcolor(15);
        }
        else
```

```
        if(p==c)
        {
        setcolor(0);
        line(p*80+70-80,215,p*80+100-80,215);
        setcolor(15);
        line(p*80+60-80,200,p*80,230);
        c—;
        }
        else
        {
        line(p*80,215,p*80+80,215);
         j=1;
        for(i=1;i<=c;++i)
        if(i!=p)
        {
        b[j]=a[i];
        j++;
        }
        c—;
        for(i=1;i<=c;++i)
        a[i]=b[i];
        }

getch();
closegraph();
}

/******************************************************************/
/* function for insertion at end of the list */
/******************************************************************/

void insatend()
{
char *inz;
clrscr();
c++;
printf("enter number to insert :");
scanf("%d",&n);
a[c]=n;
```

```
initgraph(&gd,&gm,"");
for(i=1;i<c;++i)
{
rectangle(10+(i-1)*80+20,200,10+(i-1)*80+80,230);
line(10+(i-1)*80+60,200,10+(i-1)*80+60,230);
sprintf(inz,"%d",a[i]);
outtextxy(10+(i-1)*80+25,205,inz);
}
for(i=1;i<c-1;++i)
{
line(10+(i-1)*80+70,215,10+(i-1)*80+100,215);
}

rectangle(c*80+40,300,c*80+100,330);
line(c*80+80,300,c*80+80,330);
line(c*80+80,300,c*80+100,330);
sprintf(inz,"%d",a[c]);
outtextxy(c*80+45,305,inz);


if(c>1)
{
line(c*80+40,315,c*80+20,315);
line(c*80+20,315,c*80+20,215);
line(c*80+20,215,c*80-80,215);
}
getch();
closegraph();
}

/*******************************************************************/
/* function for insertion at beginning of the list */
/*******************************************************************/

void insatbeg()
{
char *inz;
clrscr();
c++;
```

```
printf("enter number to insert :");
scanf("%d",&n);
if(c==1)
{
a[c]=n;
}
else
{
for(i=c;i>=1;—i)
a[i+1]=a[i];
a[1]=n;
}
for(i=1;i<=c;++i)
printf("%d\n",a[i]);

initgraph(&gd,&gm,"");
rectangle(100,300,160,330);
line(140,300,140,330);
if(c==1)
line(140,300,160,330);
sprintf(inz,"%d",n);
outtextxy(105,310,inz);
for(i=1;i<c;++i)
{
rectangle(100+i*80+20,200,100+i*80+80,230);
line(100+i*80+60,200,100+i*80+60,230);
sprintf(inz,"%d",a[i+1]);
outtextxy(100+i*80+25,205,inz);
}
for(i=1;i<c-1;++i)
{
line(100+i*80+70,215,100+i*80+100,215);
}

if(c>1)
{
line(100+(c-1)*80+60,200,100+(c-1)*80+80,230);
line(150,315,180,315);
line(180,315,180,215);
```

```
line(180,215,200,215);
}
getch();
closegraph();
}

/*******************************************************************/
/* function for displaying the list */
/*******************************************************************/

void display()
{
char *inz;
clrscr();
initgraph(&gd,&gm,"");
for(i=1;i<=c;++i)
{
rectangle(i*80+20,200,i*80+80,230);
line(i*80+60,200,i*80+60,230);
sprintf(inz,"%d",a[i]);
outtextxy(i*80+25,205,inz);
}
for(i=1;i<=c-1;++i)
{
line(i*80+70,215,i*80+100,215);
}

line((c)*80+60,200,(c)*80+80,230);
getch();
closegraph();
}

/*******************************************************************/
/* function for displaying the list for deletion purpose */
/*******************************************************************/

void display1()
{
char *inz;
```

```
initgraph(&gd,&gm,"");
for(i=1;i<=c;++i)
{
rectangle(i*80+20,200,i*80+80,230);
line(i*80+60,200,i*80+60,230);
sprintf(inz,"%d",a[i]);
outtextxy(i*80+25,205,inz);
}
for(i=1;i<=c-1;++i)
{
line(i*80+70,215,i*80+100,215);
}

line((c)*80+60,200,(c)*80+80,230);
getch();
}
```

5.C. v) The Doubly linked List Module

/* This module demonstrates doubly linked list and its operations. The main operations we can do are insertion deletion and display of list elements. In the insertion the elements can be inserted in the beginning of the list or at the end of the list or in the middle of the list. Similarly the elements can be deleted from beginning or end or by position. This is achieved with the help of a sub menu with eight menu options in which six for insertion and deletion one for displaying and last for taking back the program control to the main menu. */

/* This is completely independent module. to run it independently we can change the name "dllmain()" with "main()" and include all header files. */

```
/* The function declarations for each of the operations in this module */
void insatbegd();
void insatendd();
void insatposd();
void displaydl();
void displaydl1();
void delatposdl(int);

/* The global variables that are used in different functions of this module */
int ch67=0;
int c67=0;
int p68,aaa66[100],i68,b68[100],jp68,np68;
```

```
int lp68;
int gddl68=DETECT, gmdl68;

void dllmain()
{
/* creation of text oriented menu */
while(ch67!=8)
{
clrscr();
printf("\t\tDOUBLY LINKED LIST\n\n 1 INSERTION AT BEGINNING\n");
printf(" 2 INSERTION AT POSITION\n 3 INSERTION AT END\n");
printf(" 4 DELETION FROM BEGINNING\n 5 DELETION FROM POSITION\n");
printf(" 6 DELETION FROM END\n 7 DISPLAY LIST\n 8 EXIT\n");
printf("\nENTER YOUR CHOICE :");
scanf("%d",&ch67);
switch(ch67)/* activating the functions according to user request */
{
case 1:     insatbegd();
            break;
case 2:
            insatposd();
            break;

case 3:     insatendd();
            break;
case 4:     if(c67>=1)
            {
            p68=1;
            delatposdl(p68);
            closegraph();
            }
            else
            printf(" no elements in the list\n");

            break;

case 5:

            printf("\nenter position\n");
            scanf("%d",&lp68);
```

```
            if((lp68<=0)||(lp68>c67))
            printf("no valid position\n");
            else
            {
            delatposdl(lp68);
            closegraph();
            }
            break;
case 6:
            if(c67!=0)
            {
            p68=c67;
            delatposdl(p68);
            closegraph();
            }
            else
            {
            printf(" no elements in the list\n");

            }
            break;
case 7:     displaydl();
            break;
case 8:
            break;
}
getch();
}
}

/*****************************************************************/
/* function for insertion at specified position the list */
/*****************************************************************/
void insatposd()
{
            char *inz;
            clrscr();
            printf("enter position \n");
            scanf("%d",&p68);
```

```
if(p68==1)
        insatbegd();
else
if(p68==(c67+1))
        insatendd();
else
if((p68>1)&&(p68<=c67))
{
        printf("enter number to insert :");
        scanf("%d",&np68);

        initgraph(&gddl68,&gmdl68,"");
        for(i68=1;i68<=c67;++i68)
        {
                rectangle(10+(i68-1)*100+20,200,10+(i68-1)*100+100,230);
                line(10+(i68-1)*100+40,200,10+(i68-1)*100+40,230);
                line(10+(i68-1)*100+80,200,10+(i68-1)*100+80,230);
                sprintf(inz,"%d",aaa66[i68]);
                outtextxy(10+(i68-1)*100+45,205,inz);
    }
                line(30,200,50,230);
        for(i68=1;i68<c67;++i68)
        {
                line(10+(i68-1)*100+90,215,10+(i68-1)*100+130,215);
        }
        line(10+(c67-1)*100+80,200,10+(c67-1)*100+100,230);
        delay(500);

        rectangle(10+(p68-1)*100+20,300,10+(p68-1)*100+100,330);
        delay(500);
        sound(300);
        line(10+(p68-1)*100+40,300,10+(p68-1)*100+40,330);
        delay(500);
        sound(1000);
        line(10+(p68-1)*100+80,300,10+(p68-1)*100+80,330);

        delay(500);
        sound(100);
        sprintf(inz,"%d",np68);
```

```
            outtextxy(10+(p68-1)*100+40,305,inz);

            delay(500);
            sound(1500);
            line(10+(p68-1)*100+5,315,10+(p68-1)*100+30,315);
            delay(500);
            sound(100);
            line(10+(p68-1)*100+90,315,10+(p68-1)*100+110,315);
            delay(500);
            sound(500);
            setcolor(0);
            line(10+(p68-1)*100-10,215,10+(p68-1)*100+30,215);
            delay(500);
            sound(1000);
            setcolor(15);
            line(10+(p68-1)*100+15,215,10+(p68-1)*100+30,215);

            delay(500);
            sound(600);
            line(10+(p68-1)*100-10,215,10+(p68-1)*100+5,215);

            delay(500);
            sound(100);
            line(10+(p68-1)*100+5,215,10+(p68-1)*100+5,315);
            delay(500);
            sound(1600);
            line(10+(p68-1)*100+15,215,10+(p68-1)*100+15,250); /* down left*/
            delay(500);
            sound(1200);
            line(10+(p68-1)*100+110,315,10+(p68-1)*100+110,250);
            delay(500);
            sound(800);
            line(10+(p68-1)*100+15,250,10+(p68-1)*100+110,250);
            delay(500);
            nosound();
    for(i68=1;i68<p68;++i68)
            b68[i68]=aaa66[i68];

    b68[p68]=np68;
```

```
        for(i68=p68;i68<=c67;i68++)
            b68[i68+1]=aaa66[i68];
        c67++;

        for(i68=1;i68<=c67;++i68)
            aaa66[i68]=b68[i68];
        getch();

        }
        else
        {
        printf("\n position out of order\n");
        getch();

        }
         closegraph();
}

/***************************************************************/
/* function for deletion at position of the list */
/***************************************************************/

void delatposdl(int p68)
{
char *inz;
void *z;
displaydl1();
        z=malloc(imagesize(p68*100+20,200,p68*100+100,230));
        getimage(p68*100+20,200,p68*100+100,230,z);
        putimage(p68*100+20,200,z,1);
        if(p68==1)
        {
        setcolor(0);
        line(p68*100+90,215,p68*100+130,215);
        for(i68=2;i68<=c67;++i68)
        b68[i68-1]=aaa66[i68];
        c67—;
```

```
        for(i68=1;i68<=c67;++i68)
        aaa66[i68]=b68[i68];
        setcolor(15);
        }
        else
        if(p68==c67)
        {
        setcolor(0);
        line(p68*100-10,215,p68*100+30,215);
        setcolor(15);
        line(p68*100-20,200,p68*100,230);
        c67—;
        }
        else
        {
        line(p68*100,215,p68*100+100,215);
         jp68=1;
        for(i68=1;i68<=c67;++i68)
        if(i68!=p68)
        {
        b68[jp68]=aaa66[i68];
        jp68++;
        }
        c67—;
        for(i68=1;i68<=c67;++i68)
        aaa66[i68]=b68[i68];
        }

        getch();
closegraph();
}

/*******************************************************************/
/* function for insertion at end of the list */
/*******************************************************************/

void insatendd()
{
char *inz;
```

```
clrscr();
c67++;
printf("enter number to insert :");
scanf("%d",&np68);
aaa66[c67]=np68;
initgraph(&gddl68,&gmdl68,"");
for(i68=1;i68<c67;++i68)
{
rectangle(10+(i68-1)*100+20,200,10+(i68-1)*100+100,230);
line(10+(i68-1)*100+80,200,10+(i68-1)*100+80,230);
line(10+(i68-1)*100+40,200,10+(i68-1)*100+40,230);
line(30,200,50,230);
sprintf(inz,"%d",aaa66[i68]);
outtextxy(10+(i68-1)*100+45,205,inz);

}
for(i68=1;i68<c67-1;++i68)
{
line(10+(i68-1)*100+90,215,10+(i68-1)*100+130,215);
}

rectangle(c67*100+20,300,c67*100+100,330);
line(c67*100+40,300,c67*100+40,330);
line(c67*100+80,300,c67*100+80,330);
line(c67*100+80,300,c67*100+100,330);
sprintf(inz,"%d",aaa66[c67]);
outtextxy(c67*100+45,305,inz);

if(c67>1)
{
line(c67*100+30,315,c67*100+10,315);
line(c67*100+10,315,c67*100+10,215);
line(c67*100+10,215,c67*100-100,215);
}
getch();
closegraph();
}
```

```
/****************************************************************/
/* function for insertion at beginning of the list */
/****************************************************************/

void insatbegd()
{
char *inz;
clrscr();
c67++;
printf("enter number to insert :");
scanf("%d",&np68);
if(c67==1)
{
aaa66[c67]=np68;
}
else
{
for(i68=c67;i68>=1;—i68)
aaa66[i68+1]=aaa66[i68];
aaa66[1]=np68;
}
initgraph(&gddl68,&gmdl68,"");
rectangle(80,300,160,330);
line(100,300,100,330);
line(140,300,140,330);
if(c67==1)
line(140,300,160,330);
line(80,300,100,330);
sprintf(inz,"%d",np68);
outtextxy(105,310,inz);
for(i68=1;i68<c67;++i68)
{
rectangle(100+i68*100+20,200,100+i68*100+100,230);
line(100+i68*100+40,200,100+i68*100+40,230);
line(100+i68*100+80,200,100+i68*100+80,230);
sprintf(inz,"%d",aaa66[i68+1]);
outtextxy(100+i68*100+50,205,inz);
}
for(i68=1;i68<c67-1;++i68)
```

```
{
line(100+i68*100+90,215,100+i68*100+130,215);
}

if(c67>1)
{
line(100+(c67-1)*100+80,200,100+(c67-1)*100+100,230);
line(150,315,180,315);
line(180,315,180,215);
line(180,215,230,215);
}
getch();
closegraph();
}

/*************************************************************/
/* function for displaying the list */
/*************************************************************/

void displaydl()
{
char *inz;
clrscr();
initgraph(&gddl68,&gmdl68,"");
for(i68=1;i68<=c67;++i68)
{
rectangle(i68*100+20,200,i68*100+100,230);
line(i68*100+40,200,i68*100+40,230);
line(i68*100+80,200,i68*100+80,230);
sprintf(inz,"%d",aaa66[i68]);
outtextxy(i68*100+45,205,inz);
}
for(i68=1;i68<=c67-1;++i68)
{
line(i68*100+90,215,i68*100+130,215);
}
line(120,200,140,230);

line((c67)*100+80,200,(c67)*100+100,230);
```

```
getch();
closegraph();
}

/*****************************************************************/
/* function for displaying the list for deletion purpose */
/*****************************************************************/

void displaydl1()
{
char *inz;
clrscr();
initgraph(&gddl68,&gmdl68,"");
for(i68=1;i68<=c67;++i68)
{
rectangle(i68*100+20,200,i68*100+100,230);
line(i68*100+40,200,i68*100+40,230);
line(i68*100+80,200,i68*100+80,230);
sprintf(inz,"%d",aaa66[i68]);
outtextxy(i68*100+45,205,inz);
}
for(i68=1;i68<=c67-1;++i68)
{
line(i68*100+90,215,i68*100+130,215);
}
line(120,200,140,230);

line((c67)*100+80,200,(c67)*100+100,230);
getch();
closegraph();
}
```

PROJECT 6

BUILDESIGNER

(COMPLETE SOLUTION FOR RESIDENTIAL HOUSE CONSTRUCTION PLAN)

6.A) SYNOPSIS

This project deals with construction plan of residential houses. It consists of three main modules and total seven sub modules. The three main modules deal with three different dimensions namely 30 X 40ft, 40 X 50ft and 40 X 60ft. The sub modules in these main modules deal with different combination of number of rooms and with different plans for parking, compound, etc,. These are given below.

A) 30 ft X 40ft
  (i). 1 room, hall, Kitchen, car parking
  (ii). 2 rooms, hall, kitchen

B) 40ft X 50 ft
  (i). 2 rooms, hall, kitchen, car parking
  (ii). 3 rooms, hall, kitchen, car parking
  (iii). 3 rooms, hall, kitchen.

C) 40ft X 60 ft
  (i). 1 room, hall, kitchen, car parking, swimming pool
  (ii). 2 rooms, hall, kitchen, car parking, swimming pool

Each of these modules and their sub modules are explained below in detail.

6.A. i) 30 ft X 40 ft

In this module we are designing the house with different plans each with the different combinations of number of rooms, hall, kitchen, pooja room etc. The first module consists of

One room, hall, kitchen, pooja room etc. Here we are making best use of the given space by suitably constructing the plan which is more comfortable in all parts of the house. In order to demonstrate how the plan looks from different angles we are implementing three different modules for top view, front view and side view. These three views will show the clear dimensions of the design. Each of these views are explained below.

The **top view** gives the clear dimensions of the site and entrances to different parts of the house. It also shows the thickness of the walls. These are implemented with the help of lines, different labeling and styles.

The **front view** shows the elevations and look of the proposed structure from front. It shows different designs for the gate, door, windows etc. We are implementing these tasks by making use of ellipses, arcs, lines with different styles, areas with different fill styles etc.

The **side view** shows the elevations and look of the proposed structure from one of the sides. Here we have implemented left side views in some scenarios and in some other we have shown right side views. It shows designs for the windows, exhaust (if any) etc. here also we have made use of different graphical functions available with C graphics for drawing rectangles and sun sets for all the windows.

The second sub module in this module consists of

Two rooms instead of one room as explained above along with hall, kitchen, pooja room etc. Here we are adjusting the space by making smaller but comfortable sizes for all parts of the house. The three views of the design namely top view, front view and side view will show the clear dimensions of the design.

The **top view** gives the clear dimensions of the site and entrances to different parts of the house from top. It also shows the thickness of the walls.

The **front view** shows the elevations and look of the structure from the front. It shows designs for the gate, door, windows etc.

The **side view** shows the elevations and look of the structure from one of the sides. It shows designs for the windows, exhaust (if any) etc.

6.B. ii) 40 ft X 50 ft

In this module we are designing the house with three different combinations in terms of number of rooms, hall, kitchen, pooja room etc and their position.

1) The first module consists of two rooms, hall, kitchen, pooja room, car parking etc. Here we are designing the plan with more comfort by suitably adjusting the space in terms of the size, position and entrances of different blocks of the house. Taking three views of the design namely top view, front view and side view will show the clear dimensions of the design.
2) The second module deals with 3 rooms, hall, kitchen, pooja room, car paring etc. Here we are adjusting the space by making different parts of the house smaller but comfortable. Here also we are considering three views of the design namely top view; front view and side view will show the clear dimensions of the design.
3) This module has three rooms, hall, kitchen, pooja room etc. Here we are making the space for car parking by suitably reducing the sizes, shapes and positions of different parts of the house. As usual by three different views of the design namely top view, front view and side view will show the clear dimensions of the design.

The above said three modules are implemented using the graphical functions such as line drawing, rectangles, arcs, ellipses, circles, 3d bars with different color and style combinations, fill styles and effects. The appropriate texts are displayed for understanding the different parts of the designs.

6.A. iii) 40 ft X 60 ft

This module designs the luxurious houses with swimming pool, garden with greenish lawn and trees. The interior design consists of attached bathrooms, ward roofs, basins and other facilities. It consists of two sub modules for designing single and double bed room houses.

1) The first module consists of one room, hall, kitchen, pooja room, car parking swimming pool and lawn etc. The car shed is designed separately with full covering for protection from all aspects. Taking three views of the design namely top view, front view and side view will show the clear dimensions of the design.
2) The second module designs houses with two rooms, hall, kitchen, pooja room, car parking, swimming pool etc. Here also we are taking three views of the design namely top view; front view and side view will show the clear dimensions of the design.

This module is implemented with functions such as arcs, circles and ellipses. The trees and swimming pool is designed effectively by making use of different fill styles and color combinations. The designs of the gates are very beautifully done with the help of proper combinations of arcs, edges and lines. These designs give an impression of wood carvings that we could see in day-to-day wood designs of the doors and gates.

6.B) Code Details

The following are the functions used in this project.

1) main()

The build designer project consists of a main module "build0.c" which activates the function "mainscreenmain()" a module in the program file "build10.c". the "mainscreenmain()" displays the opening screen of the project with the heading of the project with little animations and after suitable delay returns back.

Next the main menu of the project will be displayed giving following options for the user to choose.

a) 30x40 feet
b) 40x50 feet
c) 40x60 feet
d) Exit

The user can choose any of these options according to their requirements. Based on the users option different functions are called from main menu. To list these functions we have,

I. **"bui30x40()"** - which is called when the user opts for the first option from the main menu. This function in turn displays sub menu with three options as given below.
   a) One room, hall, kitchen.
   b) Two room, hall, kitchen.
   c) Return to main.

Based on the users selection other functions are called from this function("bui30x40()"). If the user chooses the first option the functions "top30401r()" , "front30401r()" and "side30401r()" to view the three different views based on the users selection. The function names are self explanatory about their purpose. And if the user chooses the second option also we have three similar functions for the same purpose but for two bed room houses namely, "top30402r()", "front30402r() and "side30402r()". These functions for views of one bed room and two bed room houses are implemented in "build1.c" program file.

II. **"bui40x50()"** – which is called when the user opts for the second option from the main menu. This function in turn displays sub menu with four options as given below.

   a) Two rooms, hall, kitchen.
   b) Three rooms, hall, kitchen without car parking.
   c) Three rooms, hall, kitchen with car parking.
   d) Return to main.

Based on the users selection other functions are called from this function("bui40x50()"). If the user chooses the first option the functions "top40502r()" , "front40502r()" and "side40502r()" to view the three different views based on the users selection. The function names are self explanatory about their purpose. These three functions are present in the program file "build2.c". And if the user chooses the second option also we have three similar functions for the same purpose but for three bed room house without car parking namely, "top40503r()", "front40503r() and "side40503r()". These functions for three views are present in "build3.c" program file. Similarly if the user chooses the third option we have three similar functions for the same purpose but for three bed room house with car parking namely, "top40503rc()", "front40503rc() and "side40503rc()". These functions for three views are present in "build4.c" program file.

III. **"bui40x60()"** – which is called when the user opts for the third option from the main menu. This function in turn displays sub menu with three options as given below.

   a) One room, hall, kitchen, swimming pool.
   b) Two rooms, hall, kitchen, swimming pool.
   c) Return to main.

Based on the users selection other functions are called from this function("bui40x60()"). If the user chooses the first option the functions "top40601r()", "front40601r()" and "side40601r()" to view the three different views based on the users selection. The function names are self explanatory about their purpose. These three functions are present in the program file "build5.c". And if the user chooses the second option also we have three similar functions for the same purpose but for two bed room house with swimming pool namely, "top40602r()", "front40602r() and "side40602r()". These functions for three views are present in "build6.c" program file.

When the user opts for the fourth in the main menu module ("main ()") option the program terminates.

6.C) Source Code

6.C. i) The main module of the build designer

/* This is the main module of the build designer project. This module creates the main menu and three sub menus each for three menu items in the main menu. The first menu deals with different designs of site plans with size 30x40. It consists of two menu items for one bed room and two bed rooms. The second menu item in the main menu activates sub menu that deals with site designs with size 40x50. It consists of three sub menus for two rooms with car parking, three rooms with car parking and three rooms without car parking. The third menu item in the main menu demonstrates the designs with the size 40x60 with swimming pool and one room and two rooms. Before going to the main menu program control displays the heading of the project. */

```
/* This is build0.c program file */
/* The header files necessary for this project build designer */
#include<stdio.h>
#include<conio.h>
#include<graphics.h>
#include<stdlib.h>
#include<dos.h>

/* The program modules of this project that deal with different build options */
#include "build1.c" /* 30x40 1 room and 2 room */
#include "build2.c" /* 40x50 case 1 */
#include "build3.c" /* 40x50 case 2 */
#include "build4.c" /* 40x50 case 3 */
#include "build5.c" /* 40x60 case 1 */
#include "build6.c" /* 40x60 case 2 */
#include "build10.c" /* main screen for heading */

/* Function declarations */
void bui40x60(int, int, int, int);
void bui30x40(int, int, int, int);
void bui40x50(int, int, int, int);
void top40601r(int, int, int, int);
void front40601r(int, int, int, int);
void side40601r(int, int, int, int);

void top40602r(int, int, int, int);
```

```
void front40602r(int, int, int, int);
void side40602r(int, int, int, int);

/* Build designer project starts from here */
void main()
{
int gd=DETECT,gm,l,w,x1,x2,y1,y2;
int ch=0;
mainscreenmain(); /* The function that displays build designer heading */
while(ch!=4)/* Loop repeats until user opts for exit */
{
initgraph(&gd,&gm,"");/* Graphics is initialized */
cleardevice();
gotoxy(1,1);
printf("\n standard sizes allowed\n");
printf("\n 1 30 ft X 40 ft\n 2 40 ft X 50 ft\n 3 40 ft X 60 ft\n 4 exit\n\n enter the choice\n");
scanf("%d",&ch);
switch(ch) /* Choosing the menu options according to the user's requirements */
{
case 1:
        x1=130;
        y1=120;
        initgraph(&gd,&gm,"");
        x2=getmaxx()-130;
        y2=getmaxy()-120;

/* Calls the menu for 30x40 with boundary values as the parameters */
        bui30x40(x1,y1,x2,y2);
        closegraph();
        break;
case 2:
        x1=95;
        y1=60;
        initgraph(&gd,&gm,"");
        x2=getmaxx()-95;
        y2=getmaxy()-60;

/* Calls the menu for 40x50 with boundary values as the parameters */
        bui40x50(x1,y1,x2,y2);
```

```
            closegraph();
            break;
case 3:
            x1=30;
            y1=30;
            x2=getmaxx()-10;
            y2=getmaxy()-10;
            initgraph(&gd,&gm,"");

/* Calls the menu for 40x60 with boundary values as the parameters */
            bui40x60(x1,y1,x2,y2);
            closegraph();
            break;
case 4:     break;
default: printf("wrong choice try again....\n");
} /* end of switch */
sleep(4); /* Waits for 4 seconds before clearing the screen and terminating the program */
cleardevice();
} /* end of while */
} /* end of build designer */


/* This module gives the options for the users to design their houses within 30x40 sizes */
void bui30x40(int l1,int w1,int l2,int w2)
{
int gd=DETECT,gm,ch3040=0;
while(ch3040!=3)
{
initgraph(&gd,&gm,"");
printf("\n 1 room-1, hall, kitchen, puja room, toilet, bathroom, carparking with specious compound\n");
printf("\n 2 room-2, hall, kitchen, puja room, toilet, bathroom, with compound\n");
printf("\n 3 back to main menu\n enter your choice\n");
scanf("%d",&ch3040);
/* user can have two choices with one room and two rooms.*/
switch(ch3040)
{
case 1:     /* 30x40 with one room. User can see their house in three views */
            cleardevice();
            top30401r(l1,w1,l2,w2);/* the top view of the single room 30x40 design */
            front30401r(l1,w1,l2,w2);/* the front view of the single room 30x40 design */
```

```
            side30401r(l1,w1,l2,w2); /* the side view of the single room 30x40 design */
            break;
case 2:     /* 30x40 with two room. User can see their house in three views top, front and side */
            cleardevice();
            top30402r(l1,w1,l2,w2);
            front30402r(l1,w1,l2,w2);
            side30402r(l1,w1,l2,w2);
        break;

case 3:     break;
    }

}
}/* end of 30x40 sub menu */

/* This module demonstrates three different options for designing house in 40x50 site */
void bui40x50(int l1,int w1,int l2,int w2)
{
int gd=DETECT,gm,ch4050=0;
initgraph(&gd, &gm,"");
while(ch4050!=4)
{
cleardevice();
printf("\n 1 room 2, hall, kitchen, puja room, toilet, bathroom, carparking with specious compound\n");
printf("\n 2 room 3, hall, kitchen, puja room, toilet, bathroom, with car parking and small
compound\n");
printf("\n 3 room 3, hall, kitchen, puja room, toilet, bathroom with compound\n");
printf("\n 4 back to main menu\n enter your choice\n");
scanf("%d",&ch4050);
/* user can have three option with two and three room combinations */
switch(ch4050)
{
case 1:     cleardevice();
            initgraph(&gd, &gm,"");
            top40502r(l1,w1,l2,w2);
            cleardevice();

            front40502r(l1,w1,l2,w2);
            cleardevice();
```

```
            side40502r(l1,w1,l2,w2);
            closegraph();
        break;
case 2:     initgraph(&gd, &gm,"");
            cleardevice();
            top40503r(l1,w1,l2,w2);
            cleardevice();
            front40503r(l1,w1,l2,w2);
            cleardevice();
            side40503r(l1,w1,l2,w2);
            closegraph();
        break;

case 3:     initgraph(&gd,&gm,"");
            cleardevice();
            top40503rc(l1,w1,l2,w2);
            cleardevice();
            front40503rc(l1,w1,l2,w2);
            cleardevice();
            side40503rc(l1,w1,l2,w2);
            closegraph();
            break;
case 4:     break;
        }
}
sleep(2);
return;
}

/* within 40x60 we can build and swim. This module shows how */
void bui40x60(int l1,int w1,int l2,int w2)
{
int gd=DETECT,gm,ch4060=0;

while(ch4060!=3)
{
initgraph(&gd,&gm,"");
printf("\n 1 room-1, hall, kitchen, puja room, toilet, bathroom, carparking, swimming pool, lawn
with specious compound\n");
```

```
printf("\n 2 room-2, hall, kitchen, puja room, toilet, bathroom, carparking, swimming pool with
specious compound\n");
printf("\n 3 back to main menu\n enter your choice\n");
scanf("%d",&ch4060);
/* we have 2 options for single and double rooms with swimming pool */
switch(ch4060)
{
case 1:    initgraph(&gd,&gm,"");
           top40601r(l1,w1,l2,w2);
           front40601r(l1,w1,l2,w2);
           side40601r(l1,w1,l2,w2);
      break;
case 2:
           initgraph(&gd,&gm,"");
           top40602r(l1,w1,l2,w2);
           front40602r(l1,w1,l2,w2);
           side40602r(l1,w1,l2,w2);
      break;

case 3:    break;
      }
}
sleep(2);
return;
}/* end of the menus module */
```

6.C. ii) The Main Screen Module

```
/* Program build10.c */

/* This module displays the heading of the project "Build Designer". The different colors and fonts
        are used to make it more effective. */

void mainscreenmain()
{
int i,j,k,n,m,gd=DETECT, gm;
initgraph(&gd,&gm,"");
/* to draw a surface on both the sides of a screen. */
for(i=0;i<=getmaxx()/16+30;++i)
{
```

```
        line(i,0,i,getmaxy());
        line(getmaxx()-i,0,getmaxx()-i, getmaxy());
        setcolor(12);
        delay(10);
}
/* to check the fonts, styles and colors for the project heading */

settextstyle(1,0,6);
setcolor(9);
outtextxy(getmaxx()/7-18,120, " BUILDESIGNER ");
settextstyle(1,0,4);
setcolor(5);
outtextxy(getmaxx()/10-24,240, " COMPLETE SOLUTION FOR");
outtextxy(getmaxx()/4-40,300, "RESIDENTIAL HOUSE PLAN");
sleep(4);
} /* end of screen module */
```

6.C. iii) The module for 30 X 40 site 1 and 2 rooms house plan

```
/* Program build1.c */

/* This module deals with 30x40 site with 1 and 2 bed rooms. In each of the modules three views
namely top front and side views are demonstrated with respective labels and colors to make
demonstration more attractive. Top view is displayed and the control automatically switches to
front view and side view. The delay is maintained between the demonstrations of different views so
that user can have complete look at a particular view. */

/* Declaration of functions */
void top30401r(int, int, int, int);
void front30401r(int, int, int, int);
void side30401r(int, int, int, int);
void top30402r(int, int, int, int);
void front30402r(int, int, int, int);
void side30402r(int, int, int, int);

/* This module shows the top view of the single room design. this module takes the parameters
from its respective sub menu which is mentioned in the main module */
void top30401r(int l1,int w1, int l2,int w2)
{
                /* to draw the border with double line */
        rectangle(l1,w1,l2,w2);
```

```
rectangle(l1+3,w1+3,l2-3,w2-3);
/* design of different parts of the single room house */
rectangle(l1,w1,l2-100,w2-40);
rectangle(l1+3,w1+3,l2+3-100,w2-40-3);
rectangle(l1+3,w1+3,l2+3-100,w2-40);
l2=l2-100;
w2=w2-40;
/* design of kitchen */
rectangle(l1,w1,l1+80,w1+120);
rectangle(l1+3,w1+3,l1+77,w1+117);
/* design of room */
rectangle(l1+80,w1,l1+190,w1+100);
rectangle(l1+80,w1+3,l1+187,w1+97);
/* bath room design */
rectangle(l1+190,w1,l2-35,w1+100);
rectangle(l1+190,w1,l2-32,w1+97);
/* design of toilet */
rectangle(l2-35,w1,l2,w1+100);
rectangle(l2-35,w1+3,l2,w1+97);
/* pooja room design */
rectangle(l1,w1+120,l1+80,w2);
rectangle(l1+3,w1+120,l1+77,w2-3);

setcolor(0); /* for setting the background color for erasing certain portions to make doors
and entrances */

/* design of bedroom door */
line(l1+90,w1+100,l1+112,w1+100);
line(l1+90,w1+97,l1+112,w1+97);
setcolor(15);/* for closing door cutting edges */
line(l1+90,w1+100,l1+90,w1+97);
line(l1+112,w1+100,l1+112,w1+97);

setcolor(0);
/* bath and toilet doors */
line(l1+195,w1+100,l1+212,w1+100);
line(l1+195,w1+97,l1+212,w1+97);
setcolor(15);
line(l1+195,w1+100,l1+195,w1+97);
line(l1+212,w1+100,l1+212,w1+97);
```

```
setcolor(0);
/* toilet */
line(l2-30,w1+100,l2-15,w1+100);
line(l2-30,w1+97,l2-15,w1+97);
setcolor(15);
line(l2-30,w1+100,l2-30,w1+97);
line(l2-15,w1+100,l2-15,w1+97);

setcolor(0);
/* kitchen door */
line(l1+80,w1+101,l1+80,w1+116);
line(l1+77,w1+101,l1+77,w1+116);
setcolor(15);
line(l1+80,w1+101,l1+77,w1+101);
line(l1+80,w1+116,l1+77,w1+116);

setcolor(0);
/* pooja room door */
line(l1+80,w1+145,l1+80,w1+165);
line(l1+77,w1+145,l1+77,w1+165);
setcolor(15);
line(l1+80,w1+145,l1+77,w1+145);
line(l1+80,w1+165,l1+77,w1+165);

/* entrance to hall */
setcolor(0);
line(l1+165,w2,l1+195,w2);
line(l1+165,w2-3,l1+195,w2-3);
setcolor(15);
line(l1+165,w2,l1+165,w2-3);
line(l1+195,w2,l1+195,w2-3);

/* entrance to compound gate */
setcolor(0);
line(l1+160,w2+40,l1+200,w2+40);
line(l1+160,w2+37,l1+200,w2+37);
setcolor(15);
line(l1+160,w2+40,l1+160,w2+37);
line(l1+200,w2+40,l1+200,w2+37);
```

```
        /* car parking gate */
        setcolor(0);
        line(l2+10,w2+40,l2+90,w2+40);
        line(l2+10,w2+37,l2+90,w2+37);
        setcolor(15);
        line(l2+10,w2+40,l2+10,w2+37);
        line(l2+90,w2+40,l2+90,w2+37);

        /* labeling the different parts of the design in the respective locations */
        setcolor(9);
        outtextxy(l1+10,w1+50,"KITCHEN ");
        outtextxy(l1+90,w1+50,"BED ROOM ");
        outtextxy(l1+195,w1+50,"BATH&T");
        settextstyle(2,1,4);
        outtextxy(l2-30,w1+20,"TOILET ");
        settextstyle(2,0,4);
        outtextxy(l1+140,w1+140,"HALL ROOM ");
        outtextxy(l1+10,w1+140,"PRAYER ");
        outtextxy(l2+10,w1+50,"CAR PARKING ");
        outtextxy(l1+80,w2+10,"COMPOUND ");
        sleep(4); /* waits for 4 seconds before switching to the front view module */
        cleardevice();
    }/* end of 30x40 one room top view */

/* front view design of single room */
void front30401r(int l1,int w1,int l2,int w2)
{
            int i;
            /* boundaries of entire front view and compound with car parking */
            line(l1-10,w1+240,l2+100,w1+240);
            line(l1-10,w1+220,l1-10,w1+240);
            line(l2+100,w2-100,l2+100,w2);
            line(l2+97,w2-100,l2+97,w2);
            line(l2+100,w2-100,l2,w2-125);
            line(l1-10,w1+220,l2+100,w1+220);
            line(l1,w1+75,l1,w1+220);
            line(l1,w1+75,l2,w1+75);
            line(l2,w1+75,l2,w1+220);
            line(l1,w1+220,l2,w1+220);
            line(l1,w1+220,l1,w1+220);
```

```
        setcolor(9);
        setlinestyle(SOLID_LINE,1,3);

                /* door design */
                rectangle(l1+165,w1+160,l1+195,w1+220);
setfillstyle(11,2);
floodfill(l1+168,w1+165,9);
setcolor(15);
line(l1+165,w1+189,l1+175,w1+189);
line(l1+170,w1+189,l1+170,w1+196);

/*left windows*/
setcolor(9);
        rectangle(l1+90,w1+160,l1+120,w1+190);
        floodfill(l1+95,w1+165,9);
        line(l1+100,w1+160,l1+100,w1+190);
        line(l1+110,w1+160,l1+110,w1+190);

        /* right window */
        rectangle(l1+240,w1+160,l1+270,w1+190);
        floodfill(l1+245,w1+165,9);
        line(l1+250,w1+160,l1+250,w1+190);
        line(l1+260,w1+160,l1+260,w1+190);

        /* sunset windows and door*/
        bar3d(l1+80,w1+140,l1+280,w1+150,10,1);

/*roof sunset*/
        bar3d(l1,w1+75,l2,w1+85,10,1);
        graphdefaults();
        setfillstyle(SOLID_FILL,8);
        floodfill(l1+10,w1+223,9);

/* gate design */
setfillstyle(SOLID_FILL,13);
floodfill(l1+185,w1+100,9);
setcolor(3);
rectangle(l1+155,w1+220,l1+205,w1+240);
line(l1+178,w1+220,l1+178,w1+240);
line(l1+180,w1+220,l1+180,w1+240);
```

```
line(l1+182,w1+220,l1+182,w1+240);
ellipse(l1+166,w1+225,0,360,11,5);
ellipse(l1+166,w1+235,0,360,11,5);
ellipse(l1+194,w1+225,0,360,11,5);
ellipse(l1+194,w1+235,0,360,11,5);
rectangle(l2+10,w1+220,l2+90,w1+240);
line(l2+48,w1+220,l2+48,w1+240);
line(l2+50,w1+220,l2+50,w1+240);
line(l2+52,w1+220,l2+52,w1+240);
ellipse(l2+15,w1+223,180,0,5,4);
ellipse(l2+25,w1+223,180,0,5,4);
ellipse(l2+35,w1+223,180,0,5,4);
ellipse(l2+45,w1+223,180,0,5,4);
ellipse(l2+15,w1+229,0,180,5,4);
ellipse(l2+25,w1+229,0,180,5,4);
ellipse(l2+35,w1+229,0,180,5,4);
ellipse(l2+45,w1+229,0,180,5,4);
ellipse(l2+15,w1+232,180,0,5,4);
ellipse(l2+25,w1+232,180,0,5,4);
ellipse(l2+35,w1+232,180,0,5,4);
ellipse(l2+45,w1+232,180,0,5,4);

ellipse(l2+15,w1+238,0,180,5,4);
ellipse(l2+25,w1+238,0,180,5,4);
ellipse(l2+35,w1+238,0,180,5,4);
ellipse(l2+45,w1+238,0,180,5,4);

ellipse(l2+55,w1+223,180,0,5,4);
ellipse(l2+65,w1+223,180,0,5,4);
ellipse(l2+75,w1+223,180,0,5,4);
ellipse(l2+85,w1+223,180,0,5,4);

ellipse(l2+55,w1+229,0,180,5,4);
ellipse(l2+65,w1+229,0,180,5,4);
ellipse(l2+75,w1+229,0,180,5,4);
ellipse(l2+85,w1+229,0,180,5,4);

ellipse(l2+55,w1+232,180,0,5,4);
ellipse(l2+65,w1+232,180,0,5,4);
```

```
        ellipse(l2+75,w1+232,180,0,5,4);
        ellipse(l2+85,w1+232,180,0,5,4);

        ellipse(l2+55,w1+238,0,180,5,4);
        ellipse(l2+65,w1+238,0,180,5,4);
        ellipse(l2+75,w1+238,0,180,5,4);
        ellipse(l2+85,w1+238,0,180,5,4);

        /* compound decoration */
        setcolor(4);
        for(i=l1;i<=l1+155;i=i+10)
        {
        line(i,w1+220,i-10,w1+240);
        line(i-10,w1+220,i,w1+240);
        }
        for(i=l1+215;i<=l2+10;i=i+10)
        {
        line(i,w1+220,i-10,w1+240);
        line(i-10,w1+220,i,w1+240);
        }
        line(l2+90,w1+220,l2+100,w1+240);
        line(l2+100,w1+220,l2+90,w1+240);
        sleep(4);
        cleardevice();
}/* end of front view */

/* module for side view design for single room */
void side30401r(int l1,int w1,int l2,int w2)
{
   int i;
   l2++;
   /* boundary design */
   setcolor(9);
   rectangle(l1,w1+90,l1+150,w1+220);
   line(l1,w1+220,l1+150,w1+220);
   setlinestyle(SOLID_LINE,1,3);

   rectangle(l1+40,w1+160,l1+70,w1+190);
   setfillstyle(11,2);
   floodfill(l1+45,w1+165,9);
```

```
    line(l1+50,w1+160,l1+50,w1+190);
    line(l1+60,w1+160,l1+60,w1+190);

    /* sun sets for side windows */
    bar3d(l1+30,w1+150,l1+80,w1+156,5,1);
    bar3d(l1-10,w1+85,l1+160,w1+91,10,1);

    rectangle(l1+110,w1+100,l1+125,w1+115);
    setlinestyle(SOLID_LINE,1,1);
    line(l1+110,w1+105,l1+125,w1+105);
    line(l1+110,w1+110,l1+125,w1+110);
    setlinestyle(SOLID_LINE,1,3);

    setfillstyle(SOLID_FILL,13);

    floodfill(l1+90,w1+95,9);

    /* compound design */
    line(l1+150,w1+220,l1+150,w1+240);
    line(l1-20,w1+240,l1+150,w1+240);
    line(l1-20,w1+240,l1,w1+190);

    setfillstyle(SOLID_FILL,8);
    floodfill(l1+90,w1+230,9);
    setcolor(4);
            setlinestyle(SOLID_LINE,1,1);
            for( i=l1-4;i<=l1+150;i=i+10)
            {
            line(i,w1+220,i-10,w1+240);
            line(i-10,w1+220,i,w1+240);
            }

    sleep(4); /* waits for 4 seconds before going back to the menu */
    cleardevice();
    w2++;

} /* end of single room house */

/* The following three sub modules gives the complete demonstration of two rooms house */
```

```
void top30402r(int l1,int w1, int l2,int w2)
{
		/* boundaries */
	rectangle(l1,w1,l2,w2);
	rectangle(l1+3,w1+3,l2-3,w2-3);
	rectangle(l1,w1,l2-100,w2-40);
	rectangle(l1+3,w1+3,l2+3-100,w2-40-3);
	rectangle(l1+3,w1+3,l2+3-100,w2-40);
	l2=l2-100;
	w2=w2-40;
	/* different parts of the house */
	rectangle(l1,w1,l1+80,w1+120);
	rectangle(l1+3,w1+3,l1+77,w1+117);
	rectangle(l1+80,w1,l1+190,w1+100);/*room1 */
	rectangle(l1+80,w1+3,l1+187,w1+97);
	rectangle(l1+190,w1,l2-35,w1+100); /* bath */
	rectangle(l1+190,w1,l2-32,w1+97);

	rectangle(l2-35,w1,l2+65,w1+100); /* room2 */
	rectangle(l2-35,w1+3,l2+62,w1+97);
	line(l2+65,w1+100,l2+65,w1+200);
	line(l2+62,w1+100,l2+62,w1+200);
	line(l2+65,w1+200,l2,w1+200);
	line(l2+62,w1+197,l2,w1+197);

	line(l2,w1+142,l2+62,w1+142);
	line(l2,w1+145,l2+62,w1+145);
	line(l2,w1+112,l2+3,w1+112);
	line(l2,w1+127,l2+3,w1+127);
	line(l2,w1+162,l2+3,w1+162);
	line(l2,w1+182,l2+3,w1+182);

	/* doors */
	setcolor(0);
	line(l2,w1+112,l2,w1+127);
	line(l2+3,w1+112,l2+3,w1+127);

	line(l2,w1+162,l2,w1+182);
	line(l2+3,w1+162,l2+3,w1+182);
```

```
line(l2,w1+3,l2,w1+97);
line(l2+3,w1+3,l2+3,w1+97);

/* design of pooja room */
setcolor(15);
rectangle(l1,w1+120,l1+80,w2);
rectangle(l1+3,w1+120,l1+77,w2-3);
setcolor(0);
line(l1+90,w1+100,l1+112,w1+100);/*bed room door */
line(l1+90,w1+97,l1+112,w1+97);
setcolor(15);
line(l1+90,w1+100,l1+90,w1+97);
line(l1+112,w1+100,l1+112,w1+97);
setcolor(0);
line(l1+195,w1+100,l1+212,w1+100);/*bath & toilet*/
line(l1+195,w1+97,l1+212,w1+97);
setcolor(15);
line(l1+195,w1+100,l1+195,w1+97);
line(l1+212,w1+100,l1+212,w1+97);

setcolor(0);
line(l2-30,w1+100,l2-10,w1+100); /*room2 door*/
line(l2-30,w1+97,l2-10,w1+97);

setcolor(15);
line(l2-30,w1+100,l2-30,w1+97);
line(l2-10,w1+100,l2-10,w1+97);
setcolor(0);
line(l1+80,w1+101,l1+80,w1+116); /*kitchen door*/
line(l1+77,w1+101,l1+77,w1+116);
setcolor(15);
line(l1+80,w1+101,l1+77,w1+101);
line(l1+80,w1+116,l1+77,w1+116);
setcolor(0);
line(l1+80,w1+145,l1+80,w1+165); /*puja room door*/
line(l1+77,w1+145,l1+77,w1+165);
setcolor(15);
line(l1+80,w1+145,l1+77,w1+145);
line(l1+80,w1+165,l1+77,w1+165);
setcolor(0);
```

```
        line(l1+165,w2,l1+195,w2); /*entrance to hall door*/
        line(l1+165,w2-3,l1+195,w2-3);
        setcolor(15);
        line(l1+165,w2,l1+165,w2-3);
        line(l1+195,w2,l1+195,w2-3);
        setcolor(0);
        line(l1+160,w2+40,l1+200,w2+40); /* entrance to compound door*/
        line(l1+160,w2+37,l1+200,w2+37);
        setcolor(15);
        line(l1+160,w2+40,l1+160,w2+37);
        line(l1+200,w2+40,l1+200,w2+37);

        /* labeling of different parts in respective places */
        setcolor(9);
        outtextxy(l1+10,w1+50,"KITCHEN ");
        outtextxy(l1+90,w1+50,"BED ROOM1 ");
        outtextxy(l1+195,w1+50,"BATH&T");
        outtextxy(l2-26,w1+50,"BED ROOM2 ");
        settextstyle(2,0,4);
        outtextxy(l1+140,w1+140,"HALL ROOM ");
        outtextxy(l1+10,w1+140,"PRAYER ");
        outtextxy(l1+80,w2+10,"COMPOUND ");
        outtextxy(l2+6,w1+120,"TOILET");
        outtextxy(l2+6,w1+170,"STORE");

   sleep(4);
   cleardevice();
   }

/* front view design for two room house */
void front30402r(int l1,int w1,int l2,int w2)
{
        int i;
        int qq=1;
        /* boundaries of the front view */
        line(l1-10,w1+240,l2+100,w1+240);
        line(l1-10,w1+220,l1-10,w1+240);
        line(l2+100,w2-100,l2+100,w2);
        line(l2+97,w2-100,l2+97,w2);
        line(l2+100,w2-100,l2+75,w2-125);
```

```
line(l1-10,w1+220,l2+100,w1+220);
line(l1,w1+75,l1,w1+220);
line(l2+75,w1+219,l2+100,w1+219);
line(l1,w1+75,l2+75,w1+75);
line(l2+75,w1+75,l2+75,w1+220);
line(l1,w1+220,l2+75,w1+220);
line(l1,w1+220,l1,w1+220);

/* compound design */
setcolor(8);
for(i=w2-121;i<=w2-20;++i)
line(l2+77,i,l2+98,i+20);
setcolor(9);
setlinestyle(SOLID_LINE,1,3);

/* door design */
rectangle(l1+165,w1+160,l1+195,w1+220);
setfillstyle(8,2);
floodfill(l1+168,w1+165,9);
setcolor(15);
line(l1+165,w1+189,l1+175,w1+189);
line(l1+170,w1+189,l1+170,w1+196);

/*left windows */
setcolor(9);
rectangle(l1+80,w1+160,l1+120,w1+190);
floodfill(l1+95,w1+165,9);
line(l1+90,w1+160,l1+90,w1+190);
line(l1+100,w1+160,l1+100,w1+190);
line(l1+110,w1+160,l1+110,w1+190);

/* right window */
rectangle(l1+240,w1+160,l1+280,w1+190);
floodfill(l1+245,w1+165,9);
line(l1+250,w1+160,l1+250,w1+190);
line(l1+260,w1+160,l1+260,w1+190);
line(l1+270,w1+160,l1+270,w1+190);

/*store window*/
rectangle(l1+400,w1+160,l1+425,w1+190);
```

```
	floodfill(l1+405,w1+165,9);
	line(l1+412,w1+160,l1+412,w1+190);
	bar3d(l1+390,w1+140,l1+435,w1+150,10,1);

	/* sunset windows and door*/
	bar3d(l1+70,w1+140,l1+290,w1+150,10,1);

/*roof sunset*/
	bar3d(l1,w1+75,l2+75,w1+85,10,1);
	graphdefaults();
	setfillstyle(SOLID_FILL,8);
	floodfill(l1+10,w1+223,9);
	setfillstyle(SOLID_FILL,7);
	floodfill(l1+185,w1+100,9);

	/* compound design */
	setcolor(4);
	for(i=l1;i<=l1+155;i=i+10)
	{
	rectangle(i-10,w1+220,i,w1+240);
	if(qq%2==0)
	line(i-10,w1+225,i,w1+225);
	else
	line(i-10,w1+235,i,w1+235);
	qq++;
	}

	for(i=l1+215;i<=l2+100;i=i+10)
	{
	rectangle(i-10,w1+220,i,w1+240);
	if(qq%2==0)
	line(i-10,w1+225,i,w1+225);
	else
	line(i-10,w1+235,i,w1+235);
	qq++;
	}

	/* main gate design for the compound */
	setcolor(2);
```

```
        rectangle(l1+155,w1+220,l1+205,w1+240);
        line(l1+178,w1+220,l1+178,w1+240);
        line(l1+180,w1+220,l1+180,w1+240);
        line(l1+182,w1+220,l1+182,w1+240);

        ellipse(l1+165,w1+223,180,0,5,4);
        ellipse(l1+175,w1+223,180,0,5,4);

        ellipse(l1+165,w1+229,0,180,5,4);
        ellipse(l1+175,w1+229,0,180,5,4);

        ellipse(l1+165,w1+232,180,0,5,4);
        ellipse(l1+175,w1+232,180,0,5,4);

        ellipse(l1+165,w1+238,0,180,5,4);
        ellipse(l1+175,w1+238,0,180,5,4);

        ellipse(l1+185,w1+223,180,0,5,4);
        ellipse(l1+195,w1+223,180,0,5,4);

        ellipse(l1+185,w1+229,0,180,5,4);
        ellipse(l1+195,w1+229,0,180,5,4);

        ellipse(l1+185,w1+232,180,0,5,4);
        ellipse(l1+195,w1+232,180,0,5,4);

        ellipse(l1+185,w1+238,0,180,5,4);
        ellipse(l1+195,w1+238,0,180,5,4);

        sleep(4);
        cleardevice();
}

/* side view design of two bed room house */
void side30402r(int l1,int w1,int l2,int w2)
{
    int pp=1,i;

    /* boundary design */
    setcolor(9);
```

```
rectangle(l1,w1+90,l1+150,w1+220);
line(l1,w1+220,l1+150,w1+220);
setlinestyle(SOLID_LINE,1,3);
rectangle(l1+90,w1+160,l1+130,w1+190);
setfillstyle(8,2);
floodfill(l1+100,w1+165,9);
line(l1+100,w1+160,l1+100,w1+190);
line(l1+110,w1+160,l1+110,w1+190);
line(l1+120,w1+160,l1+120,w1+190);

/* sun set */
bar3d(l1+80,w1+150,l1+140,w1+156,5,1);
bar3d(l1-10,w1+85,l1+160,w1+91,10,1);
rectangle(l1+45,w1+100,l1+60,w1+115);
setlinestyle(SOLID_LINE,1,1);
floodfill(l1+50,w1+105,9);
line(l1+45,w1+105,l1+60,w1+105);
line(l1+45,w1+110,l1+60,w1+110);
setlinestyle(SOLID_LINE,1,3);
setfillstyle(SOLID_FILL,7);

floodfill(l1+90,w1+95,9);
line(l1+150,w1+220,l1+150,w1+240);
line(l1-20,w1+240,l1+150,w1+240);
line(l1-20,w1+240,l1,w1+190);

setfillstyle(SOLID_FILL,8);
floodfill(l1+90,w1+230,9);
setcolor(4);
setlinestyle(SOLID_LINE,1,1);

/* windows */
for( i=l1-4;i<=l1+150;i=i+10)
    {
    rectangle(i,w1+220,i-10,w1+240);
    if(pp%2==0)
    line(i-10,w1+225,i,w1+225);
    else
    line(i-10,w1+235,i,w1+235);
    pp++;
```

```
        }
        sleep(4);
        cleardevice();
l2++;
w2++;
} /* end of 30x40 designs */
```

6.C. iv) The module for 2 bed room in 40X 50 site

```
/* Program build2.c */

/* This module deals with two bed room and car parking in 40x50 site. Here also top, side and front
views are drawn to get the actual effect in terms of size and look from front, top and side views by
the user. */

/* Function declarations */
void top40502r(int, int, int, int);
void front40502r(int, int, int, int);
void side40502r(int, int, int, int);

/* side view module of two bed room house */
void side40502r(int l1,int w1,int l2,int w2)
{
    l2++;
    setcolor(9);
    rectangle(l1,w1+90,l1+250,w1+220);
    line(l1-40,w1+220,l1,w1+220);
    line(l1-40,w1+220,l1,w1+150);
    setfillstyle(10,7);
    floodfill(l1-10,w1+200,9);

    line(l1,w1+220,l1+150,w1+220);
    setlinestyle(SOLID_LINE,1,3);

    rectangle(l1+50,w1+100,l1+65,w1+115);
    setlinestyle(SOLID_LINE,1,1);
    line(l1+50,w1+105,l1+65,w1+105);
    line(l1+50,w1+110,l1+65,w1+110);
    setlinestyle(SOLID_LINE,1,3);
```

```
    rectangle(l1+200,w1+100,l1+215,w1+115);
    setlinestyle(SOLID_LINE,1,1);
    line(l1+200,w1+105,l1+215,w1+105);
    line(l1+200,w1+110,l1+215,w1+110);
    setlinestyle(SOLID_LINE,1,3);
    setfillstyle(SOLID_FILL,11);
    floodfill(l1+63,w1+200,9);
    setfillstyle(11,1);
    bar3d(l1-10,w1+80,l1+255,w1+90,10,1);
    sleep(4);
    cleardevice();
    w2++;

}

/* front view of two bedroom house */
void front40502r(int l1,int w1,int l2,int w2)
{
    /* borders */
    rectangle(l1-40,w1+50,l2+40,w2-70);
    line(l1-40,w2-138,l2+40,w2-138);
    line(l2-60,w1+50,l2-60,w2-138);
    setcolor(9);
    setlinestyle(SOLID_LINE,1,3);
    /* door */
    rectangle(l1+165,w1+160,l1+195,w1+220);
    setfillstyle(11,1);
    floodfill(l1+168,w1+165,9);
    setcolor(15);
    line(l1+165,w1+189,l1+175,w1+189);
    line(l1+170,w1+189,l1+170,w1+196);

    /* left windows */
        setcolor(9);
        rectangle(l1+90,w1+160,l1+120,w1+190);
        floodfill(l1+95,w1+165,9);
        line(l1+100,w1+160,l1+100,w1+190);
        line(l1+110,w1+160,l1+110,w1+190);

        /* right window */
```

```
        rectangle(l1+240,w1+160,l1+270,w1+190);
        floodfill(l1+245,w1+165,9);
        line(l1+250,w1+160,l1+250,w1+190);
        line(l1+260,w1+160,l1+260,w1+190);

        /* sunset windows and door */
        bar3d(l1+80,w1+140,l1+280,w1+150,10,1);
/* roof sunset */
        bar3d(l1-40,w1+40,l2+50,w1+50,10,1);
        graphdefaults();
        setfillstyle(SOLID_FILL,8);
        setfillstyle(SOLID_FILL,11);
        floodfill(l1+185,w1+100,9);

        /* exhaust */
        setcolor(7);
        rectangle(l1-40,w2-90,l1+155,w2-70);
        rectangle(l1+205,w2-90,l2-50,w2-70);
        setfillstyle(8,8);
        floodfill(l1-30,w2-80,7);
        floodfill(l1+210,w2-80,7);

        line(l1+155,w2-90,l1+165,w2-140);
        line(l1+205,w2-90,l1+195,w2-140);
        line(l1+155,w2-71,l1+205,w2-71);
        line(l1+165,w2-139,l1+195,w2-139);
        setfillstyle(10,7);
        floodfill(l1+180,w2-100,7);

        /* Gate design */
        setcolor(3);
        rectangle(l1+155,w2-90,l1+205,w2-70);
        line(l1+178,w2-90,l1+178,w2-70);
        line(l1+180,w2-90,l1+180,w2-70);
        line(l1+182,w2-90,l1+182,w2-70);

        ellipse(l1+166,w2-85,0,360,11,5);
        ellipse(l1+166,w2-75,0,360,11,5);

        ellipse(l1+194,w2-85,0,360,11,5);
```

```
ellipse(l1+194,w2-75,0,360,11,5);
setcolor(8);
setfillstyle(SOLID_FILL,8);
floodfill(l2+30,w2-200,9);
line(l2-60,w2-138,l2+39,w2-138);

setcolor(8);
rectangle(l2-120,w1+70,l2-100,w1+90);
floodfill(l2-110,w1+80,8);

setfillstyle(11,2);
setcolor(9);

line(l1+154,w2-91,l1+164,w2-137);
line(l1-39,w2-91,l1+154,w2-91);
line(l1-39,w2-137,l1+164,w2-137);
line(l1-39,w2-137,l1-39,w2-91);

floodfill(l1-10,w2-120,9);
line(l1+205,w2-90,l1+195,w2-140);
line(l1+205,w2-90,l2-50,w2-90);
line(l1+195,w2-138,l2-60,w2-138);
line(l2-60,w2-138,l2-50,w2-90);
floodfill(l1+210,w2-100,9);
line(l2-50,w2-90,l2-50,w2-70);
line(l2-50,w2-70,l2+39,w2-70);
line(l2-60,w2-138,l2+39,w2-138);
setfillstyle(10,7);
floodfill(l2-40,w2-100,9);
setcolor(3);

rectangle(l2-50,w2-90,l2+39,w2-70);
line(l2-9,w2-90,l2-9,w2-70);
line(l2-7,w2-90,l2-7,w2-70);
line(l2-5,w2-90,l2-5,w2-70);

ellipse(l2-40,w2-85,0,360,11,5);
ellipse(l2-40,w2-75,0,360,11,5);
```

```
        ellipse(l2+5,w2-85,0,360,11,5);
        ellipse(l2+5,w2-75,0,360,11,5);

        ellipse(l2-30,w2-85,0,360,11,5);
        ellipse(l2-30,w2-75,0,360,11,5);

        ellipse(l2+15,w2-85,0,360,11,5);
        ellipse(l2+15,w2-75,0,360,11,5);

        ellipse(l2-20,w2-85,0,360,11,5);
        ellipse(l2-20,w2-75,0,360,11,5);

        ellipse(l2+25,w2-85,0,360,11,5);
        ellipse(l2+25,w2-75,0,360,11,5);

        sleep(4);
        cleardevice();
}

/* top view of two bed room house */
void top40502r(int l1,int w1, int l2,int w2)
{
    cleardevice();
    rectangle(l1,w1,l2,w2);
    rectangle(l1+3,w1+3,l2-3,w2-3);
    rectangle(l1,w1,l2-100,w2-70);
    rectangle(l1+3,w1+3,l2+3-100,w2-70-3);
    rectangle(l1+3,w1+3,l2+3-100,w2-70);

    rectangle(l1,w1,l1+100,w1+150);/*kitchen */
    rectangle(l1+3,w1+3,l1+97,w1+147);

    rectangle(l1+100,w1,l1+200,w1+150);/*room*/
    rectangle(l1+100,w1+3,l1+197,w1+147);

    rectangle(l1+200,w1,l1+250,w1+150); /* bath */
    rectangle(l1+200,w1,l1+247,w1+147);
    line(l1+200,w1+73,l1+247,w1+73);
    line(l1+200,w1+76,l1+247,w1+76);
```

```
rectangle(l2-200,w1,l2-100,w1+150); /* room2 */
rectangle(l2-200,w1+3,l2-97,w1+147);

rectangle(l2-100,w1,l2,w1+110);/* store */
rectangle(l2-100,w1+3,l2-3,w1+107);

rectangle(l1,w1+190,l1+100,w2-70);/* puja */
rectangle(l1+3,w1+187,l1+97,w2-70);

rectangle(l1+100,w1+150,l2-160,w2-70);/* hall */
rectangle(l1+100,w1+150,l2-157,w2-70);

line(l2-160,w2-130,l2-100,w2-130);
line(l2-160,w2-133,l2-100,w2-133);


setcolor(0);
line(l1+102,w1+147,l1+132,w1+147);
line(l1+102,w1+150,l1+132,w1+150);
setcolor(15);
line(l1+102,w1+147,l1+102,w1+150);
line(l1+132,w1+147,l1+132,w1+150);


rectangle(l1+140,w1+125,l1+197,w1+150);/*room 1 store*/
rectangle(l1+137,w1+122,l1+197,w1+150);

rectangle(l2-160,w1+122,l2-100,w1+150);/*room 2 store */
rectangle(l2-157,w1+125,l2-100,w1+150);

rectangle(l1+3,w1+161,l1+16,w1+175); /* basin*/

/* cuttings for doors of different parts in the house */
setcolor(0);
line(l1+252,w1+147,l1+282,w1+147);
line(l1+252,w1+150,l1+282,w1+150);
setcolor(15);
line(l1+252,w1+147,l1+252,w1+150);
line(l1+282,w1+147,l1+282,w1+150);
```

```
setcolor(0);
line(l2-65,w1+110,l2-35,w1+110);
line(l2-65,w1+107,l2-35,w1+107);
setcolor(15);
line(l2-65,w1+107,l2-65,w1+110);
line(l2-35,w1+107,l2-35,w1+110);

setcolor(0);
line(l1+200,w1+5,l1+200,w1+28);
line(l1+197,w1+5,l1+197,w1+28);
setcolor(15);
line(l1+197,w1+5,l1+200,w1+5);
line(l1+197,w1+28,l1+200,w1+28);


setcolor(0);
line(l1+250,w1+122,l1+250,w1+145);
line(l2-200,w1+122,l2-200,w1+145);
line(l1+247,w1+122,l1+247,w1+145);
setcolor(15);
line(l1+247,w1+122,l1+250,w1+122);
line(l1+247,w1+145,l1+250,w1+145);


setcolor(0);
line(l1+100,w1+150,l1+100,w2-170);

setcolor(0);
line(l1+35,w1+147,l1+65,w1+147);
line(l1+35,w1+150,l1+65,w1+150);
setcolor(15);
line(l1+35,w1+147,l1+35,w1+150);
line(l1+65,w1+147,l1+65,w1+150);

    setcolor(0);
line(l1+35,w1+187,l1+65,w1+187);
line(l1+35,w1+190,l1+65,w1+190);
setcolor(15);
line(l1+35,w1+187,l1+35,w1+190);
line(l1+65,w1+187,l1+65,w1+190);
```

```
        setcolor(0); //gate to hall
line(l1+175,w2-70,l1+215,w2-70);
line(l1+175,w2-73,l1+215,w2-73);
setcolor(15);
line(l1+175,w2-73,l1+175,w2-70);
line(l1+215,w2-73,l1+215,w2-70);

        setcolor(0);
line(l2-160,w2-206,l2-160,w2-176);
line(l2-157,w2-206,l2-157,w2-176);
setcolor(15);
line(l2-157,w2-206,l2-160,w2-206);
line(l2-157,w2-176,l2-160,w2-176);

setcolor(0);
line(l2-100,w2-100,l2-100,w2-75);
line(l2-97,w2-100,l2-97,w2-75);
setcolor(15);
line(l2-100,w2 100,l2-97,w2-100);
line(l2-100,w2-75,l2-97,w2-75);


        setcolor(0); /*compound entrance*/
        line(l1+165,w2,l1+225,w2);
line(l1+165,w2-3,l1+225,w2-3);
setcolor(15);
line(l1+165,w2,l1+165,w2-3);
line(l1+225,w2,l1+225,w2-3);


        setcolor(0); /*car entrance */
line(l2-90,w2,l2-10,w2);
line(l2-90,w2-3,l2-10,w2-3);
setcolor(15);
line(l2-90,w2,l2-90,w2-3);
line(l2-10,w2,l2-10,w2-3);

/* labeling of different parts in the house */
setcolor(9);
```

```
    outtextxy(l1+10,w1+60,"KITCHEN");
    outtextxy(l1+140,w2-15,"ENTRANCE TO COMPOUND");
    outtextxy(l1+147,w1+137,"WARE");
    outtextxy(l1+297,w1+137,"WARE");
    outtextxy(l1+18,w1+165,"<- BASIN");
    outtextxy(l1+110,w1+60,"BED ROOM 1");
    outtextxy(l1+260,w1+60,"BED ROOM 2");
    outtextxy(l2-90,w1+60,"STORE ROOM");
    outtextxy(l2-90,w1+160,"CAR PARKING");
    outtextxy(l2-120,w2-20,"GATE FOR CAR");
    outtextxy(l1+160,w2-45,"FRONT COMPOUND");
    outtextxy(l1+10,w2-140,"PRAYER ROOM");
    outtextxy(l1+205,w1+40," T&B");
    outtextxy(l1+205,w1+90," T&B");
    outtextxy(l2-150,w1+160,"BATH");
    outtextxy(l2-150,w2-85,"TOILET");
    outtextxy(l1+140,w2-140,"HALL ROOM");
    outtextxy(l1+140,w2-85,"ENTRANCE TO HALL");

    sleep(4);
    cleardevice();
  } /* end of 2 bed room in 40 X 50 */
```

6.C. v) The module for 3 Bed room in 40 X 50 without car parking

/* Program name build3.c */

/* This module deals with three bed room house without car parking. As usual here also three different views of the house are implemented. */

```
void side40503r(int l1,int w1,int l2,int w2)
{
    l2++;
    cleardevice();
    setcolor(9);
    rectangle(l1,w1+90,l1+250,w1+220);

    line(l1-40,w1+220,l1,w1+150);
    line(l1-40,w1+220,l1-40,w1+240);
    line(l1-40,w1+240,l1+265,w1+240);
    line(l1+265,w1+240,l1+250,w1+160);
```

```
    setfillstyle(10,7);
    floodfill(l1-10,w1+200,9);

    line(l1,w1+220,l1+150,w1+220);
    setlinestyle(SOLID_LINE,1,3);

    /*ventilation for toilet*/
    rectangle(l1+85,w1+100,l1+100,w1+115);
    setlinestyle(SOLID_LINE,1,1);
    line(l1+85,w1+105,l1+100,w1+105);
    line(l1+85,w1+110,l1+100,w1+110);
    setlinestyle(SOLID_LINE,1,3);

    /* window */
    rectangle(l1+125,w1+150,l1+165,w1+180);
    line(l1+135,w1+150,l1+135,w1+180);
    line(l1+145,w1+150,l1+145,w1+180);
    line(l1+155,w1+150,l1+155,w1+180);

    /* ventilation for general bath */
    rectangle(l1+200,w1+100,l1+215,w1+115);
    setlinestyle(SOLID_LINE,1,1);

    line(l1+200,w1+105,l1+215,w1+105);
    line(l1+200,w1+110,l1+215,w1+110);

    setlinestyle(SOLID_LINE,1,3);
    setfillstyle(SOLID_FILL,11);
    floodfill(l1+63,w1+200,9);
    setfillstyle(11,2);
    /* sunset for window */
    bar3d(l1-10,w1+80,l1+255,w1+90,10,1);
    sleep(4);
    w2++;
}

/* front view */
void front40503r(int l1,int w1,int l2,int w2)
{
```

```
cleardevice();
rectangle(l1-40,w1+50,l2+40,w2-70);
 line(l1-40,w2-138,l2+40,w2-138);
 line(l2,w1+50,l2,w2-138);
 setcolor(9);
 setlinestyle(SOLID_LINE,1,3);
 /* door*/
 rectangle(l1+165,w1+160,l1+195,w1+220);
 setfillstyle(11,1);
 floodfill(l1+168,w1+165,9);
 setcolor(15);
 line(l1+165,w1+189,l1+175,w1+189);
 line(l1+170,w1+189,l1+170,w1+196);

 /*left windows*/
        setcolor(9);
        rectangle(l1+90,w1+160,l1+120,w1+190);
        floodfill(l1+95,w1+165,9);
        line(l1+100,w1+160,l1+100,w1+190);
        line(l1+110,w1+160,l1+110,w1+190);

        /* right window*/
        rectangle(l1+240,w1+160,l1+270,w1+190);
        floodfill(l1+245,w1+165,9);
        line(l1+250,w1+160,l1+250,w1+190);
        line(l1+260,w1+160,l1+260,w1+190);

        /* room3 window*/
        rectangle(l1+320,w1+160,l1+350,w1+190);
        floodfill(l1+325,w1+165,9);
        line(l1+330,w1+160,l1+330,w1+190);
        line(l1+340,w1+160,l1+340,w1+190);

        /* sunset windows and door*/
        bar3d(l1+80,w1+140,l1+360,w1+150,10,1);
 /*roof sunset*/
        bar3d(l1-40,w1+40,l2+10,w1+50,10,1);
        graphdefaults();
        setfillstyle(SOLID_FILL,8);
```

```
setfillstyle(SOLID_FILL,11);
floodfill(l1+185,w1+100,9);

setcolor(7);
rectangle(l1-40,w2-90,l1+155,w2-70);
rectangle(l1+205,w2-90,l2+40,w2-70);
setfillstyle(8,8);
floodfill(l1-30,w2-80,7);
floodfill(l1+210,w2-80,7);

line(l1+155,w2-90,l1+165,w2-140);
line(l1+205,w2-90,l1+195,w2-140);
line(l1+155,w2-71,l1+205,w2-71);
line(l1+165,w2-139,l1+195,w2-139);
setfillstyle(10,7);
floodfill(l1+180,w2-100,7);
/* gates design*/
setcolor(3);
rectangle(l1+155,w2-90,l1+205,w2-70);
line(l1+178,w2-90,l1+178,w2-70);
line(l1+180,w2-90,l1+180,w2-70);
line(l1+182,w2-90,l1+182,w2-70);

ellipse(l1+166,w2-85,0,360,11,5);
ellipse(l1+166,w2-75,0,360,11,5);

ellipse(l1+194,w2-85,0,360,11,5);
ellipse(l1+194,w2-75,0,360,11,5);

setcolor(8);
setfillstyle(SOLID_FILL,8);
floodfill(l2+30,w2-200,9);
line(l2-60,w2-138,l2+39,w2-138);

setcolor(8);
rectangle(l2-120,w1+70,l2-100,w1+90);
floodfill(l2-110,w1+80,8);

setfillstyle(11,2);
setcolor(9);
```

```
        line(l1+154,w2-91,l1+164,w2-137);
        line(l1-39,w2-91,l1+154,w2-91);
        line(l1-39,w2-137,l1+164,w2-137);
        line(l1-39,w2-137,l1-39,w2-91);

        floodfill(l1-10,w2-120,9);
        line(l1+205,w2-90,l1+195,w2-140);
        line(l1+205,w2-90,l2-50,w2-90);
        line(l1+195,w2-138,l2,w2-138);
        line(l2-50,w2-90,l2+40,w2-90);
        floodfill(l1+210,w2-100,9);

        sleep(4);
        cleardevice();
}

/* top view */
void top40503r(int l1,int w1, int l2,int w2)
{
    cleardevice();
    line(l1+3,w1-10,l2-3,w1-10);
    line(l1,w1-12,l2,w1-12);
    line(l2-3,w1-10,l2-3,w1+3);
    line(l2,w1-12,l2,w1);
    line(l1+3,w1-10,l1+3,w1);
    line(l1,w1-12,l1,w1);

    rectangle(l1,w1,l2,w2);
    rectangle(l1+3,w1+3,l2-3,w2-3);
    rectangle(l1,w1,l2-100,w2-70);
    rectangle(l1+3,w1+3,l2+3-100,w2-70-3);
    rectangle(l1+3,w1+3,l2+3-100,w2-70);
    setcolor(0);
    line(l2-39,w1,l2-4,w1);
    line(l2-39,w1+3,l2-4,w1+3);

    setcolor(15);

    rectangle(l1,w1,l1+100,w1+150);/*kitchen*/
    rectangle(l1+3,w1+3,l1+97,w1+147);
```

```
rectangle(l1+100,w1,l1+200,w1+150);/*room */
rectangle(l1+100,w1+3,l1+197,w1+147);

rectangle(l1+200,w1,l1+250,w1+150); /* bath*/
rectangle(l1+200,w1,l1+247,w1+147);

line(l1+200,w1+73,l1+247,w1+73);
line(l1+200,w1+76,l1+247,w1+76);

rectangle(l2-200,w1,l2-100,w1+150); /* room2*/
rectangle(l2-200,w1+3,l2-97,w1+147);

rectangle(l2-100,w1,l2-40,w1+90);/* bath general*/
rectangle(l2-100,w1+3,l2-43,w1+87);

line(l2-40,w1+90,l2-40,w2-70); /* side compound */
line(l2-43,w1+90,l2-43,w2-70);

line(l2-80,w2-70,l2-40,w2-70);
line(l2-80,w2-73,l2-43,w2-73);

rectangle(l1,w1+190,l1+100,w2-70);/* pooja room*/
rectangle(l1+3,w1+187,l1+97,w2-70);

rectangle(l1+100,w1+150,l2-160,w2-70);/* hall */
rectangle(l1+100,w1+150,l2-157,w2-70);

/* entrance cuttings */
setcolor(0);
line(l2-97,w1+150,l2-97,w2-70);
line(l2-100,w1+150,l2-100,w2-70);

line(l2-160,w1+151,l2-160,w1+153);
line(l2-157,w1+151,l2-157,w1+153);

/* entrance edges */
setcolor(15);
rectangle(l2-160,w1+183,l2-80,w2-70);
rectangle(l2-160,w1+186,l2-83,w2-73);
```

```
/*room 3 door*/
setcolor(0);
line(l2-160,w1+188,l2-160,w1+215);
line(l2-157,w1+188,l2-157,w1+215);
setcolor(15);
line(l2-160,w1+188,l2-157,w1+188);
line(l2-160,w1+215,l2-157,w1+215);

/* toilet general*/
line(l2-80,w1+183,l2-40,w1+183);
line(l2-80,w1+186,l2-40,w1+186);
        setcolor(0);
line(l2-70,w1+183,l2-50,w1+183);
line(l2-70,w1+186,l2-50,w1+186);

setcolor(15);
line(l2-70,w1+183,l2-70,w1+186);
line(l2-50,w1+183,l2-50,w1+186);

/*partition*/
line(l2-80,w1+236,l2-40,w1+236);
line(l2-80,w1+239,l2-40,w1+239);

setcolor(0);
line(l1+102,w1+147,l1+132,w1+147);
line(l1+102,w1+150,l1+132,w1+150);

setcolor(15);
line(l1+102,w1+147,l1+102,w1+150);
line(l1+132,w1+147,l1+132,w1+150);

rectangle(l1+140,w1+125,l1+197,w1+150);/*room 1 store*/
rectangle(l1+137,w1+122,l1+197,w1+150);

rectangle(l2-160,w1+122,l2-100,w1+150);/*room 2 store */
rectangle(l2-157,w1+125,l2-100,w1+150);

rectangle(l1+3,w1+161,l1+16,w1+175); /* basin*/
```

```
/* entrance cuttings for different parts of the house */
setcolor(0);
line(l1+252,w1+147,l1+282,w1+147);
line(l1+252,w1+150,l1+282,w1+150);
setcolor(15);
line(l1+252,w1+147,l1+252,w1+150);
line(l1+282,w1+147,l1+282,w1+150);

setcolor(0);
line(l2-65,w1+110,l2-35,w1+110);
line(l2-65,w1+107,l2-35,w1+107);

line(l1+200,w1+5,l1+200,w1+28);
line(l1+197,w1+5,l1+197,w1+28);
setcolor(15);
line(l1+197,w1+5,l1+200,w1+5);
line(l1+197,w1+28,l1+200,w1+28);

setcolor(0);
line(l1+250,w1+122,l1+250,w1+145);
line(l2-200,w1+122,l2-200,w1+145);
line(l1+247,w1+122,l1+247,w1+145);
setcolor(15);
line(l1+247,w1+122,l1+250,w1+122);
line(l1+247,w1+145,l1+250,w1+145);


setcolor(0);
line(l1+100,w1+150,l1+100,w2-170);

setcolor(0);
line(l1+35,w1+147,l1+65,w1+147);
line(l1+35,w1+150,l1+65,w1+150);
setcolor(15);
line(l1+35,w1+147,l1+35,w1+150);
line(l1+65,w1+147,l1+65,w1+150);

    setcolor(0);
line(l1+35,w1+187,l1+65,w1+187);
line(l1+35,w1+190,l1+65,w1+190);
```

```
setcolor(15);
line(l1+35,w1+187,l1+35,w1+190);
line(l1+65,w1+187,l1+65,w1+190);

    setcolor(0); //gate to hall
line(l1+175,w2-70,l1+215,w2-70);
line(l1+175,w2-73,l1+215,w2-73);
setcolor(15);
line(l1+175,w2-73,l1+175,w2-70);
line(l1+215,w2-73,l1+215,w2-70);

    setcolor(0);
line(l2-160,w2-206,l2-160,w2-176);
line(l2-157,w2-206,l2-157,w2-176);

line(l2-100,w2-100,l2-100,w2-75);
line(l2-97,w2-100,l2-97,w2-75);
setcolor(15);

    setcolor(0);
line(l1+165,w2,l1+225,w2);
line(l1+165,w2-3,l1+225,w2-3);
setcolor(15);
line(l1+165,w2,l1+165,w2-3);
line(l1+225,w2,l1+225,w2-3);

/* labeling in different parts of the house */
setcolor(9);
outtextxy(l1+10,w1+60,"KITCHEN");
outtextxy(l1+140,w2-15,"ENTRANCE TO COMPOUND");
outtextxy(l1+147,w1+137,"WARE");
outtextxy(l1+297,w1+137,"WARE");
outtextxy(l1+18,w1+165,"<- BASIN");
outtextxy(l1+110,w1+60,"BED ROOM 1");
outtextxy(l1+260,w1+60,"BED ROOM 2");
outtextxy(l2-90,w1+60,"GBATH");
outtextxy(l2-75,w1+195,"GTOI");
outtextxy(l2-75,w2-100,"WARE");
outtextxy(l1+160,w2-45,"FRONT COMPOUND");
outtextxy(l1+10,w2-140,"PRAYER ROOM");
```

```
    outtextxy(l1+205,w1+40," T&B");
    outtextxy(l1+205,w1+90," T&B");
    outtextxy(l2-150,w2-85,"ROOM3");
    outtextxy(l1+140,w2-140,"HALL ROOM");
    outtextxy(l1+140,w2-85,"ENTRANCE TO HALL");

    sleep(4);
    cleardevice();
} /* end of 3 bed without car parking in 40 X 50 */
```

6.C. vi) The module for 3 bed room in 40 X 50 with car parking

```
/* Program name: Build4.c */
/* This module deals with three bed room with car parking in 40x50 site */

/* function declarations */
void top40503rc(int, int, int, int);
void front40503rc(int, int, int, int);
void side40503rc(int, int, int, int);

/* side view of the three bed room with car parking */
void side40503rc(int l1,int w1,int l2,int w2)
{
    l2++;
    setcolor(9);
    line(l1+250,w1+220,l1+260,w1+220);
    line(l1+260,w1+220,l1+250,w1+160);


    rectangle(l1,w1+90,l1+250,w1+220);
    line(l1-40,w1+220,l1,w1+220);
    line(l1-40,w1+220,l1,w1+150);
    setfillstyle(11,8);
    floodfill(l1-10,w1+200,9);
    line(l1,w1+220,l1+150,w1+220);
    setlinestyle(SOLID_LINE,1,3);
    rectangle(l1+50,w1+100,l1+65,w1+115);
    setlinestyle(SOLID_LINE,1,1);
    line(l1+50,w1+105,l1+65,w1+105);
```

```
    line(l1+50,w1+110,l1+65,w1+110);
    setlinestyle(SOLID_LINE,1,3);

    rectangle(l1+200,w1+100,l1+215,w1+115);
    setlinestyle(SOLID_LINE,1,1);
    line(l1+200,w1+105,l1+215,w1+105);
    line(l1+200,w1+110,l1+215,w1+110);
    setlinestyle(SOLID_LINE,1,3);
    setfillstyle(SOLID_FILL,7);
    floodfill(l1+63,w1+200,9);
    setfillstyle(11,1);
    bar3d(l1-10,w1+80,l1+255,w1+90,10,1);
    setfillstyle(11,8);
    floodfill(l1+252,w1+218,9);
    sleep(4);
    w2++;
    cleardevice();
}

/* front view of three bed room house with car parking */
void front40503rc(int l1,int w1,int l2,int w2)
{
    cleardevice();
    rectangle(l1-40,w1+50,l2+40,w2-70);
    line(l1-40,w2-138,l2+40,w2-138);
    line(l2-60,w1+50,l2-60,w2-138);
    setcolor(9);
    setlinestyle(SOLID_LINE,1,3);

    /* door*/
    rectangle(l1+165,w1+160,l1+195,w1+220);
    setfillstyle(8,8);
    floodfill(l1+168,w1+165,9);
    setcolor(15);
    line(l1+165,w1+189,l1+175,w1+189);
    line(l1+170,w1+189,l1+170,w1+196);

/*room3 windows*/
        setcolor(9);
        rectangle(l1-10,w1+160,l1+30,w1+190);
```

```
floodfill(l1-5,w1+165,9);
line(l1,w1+160,l1,w1+190);
line(l1+10,w1+160,l1+10,w1+190);
line(l1+20,w1+160,l1+20,w1+190);

/*left windows*/
setcolor(9);
rectangle(l1+80,w1+160,l1+120,w1+190);
floodfill(l1+95,w1+165,9);
line(l1+90,w1+160,l1+90,w1+190);
line(l1+100,w1+160,l1+100,w1+190);
line(l1+110,w1+160,l1+110,w1+190);

/* right window*/
rectangle(l1+240,w1+160,l1+280,w1+190);
floodfill(l1+245,w1+165,9);
line(l1+250,w1+160,l1+250,w1+190);
line(l1+260,w1+160,l1+260,w1+190);
line(l1+270,w1+160,l1+270,w1+190);

/* sunset windows and door*/
bar3d(l1-20,w1+140,l1+285,w1+150,10,1);
bar3d(l1-40,w1+40,l2+50,w1+50,10,1);
graphdefaults();
setfillstyle(SOLID_FILL,7);
floodfill(l1+185,w1+100,9);

/* gate and door design */
setcolor(7);
rectangle(l1-40,w2-90,l1+155,w2-70);
rectangle(l1+205,w2-90,l2-50,w2-70);
setfillstyle(11,1);
floodfill(l1-30,w2-80,7);
floodfill(l1+210,w2-80,7);

line(l1+155,w2-90,l1+165,w2-140);
line(l1+205,w2-90,l1+195,w2-140);
line(l1+155,w2-71,l1+205,w2-71);
line(l1+165,w2-139,l1+195,w2-139);
```

```
setfillstyle(10,8);
floodfill(l1+180,w2-100,7);
setcolor(6);

rectangle(l1+155,w2-90,l1+205,w2-70);
line(l1+178,w2-90,l1+178,w2-70);
line(l1+180,w2-90,l1+180,w2-70);
line(l1+182,w2-90,l1+182,w2-70);
setlinestyle(SOLID_LINE,1,1);
ellipse(l1+166,w2-85,0,360,11,5);
ellipse(l1+166,w2-75,0,360,11,5);

ellipse(l1+194,w2-85,0,360,11,5);
ellipse(l1+194,w2-75,0,360,11,5);
setcolor(8);
setfillstyle(SOLID_FILL,8);
floodfill(l2+30,w2-200,9);
line(l2-60,w2-138,l2+39,w2-138);

setcolor(8);
rectangle(l2-120,w1+70,l2-100,w1+90);
floodfill(l2-110,w1+80,8);

setfillstyle(11,2);
setcolor(9);
setlinestyle(SOLID_LINE,1,1);
line(l1+154,w2-91,l1+164,w2-137);
line(l1-39,w2-91,l1+154,w2-91);
line(l1-39,w2-137,l1+164,w2-137);
line(l1-39,w2-137,l1-39,w2-91);


floodfill(l1-10,w2-120,9);
line(l1+205,w2-90,l1+195,w2-140);
line(l1+205,w2-90,l2-50,w2-90);
line(l1+195,w2-138,l2-60,w2-138);
line(l2-60,w2-138,l2-50,w2-90);
floodfill(l1+210,w2-100,9);
line(l2-50,w2-90,l2-50,w2-70);
line(l2-50,w2-70,l2+39,w2-70);
```

```
        line(l2-60,w2-138,l2+39,w2-138);
        setfillstyle(10,8);
        floodfill(l2-40,w2-100,9);
        setcolor(6);

        rectangle(l2-50,w2-90,l2+39,w2-70);
        line(l2-9,w2-90,l2-9,w2-70);
        line(l2-7,w2-90,l2-7,w2-70);
        line(l2-5,w2-90,l2-5,w2-70);
        ellipse(l2-40,w2-85,0,360,11,5);
        ellipse(l2-40,w2-75,0,360,11,5);

        ellipse(l2+5,w2-85,0,360,11,5);
        ellipse(l2+5,w2-75,0,360,11,5);


        ellipse(l2-30,w2-85,0,360,11,5);
        ellipse(l2-30,w2-75,0,360,11,5);

        ellipse(l2+15,w2-85,0,360,11,5);
        ellipse(l2+15,w2-75,0,360,11,5);


        ellipse(l2-20,w2-85,0,360,11,5);
        ellipse(l2-20,w2-75,0,360,11,5);

        ellipse(l2+25,w2-85,0,360,11,5);
        ellipse(l2+25,w2-75,0,360,11,5);

        sleep(4);
        cleardevice();
}

/* top view */
void top40503rc(int l1,int w1, int l2,int w2)
{
    cleardevice();
    rectangle(l1,w1,l2,w2);
    rectangle(l1+3,w1+3,l2-3,w2-3);
    rectangle(l1,w1,l2-100,w2-70);
```

```
rectangle(l1+3,w1+3,l2+3-100,w2-70-3);
rectangle(l1+3,w1+3,l2+3-100,w2-70);

rectangle(l1,w1,l1+100,w1+150);/*kitchen*/
rectangle(l1+3,w1+3,l1+97,w1+147);

rectangle(l1+100,w1,l1+200,w1+150);/*room*/
rectangle(l1+100,w1+3,l1+197,w1+147);

rectangle(l1+200,w1,l1+250,w1+150); /* bath*/
rectangle(l1+200,w1,l1+247,w1+147);
line(l1+200,w1+73,l1+247,w1+73);
line(l1+200,w1+76,l1+247,w1+76);

rectangle(l2-200,w1,l2-100,w1+150); /* room2*/
rectangle(l2-200,w1+3,l2-97,w1+147);

rectangle(l2-100,w1,l2,w1+110);/* store*/
rectangle(l2-100,w1+3,l2-3,w1+107);

rectangle(l1,w1+190,l1+100,w2-70);/* puja*/
rectangle(l1+3,w1+187,l1+97,w2-70);

rectangle(l1+100,w1+150,l2-160,w2-70);/* hall*/
rectangle(l1+100,w1+150,l2-157,w2-70);

line(l2-160,w2-130,l2-100,w2-130);
line(l2-160,w2-133,l2-100,w2-133);

setcolor(0);
line(l1+102,w1+147,l1+132,w1+147);
line(l1+102,w1+150,l1+132,w1+150);
setcolor(15);
line(l1+102,w1+147,l1+102,w1+150);
line(l1+132,w1+147,l1+132,w1+150);


rectangle(l1+140,w1+125,l1+197,w1+150);/*room 1 store*/
rectangle(l1+137,w1+122,l1+197,w1+150);
```

```
rectangle(l2-160,w1+122,l2-100,w1+150);/*room 2 store*/
rectangle(l2-157,w1+125,l2-100,w1+150);

rectangle(l1+3,w1+161,l1+16,w1+175); /* basin*/

/* cuttings for entrances for different parts of the house */
setcolor(0);
line(l1+252,w1+147,l1+282,w1+147);
line(l1+252,w1+150,l1+282,w1+150);
setcolor(15);
line(l1+252,w1+147,l1+252,w1+150);
line(l1+282,w1+147,l1+282,w1+150);

setcolor(0);
line(l2-65,w1+110,l2-35,w1+110);
line(l2-65,w1+107,l2-35,w1+107);
setcolor(15);
line(l2-65,w1+107,l2-65,w1+110);
line(l2-35,w1+107,l2-35,w1+110);

setcolor(0);
line(l1+200,w1+5,l1+200,w1+28);
line(l1+197,w1+5,l1+197,w1+28);
setcolor(15);
line(l1+197,w1+5,l1+200,w1+5);
line(l1+197,w1+28,l1+200,w1+28);

setcolor(0);
line(l1+210,w1+150,l1+240,w1+150);
line(l1+210,w1+147,l1+240,w1+147);
setcolor(15);
line(l1+210,w1+147,l1+210,w1+150);
line(l1+240,w1+147,l1+240,w1+150);


setcolor(0);
line(l1+100,w1+150,l1+100,w2-170);

setcolor(0);
line(l1+35,w1+147,l1+65,w1+147);
```

```
line(l1+35,w1+150,l1+65,w1+150);
setcolor(15);
line(l1+35,w1+147,l1+35,w1+150);
line(l1+65,w1+147,l1+65,w1+150);

    setcolor(0);
line(l1+35,w1+187,l1+65,w1+187);
line(l1+35,w1+190,l1+65,w1+190);
setcolor(15);
line(l1+35,w1+187,l1+35,w1+190);
line(l1+65,w1+187,l1+65,w1+190);

    setcolor(0); //gate to hall
line(l1+175,w2-70,l1+215,w2-70);
line(l1+175,w2-73,l1+215,w2-73);
setcolor(15);
line(l1+175,w2-73,l1+175,w2-70);
line(l1+215,w2-73,l1+215,w2-70);

    setcolor(0);
line(l2-160,w2-185,l2-160,w2-155);
line(l2-157,w2-185,l2-157,w2-155);
setcolor(15);
line(l2-157,w2-185,l2-160,w2-185);
line(l2-157,w2-155,l2-160,w2-155);

setcolor(0);
line(l2-100,w2-100,l2-100,w2-75);
line(l2-97,w2-100,l2-97,w2-75);
setcolor(15);
line(l2-100,w2-100,l2-97,w2-100);
line(l2-100,w2-75,l2-97,w2-75);

    setcolor(0);
    line(l1+165,w2,l1+225,w2);
line(l1+165,w2-3,l1+225,w2-3);
setcolor(15);
line(l1+165,w2,l1+165,w2-3);
line(l1+225,w2,l1+225,w2-3);
```

```
        setcolor(0); /*car entrance*/
    line(l2-90,w2,l2-10,w2);
    line(l2-90,w2-3,l2-10,w2-3);
    setcolor(15);
    line(l2-90,w2,l2-90,w2-3);
    line(l2-10,w2,l2-10,w2-3);

    /* labeling */
    setcolor(9);
    outtextxy(l1+10,w1+60,"KITCHEN");
    outtextxy(l1+140,w2-15,"ENTRANCE TO COMPOUND");
    outtextxy(l1+147,w1+137,"WARE");
    outtextxy(l1+297,w1+137,"WARE");
    outtextxy(l1+18,w1+165,"<- BASIN");
    outtextxy(l1+110,w1+60,"BED ROOM 1");
    outtextxy(l1+260,w1+60,"BED ROOM 2");
    outtextxy(l2-90,w1+60,"STORE ROOM");
    outtextxy(l2-90,w1+160,"CAR PARKING");
    outtextxy(l2-120,w2-20,"GATE FOR CAR");
    outtextxy(l1+160,w2-45,"FRONT COMPOUND");
    outtextxy(l1+10,w2-140,"BED ROOM 3");
    outtextxy(l1+205,w1+40," T&B");
    outtextxy(l1+205,w1+90,"GB");
    outtextxy(l2-150,w1+160,"PUJA");
    outtextxy(l2-150,w2-85,"TOILET");
    outtextxy(l1+140,w2-140,"HALL ROOM");
    outtextxy(l1+140,w2-85,"ENTRANCE TO HALL");

    sleep(4);
    cleardevice();
  } /* End of 40 X 50 site modules */
```

6.C. vii) The module for 40 X 60 with one room and swimming pool

/* Program name: build5.c */

/* This module deals with single bed room house with car parking and swimming pool in a 60x40 site. The swimming pool is designed with greenish lawn which we can observe at the time of top view. The front view shows the house with closed car parking and trees around the swimming pool. The luxurious compound with garden is implemented */

```
/* side view */
void side40601r(int l1,int w1, int l2,int w2)
{

cleardevice();
setfillstyle(11,7);

rectangle(l1+410,w1+220,l1+510,w2-100);
bar3d(l1+410,w1+210,l1+520,w1+220,10,1);
rectangle(l1+445,w2-180,l1+475,w2-150);
floodfill(l1+450,w2-160,15);
line(l1+455,w2-180,l1+455,w2-150);
line(l1+465,w2-180,l1+465,w2-150);
bar3d(l1+435,w2-195,l1+480,w2-185,10,1);

rectangle(l1+100,w1+150,l1+410,w2-100);
bar3d(l1+90,w1+140,l1+420,w1+150,10,1);
rectangle(l1+135,w2-180,l1+165,w2-150);
floodfill(l1+145,w2-160,15);
line(l1+150,w2-180,l1+150,w2-150);
rectangle(l1+140,w2-270,l1+160,w2-250);
floodfill(l1+145,w2-260,15);
rectangle(l1+210,w2-180,l1+255,w2-150);
floodfill(l1+215,w2-160,15);
line(l1+240,w2-180,l1+240,w2-150);
line(l1+225,w2-180,l1+225,w2-150);
bar3d(l1+125,w2-195,l1+265,w2-185,10,1);

rectangle(l1+300,w2-270,l1+320,w2-250);
floodfill(l1+310,w2-260,15);
setfillstyle(7,8);
floodfill(l1+420,w2-120,15);

setfillstyle(7,11);
floodfill(l1+120,w2-120,15);
rectangle(l1+80,w2-80,l1+540,w2-50);

line(l1+540,w2-80,l1+510,w2-200);
line(l1+80,w2-80,l1+100,w2-200);
setfillstyle(8,3);
```

```
floodfill(l1+85,w2-75,15);
setfillstyle(11,2);
floodfill(l1+85,w2-85,15);
l2++;
sleep(4);
cleardevice();
}

/* front view */
void front40601r(int l1,int w1,int l2,int w2)
{

cleardevice();
setfillstyle(11,7);
rectangle(l1,w1+100,l2-20,w2-100);
line(l1+300,w1+100,l1+300,w2-120);
bar3d(l1-10,w1+90,l1+310,w1+100,10,1);

/* gate design */
ellipse(l1+440,w1+169,0,180,61,55);
ellipse(l1+440,w1+169,0,180,64,58);


ellipse(l1+362,w1+171+65,0,72,51,70);
ellipse(l1+359,w1+171+65,0,72,51,70);

ellipse(l1+518,w1+171+65,110,180,51,73);
ellipse(l1+521,w1+171+65,110,180,51,73);
line(l1+410,w1+171+64,l1+470,w1+171+64);


/* left tree design */
ellipse(l1+340,w1+260,50,210,15,6);
ellipse(l1+340,w1+260,210,50,15,6);

ellipse(l1+380,w1+260,50,210,15,6);
ellipse(l1+380,w1+260,210,50,15,6);

ellipse(l1+340,w1+285,50,210,15,6);
ellipse(l1+340,w1+285,210,50,15,6);
```

```
ellipse(l1+380,w1+285,50,210,15,6);
ellipse(l1+380,w1+285,210,50,15,6);


ellipse(l1+360,w1+230,50,210,6,15);
ellipse(l1+360,w1+230,210,50,6,15);
line(l1+360,w1+245,l1+360,w1+318);
line(l1+355,w1+260,l1+365,w1+260);
line(l1+355,w1+285,l1+365,w1+285);

setfillstyle(SOLID_FILL,2);
floodfill(l1+340,w1+260,15);
floodfill(l1+360,w1+230,15);
floodfill(l1+380,w1+260,15);
floodfill(l1+340,w1+285,15);
floodfill(l1+380,w1+285,15);

/* tree right */
ellipse(l1+510,w1+260,50,210,15,6);
ellipse(l1+510,w1+260,210,50,15,6);

ellipse(l1+550,w1+260,50,210,15,6);
ellipse(l1+550,w1+260,210,50,15,6);

ellipse(l1+510,w1+285,50,210,15,6);
ellipse(l1+510,w1+285,210,50,15,6);

ellipse(l1+550,w1+285,50,210,15,6);
ellipse(l1+550,w1+285,210,50,15,6);

ellipse(l1+530,w1+230,50,210,6,15);
ellipse(l1+530,w1+230,210,50,6,15);
line(l1+530,w1+245,l1+530,w1+318);
line(l1+525,w1+260,l1+535,w1+260);
line(l1+525,w1+285,l1+535,w1+285);
setfillstyle(SOLID_FILL,2);
floodfill(l1+510,w1+260,15);
floodfill(l1+530,w1+230,15);
floodfill(l1+550,w1+260,15);
```

```
floodfill(l1+550,w1+285,15);
floodfill(l1+510,w1+285,15);

/* other parts of the house design */
setfillstyle(SOLID_FILL,9);
floodfill(l2-167,w1+170,15);
setfillstyle(11,7);
rectangle(l1,w1+180,l1+100,w2-100);/*car park room*/

rectangle(l1+185,w2-160,l1+220,w2-230);/*door*/
floodfill(l1+188,w2-180,15);

rectangle(l1+130,w2-230,l1+160,w2-195);/*left window*/
floodfill(l1+135,w2-220,15);
line(l1+140,w2-230,l1+140,w2-195);
line(l1+150,w2-230,l1+150,w2-195);

rectangle(l1+245,w2-230,l1+275,w2-195);/*right window*/
floodfill(l1+250,w2-220,15);
line(l1+255,w2-230,l1+255,w2-195);
line(l1+265,w2-230,l1+265,w2-195);
bar3d(l1+120,w2-245,l1+280,w2-235,10,1);
line(l1+100,w2-120,l2-20,w2-120);
line(l1+100,w2-160,l1+300,w2-160);
setfillstyle(10,2);
floodfill(l1+310,w1+105,15);
setfillstyle(7,11);
floodfill(l1+10,w1+105,15);
setfillstyle(7,8);
floodfill(l1+10,w2-110,15);

setfillstyle(8,3);
floodfill(l1+110,w2-110,15);
floodfill(l1+310,w2-110,15);
//gate
line(l1+170,w2-120,l1+170,w2-100);
line(l1+235,w2-120,l1+235,w2-100);

line(l1+167,w2-120,l1+167,w2-100);
line(l1+238,w2-120,l1+238,w2-100);
```

```
line(l1+201,w2-120,l1+201,w2-100);
line(l1+203,w2-120,l1+203,w2-100);
line(l1+205,w2-120,l1+205,w2-100);
setfillstyle(2,6);

floodfill(l1+172,w2-118,15);
setfillstyle(2,6);
floodfill(l1+208,w2-118,15);

setfillstyle(SOLID_FILL,8);
floodfill(l1+208,w2-128,15);
sleep(4);
cleardevice();
}


/* top view of the house */
void top40601r(int l1,int w1,int l2,int w2)
{
cleardevice();
rectangle(l1,w1,l2-10,w2-10); /*Border */
rectangle(l1+3,w1+3,l2-13,w2-13);

line(l1+3,w1+100,l1+77,w1+100); /*kitchen */
line(l1+3,w1+97,l1+80,w1+97);

rectangle(l1+103,w1,l1+240,w1+150); /*room1*/
rectangle(l1+106,w1+3,l1+237,w1+147); /*inside*/

rectangle(l1+240,w1,l1+290,w1+150); /*room1 toilet*/
rectangle(l1+240,w1,l1+287,w1+147); /*inside*/

rectangle(l1,w1+97,l1+80,w1+180); /*Dinning*/
rectangle(l1,w1+100,l1+77,w1+177);


rectangle(l1,w1+180,l1+80,w1+230); /*bath1*/
rectangle(l1+3,w1+180,l1+77,w1+227);
```

```
rectangle(l1,w1+227,l1+80,w1+310); /*puja*/
rectangle(l1+3,w1+230,l1+77,w1+307); /*inside*/

rectangle(l1,w1,l1+290,w1+310); /*hall*/
rectangle(l1+3,w1+3,l1+287,w1+307);

rectangle(l1,w1,l2-33,w2-30); /*inner compound*/
rectangle(l1+3,w1+3,l2-36,w2-33);
setcolor(0);
line(l2-33,w1+4,l2-33,w1+30);
line(l2-36,w1+4,l2-36,w1+30);
setcolor(15);

/* car parking design */
line(l1+130,w2-130,l1+130,w2-110);
line(l1+127,w2-130,l1+127,w2-110);
line(l1+130,w2-50,l1+130,w2-30);
line(l1+127,w2-50,l1+127,w2-30);
line(l1+127,w2-110,l1+130,w2-110);
line(l1+127,w2-50,l1+130,w2-50);

/* swimming pool compound */
rectangle(l1+320,w1+30,l2-33,w2-130);
rectangle(l1+323,w1+33,l2-36,w2-130);
line(l2-32,w1+409,l2-10,w1+409);

/* cuttings for doors of different parts of the house */
setcolor(0);
line(l1+240,w1+5,l1+240,w1+25); /*room toilet*/
line(l1+237,w1+5,l1+237,w1+25);

line(l1+262,w1+150,l1+285,w1+150); /* g toilet */
line(l1+262,w1+147,l1+285,w1+147);

line(l1+150,w1+150,l1+185,w1+150); /*room*/
line(l1+150,w1+147,l1+185,w1+147);

line(l1+80,w1+120,l1+80,w1+160); /*dinning*/
line(l1+77,w1+120,l1+77,w1+160);
```

```
line(l1+80,w1+185,l1+80,w1+205); /*gbath*/
line(l1+77,w1+185,l1+77,w1+205);

line(l1+80,w1+255,l1+80,w1+280); /*pooja */
line(l1+77,w1+255,l1+77,w1+280);

line(l1+185,w1+310,l1+230,w1+310); /*hall*/
line(l1+185,w1+307,l1+230,w1+307);

line(l1+175,w1+409,l1+245,w1+409); /*room entrance*/
line(l1+175,w1+406,l1+245,w1+406);
line(l1+175,w1+429,l1+245,w1+429);
line(l1+175,w1+426,l1+245,w1+426);

setcolor(15);
line(l1+185,w1+310,l1+185,w1+307); /*hall*/
line(l1+230,w1+310,l1+230,w1+307);

line(l1+175,w1+406,l1+175,w1+429); /*compound entrance */
line(l1+245,w1+406,l1+245,w1+429);
line(l1+175,w1+426,l1+175,w1+429);
line(l1+245,w1+426,l1+245,w1+429);


line(l1+150,w1+150,l1+150,w1+147); /*dining hall*/
line(l1+185,w1+147,l1+185,w1+150);

line(l1+80,w1+120,l1+77,w1+120);
line(l1+80,w1+160,l1+77,w1+160);


line(l1+80,w1+185,l1+77,w1+185);
line(l1+80,w1+205,l1+77,w1+205);

line(l1+80,w1+255,l1+77,w1+255);
line(l1+80,w1+280,l1+77,w1+280);

line(l1+262,w1+150,l1+262,w1+147);
line(l1+285,w1+150,l1+285,w1+147);
```

```
line(l1+240,w1+5,l1+237,w1+5);
line(l1+240,w1+25,l1+237,w1+25);


line(l1+240,w1+72,l1+287,w1+72);
line(l1+240,w1+75,l1+287,w1+75);

/*swimming pool design
 area l1+323,w1+33, l2-36, w2-130 261 X 287 */
ellipse(l1+440,w1+104,0,180,61,55);
ellipse(l1+440,w1+104,0,180,64,58);

ellipse(l1+440,w2-201,178,0,61,55);
ellipse(l1+440,w2-201,178,0,64,58);

ellipse(l1+362,w1+171,289,72,51,70);
ellipse(l1+359,w1+171,289,72,51,70);

ellipse(l1+518,w1+171,110,251,51,73);
ellipse(l1+521,w1+171,110,251,51,73);
setfillstyle(SOLID_FILL,9);
floodfill(l1+440,w1+104,15);

setfillstyle(8,2);
floodfill(l1+360,w1+104,15);
line(l1+290,w2-130,l1+290,w2-30);
setfillstyle(11,2);
floodfill(l1+360,w1+10,15);

rectangle(l1+430,w2-201+35,l1+450,w2-201+55);
line(l1+430,w2-201+42,l1+450,w2-201+42);
line(l1+430,w2-201+49,l1+450,w2-201+49);

/* labeling */
setcolor(9);
outtextxy(l1+10,w1+50,"KITCHEN");
outtextxy(l1+110,w1+50,"BED ROOM");
outtextxy(l1+245,w1+50,"T&B");
outtextxy(l1+245,w1+125,"T");
```

```
outtextxy(l1+10,w1+125,"DINNING");
outtextxy(l1+10,w1+200,"GB");
outtextxy(l1+10,w1+250,"PRAYER");
outtextxy(l1+130,w1+250,"HALL ROOM");
outtextxy(l1+10,w1+350,"CAR PARKING");

setcolor(15);
sleep(4);
cleardevice();
}
```

6.C. viii) The module for two bed rooms house with swimming pool in 40 X 60 site

```
/* Program name: build6.c */
/* This module deals with two bed room luxurious house with swimming pool and greenish lawn */

void side40602r(int l1,int w1, int l2,int w2)
{
cleardevice();
setfillstyle(11,7);
rectangle(l1+410,w1+220,l1+510,w2-100); /*car parking*/
bar3d(l1+410,w1+210,l1+520,w1+220,10,1); /*car roof*/
rectangle(l1+440,w2-180,l1+480,w2-150); /*car window*/
floodfill(l1+450,w2-160,15); /*flood fill for window*/
line(l1+450,w2-180,l1+450,w2-150);
line(l1+460,w2-180,l1+460,w2-150);
line(l1+470,w2-180,l1+470,w2-150);
bar3d(l1+435,w2-195,l1+480,w2-185,10,1); /*bar for window*/

rectangle(l1+100,w1+150,l1+410,w2-100);/*border other than car*/
bar3d(l1+90,w1+140,l1+420,w1+150,10,1); /*roof*/
rectangle(l1+135,w2-180,l1+165,w2-150); /*kitchen window*/
floodfill(l1+145,w2-160,15);
line(l1+145,w2-180,l1+145,w2-150);
line(l1+155,w2-180,l1+155,w2-150);
rectangle(l1+140,w2-270,l1+160,w2-250); /*kitchen ventilation*/
floodfill(l1+145,w2-260,15);
rectangle(l1+210,w2-180,l1+250,w2-150); /*win for dinning*/
floodfill(l1+215,w2-160,15);
```

```
line(l1+220,w2-180,l1+220,w2-150);
line(l1+230,w2-180,l1+230,w2-150);
line(l1+240,w2-180,l1+240,w2-150);
bar3d(l1+125,w2-195,l1+265,w2-185,10,1); /*sunset for kitchen and dining*/

rectangle(l1+300,w2-270,l1+320,w2-250); /*ventilation for bath*/
floodfill(l1+310,w2-260,15);
setfillstyle(10,3);
floodfill(l1+420,w2-120,15); /*for car parking*/

setfillstyle(10,5);
floodfill(l1+120,w2-120,15);/*fill for entire house*/
rectangle(l1+80,w2-80,l1+540,w2-50);/*side*/

line(l1+540,w2-80,l1+510,w2-200);/*right line towards car*/
line(l1+80,w2-80,l1+100,w2-200); /*left line towards house */
setfillstyle(7,8);
floodfill(l1+85,w2-75,15);/*outside wall */
setfillstyle(11,2);
floodfill(l1+85,w2-85,15); /*compound fill */
l2++;
sleep(4);
cleardevice();
}


void front40602r(int l1,int w1,int l2,int w2)
{

cleardevice();
setfillstyle(11,7);

rectangle(l1+35,w1+250,l1+65,w1+285); /*window for car*/
bar3d(l1+25,w1+235,l1+75,w1+245,10,1);
floodfill(l1+40,w1+260,15);
line(l1+45,w1+250,l1+45,w1+285);
line(l1+55,w1+250,l1+55,w1+285);

rectangle(l1,w1+100,l2-20,w2-100); /*border*/
```

```
line(l1+370,w1+100,l1+370,w2-120);/*divider house& swimming*/
bar3d(l1-10,w1+90,l1+380,w1+100,10,1); /*roof*/

/* swimming pool design */
ellipse(l1+490,w1+169,0,180,61,55); /*up ellipse*/
ellipse(l1+490,w1+169,0,180,64,58);

ellipse(l1+412,w1+171+65,0,72,51,70); /*left ellipse*/
ellipse(l1+409,w1+171+65,0,72,51,70);

ellipse(l1+568,w1+171+65,110,180,51,73); /*right ellipse*/
ellipse(l1+571,w1+171+65,110,180,51,73);
line(l1+460,w1+171+64,l1+520,w1+171+64); /*down line to join ellipse*/

/*tree left*/
ellipse(l1+390,w1+260,50,210,15,6); /*left leaf1*/
ellipse(l1+390,w1+260,210,50,15,6);

ellipse(l1+430,w1+260,50,210,15,6); /*right leaf1*/
ellipse(l1+430,w1+260,210,50,15,6);

ellipse(l1+390,w1+285,50,210,15,6);/*left leaf2*/
ellipse(l1+390,w1+285,210,50,15,6);

ellipse(l1+430,w1+285,50,210,15,6); /*right leaf2*/
ellipse(l1+430,w1+285,210,50,15,6);

ellipse(l1+410,w1+230,50,210,6,15); /*top leaf*/
ellipse(l1+410,w1+230,210,50,6,15);
line(l1+410,w1+245,l1+410,w1+318); /* stem*/
line(l1+405,w1+260,l1+415,w1+260); /*up*/

line(l1+405,w1+285,l1+415,w1+285); /*down*/

setfillstyle(SOLID_FILL,2);
floodfill(l1+390,w1+260,15); /*tree flood fill*/
floodfill(l1+410,w1+230,15);
floodfill(l1+430,w1+260,15);
floodfill(l1+390,w1+285,15);
floodfill(l1+430,w1+285,15);
```

```
/*right tree design*/
ellipse(l1+515,w1+260,50,210,15,6); /*left leaf1*/
ellipse(l1+515,w1+260,210,50,15,6);

ellipse(l1+555,w1+260,50,210,15,6); /*right leaf1*/
ellipse(l1+555,w1+260,210,50,15,6);

ellipse(l1+515,w1+285,50,210,15,6);/*left leaf2*/
ellipse(l1+515,w1+285,210,50,15,6);

ellipse(l1+555,w1+285,50,210,15,6); //right leaf2*/
ellipse(l1+555,w1+285,210,50,15,6);

ellipse(l1+535,w1+230,50,210,6,15);
ellipse(l1+535,w1+230,210,50,6,15);
line(l1+535,w1+245,l1+535,w1+318);
line(l1+530,w1+260,l1+540,w1+260);
line(l1+530,w1+285,l1+540,w1+285);
setfillstyle(SOLID_FILL,2);
floodfill(l1+510,w1+260,15);
floodfill(l1+530,w1+230,15);
floodfill(l1+550,w1+260,15);
floodfill(l1+510,w1+285,15);
floodfill(l1+550,w1+285,15);

setfillstyle(SOLID_FILL,9);
floodfill(l2-117,w1+170,15); /*inside swimming pool*/
setfillstyle(11,7);
rectangle(l1,w1+180,l1+100,w2-100);/*car parking(garage)*/

rectangle(l1+185,w2-160,l1+220,w2-230);/*door*/
floodfill(l1+188,w2-180,15);

rectangle(l1+130,w2-230,l1+160,w2-195);/*left window*/
floodfill(l1+135,w2-220,15);
line(l1+140,w2-230,l1+140,w2-195);
line(l1+150,w2-230,l1+150,w2-195);

rectangle(l1+245,w2-230,l1+275,w2-195);/*right window*/
```

```
floodfill(l1+250,w2-220,15);
line(l1+255,w2-230,l1+255,w2-195);
line(l1+265,w2-230,l1+265,w2-195);
bar3d(l1+120,w2-245,l1+280,w2-235,10,1); /*sunset for door and window*/
line(l1+100,w2-120,l2-20,w2-120);/*above gate*/
line(l1+100,w2-160,l1+370,w2-160); /*hall down line*/
setfillstyle(10,3);
floodfill(l1+310,w1+105,15);
setfillstyle(10,5);
floodfill(l1+10,w1+105,15);
setfillstyle(10,3);
floodfill(l1+10,w2-110,15);

setfillstyle(11,2);
floodfill(l1+380,w1+300,15); /*compound of swimming pool*/

setfillstyle(7,8);
floodfill(l1+110,w2-110,15);
floodfill(l1+310,w2-110,15);
//gate
line(l1+170,w2-120,l1+170,w2-100);
line(l1+235,w2-120,l1+235,w2-100);

line(l1+167,w2-120,l1+167,w2-100);
line(l1+238,w2-120,l1+238,w2-100);

line(l1+201,w2-120,l1+201,w2-100);
line(l1+203,w2-120,l1+203,w2-100);
line(l1+205,w2-120,l1+205,w2-100);
setfillstyle(2,9);

floodfill(l1+172,w2-118,15); /*gate left part*/
setfillstyle(2,9);
floodfill(l1+28,w2-118,15); /*gate right part*/

setfillstyle(SOLID_FILL,8);
floodfill(l1+208,w2-128,15); /*compound bellow gate*/

rectangle(l1+340,w2-325,l1+360,w2-305);/*toilet ventilation*/
```

```
setfillstyle(SOLID_FILL,8);
floodfill(l1+350,w2-320,15);


sleep(4);
cleardevice();
}


void top40602r(int l1,int w1,int l2,int w2)
{
graphdefaults();
cleardevice();
rectangle(l1,w1,l2-10,w2-10); /*Border*/
rectangle(l1+3,w1+3,l2-13,w2-13);

line(l1+3,w1+100,l1+77,w1+100); /*kitchen*/
line(l1+3,w1+97,l1+80,w1+97);

rectangle(l1+103,w1,l1+220,w1+150); /*room1*/
rectangle(l1+106,w1+3,l1+217,w1+147);

line(l1+270,w1+150,l1+370,w1+150);/*room2*/
line(l1+270,w1+147,l1+370,w1+147);

rectangle(l1+220,w1,l1+270,w1+150); /*room1 toilet*/
rectangle(l1+220,w1,l1+267,w1+147);

rectangle(l1,w1+97,l1+80,w1+180); /*Dining*/
rectangle(l1,w1+100,l1+77,w1+177); /*inside*/

rectangle(l1+320,w1+150,l1+370,w1+310); /*store & Toilet*/
rectangle(l1+317,w1+150,l1+370,w1+310);

line(l1+320,w1+237,l1+370,w1+237); /*partition*/
line(l1+320,w1+240,l1+370,w1+240);

rectangle(l1,w1+180,l1+80,w1+230); /*bath1*/
rectangle(l1+3,w1+180,l1+77,w1+227);
```

```
rectangle(l1,w1+227,l1+80,w1+310); /*puja*/
rectangle(l1+3,w1+230,l1+77,w1+307); /*inside*/

rectangle(l1,w1,l1+370,w1+310); /*hall*/
rectangle(l1+3,w1+3,l1+367,w1+307); /*inside*/

rectangle(l1,w1,l2-33,w2-30); /*inner compound*/
rectangle(l1+3,w1+3,l2-36,w2-33); /*inside*/

setcolor(0);

line(l2-33,w1+4,l2-33,w1+30); /*car gate cuttings*/
line(l2-36,w1+4,l2-36,w1+30);

/* car parking design */
setcolor(15);

line(l1+130,w2-130,l1+130,w2-110);
line(l1+127,w2-130,l1+127,w2-110);
line(l1+130,w2-50,l1+130,w2-30);
line(l1+127,w2-50,l1+127,w2-30);
line(l1+127,w2-110,l1+130,w2-110);
line(l1+127,w2-50,l1+130,w2-50);

rectangle(l1+385,w1+30,l2-33,w2-130);/* swimming pool compound*/
rectangle(l1+388,w1+33,l2-36,w2-130);
line(l2-32,w1+409,l2-10,w1+409);

setcolor(0);

line(l1+320,w1+235,l1+320,w1+210); /*door cutting for store*/
line(l1+317,w1+235,l1+317,w1+210);

line(l1+320,w1+303,l1+320,w1+280); /*door for general toilet*/
line(l1+317,w1+303,l1+317,w1+280);

line(l1+220,w1+5,l1+220,w1+25); /*room1 toilet*/
line(l1+217,w1+5,l1+217,w1+25); /*room1 toilet*/
```

```
line(l1+270,w1+144,l1+270,w1+120); /*room2 toilet*/
line(l1+267,w1+144,l1+267,w1+120); /*room2 toilet*/

line(l1+150,w1+150,l1+185,w1+150); /*room 1*/
line(l1+150,w1+147,l1+185,w1+147);

line(l1+275,w1+150,l1+310,w1+150);
line(l1+275,w1+147,l1+310,w1+147);

line(l1+80,w1+120,l1+80,w1+160); /*dinning*/
line(l1+77,w1+120,l1+77,w1+160);

line(l1+80,w1+185,l1+80,w1+205); /*general bath*/
line(l1+77,w1+185,l1+77,w1+205);

line(l1+80,w1+255,l1+80,w1+280); /*prayer*/
line(l1+77,w1+255,l1+77,w1+280);

line(l1+185,w1+310,l1+230,w1+310); /*hall*/
line(l1+185,w1+307,l1+230,w1+307);

line(l1+175,w1+409,l1+245,w1+409); /*Entrance*/
line(l1+175,w1+406,l1+245,w1+406);
line(l1+175,w1+429,l1+245,w1+429);
line(l1+175,w1+426,l1+245,w1+426);

setcolor(15);

line(l1+320,w1+303,l1+317,w1+303); /*door for store */
line(l1+320,w1+280,l1+317,w1+280);

line(l1+320,w1+235,l1+317,w1+235); /*door cutting for store */
line(l1+320,w1+210,l1+317,w1+210);

line(l1+267,w1+144,l1+270,w1+144); /*room2 toilet*/
line(l1+267,w1+120,l1+270,w1+120);

line(l1+275,w1+150,l1+275,w1+147);
line(l1+310,w1+150,l1+310,w1+147);
```

```
line(l1+185,w1+310,l1+185,w1+307); /*hall*/
line(l1+230,w1+310,l1+230,w1+307);

line(l1+175,w1+406,l1+175,w1+429); /*entrance compound*/
line(l1+245,w1+406,l1+245,w1+429);
line(l1+175,w1+426,l1+175,w1+429);
line(l1+245,w1+426,l1+245,w1+429);

line(l1+150,w1+150,l1+150,w1+147); /*room*/
line(l1+185,w1+147,l1+185,w!+150);

line(l1+80,w1+120,l1+77,w1+120); /*dining*/
line(l1+80,w1+160,l1+77,w1+160);

line(l1+80,w1+185,l1+77,w1+185); /*general bath*/
line(l1+80,w1+205,l1+77,w1+205);

line(l1+80,w1+255,l1+77,w1+255); /*prayer*/
line(l1+80,w1+280,l1+77,w1+280);

line(l1+220,w1+5,l1+217,w1+5); /*room toilet*/
line(l1+220,w1+25,l1+217,w1+25);

line(l1+220,w1+72,l1+267,w1+72); /*room1 toilet partition*/
line(l1+220,w1+75,l1+267,w1+75);

/*swimming pool design*/
/* area l1+323,w1+33, l2-36, w2-130 261 X 287*/
ellipse(l1+480,w1+104,0,180,61,55); /*up ellipse*/
ellipse(l1+480,w1+104,0,180,64,58);

ellipse(l1+480,w2-201,178,0,61,55); /*down ellipse*/
ellipse(l1+480,w2-201,178,0,64,58);

ellipse(l1+402,w1+171,289,72,51,70); /*left ellipse*/
ellipse(l1+399,w1+171,289,72,51,70);

ellipse(l1+558,w1+171,110,251,51,73); /*right ellipse */
ellipse(l1+560,w1+171,110,251,51,73);
```

```
setfillstyle(SOLID_FILL,9);
floodfill(l1+485,w1+104,15); /*inside swimming pool*/

setfillstyle(8,2);
floodfill(l1+389,w1+104,15);
line(l1+370,w2-130,l1+370,w2-30);
setfillstyle(11,2);
floodfill(l1+380,w1+10,15); /*lawn*/

rectangle(l1+470,w2-201+35,l1+490,w2-201+55); /*swimming pool straight.*/
line(l1+470,w2-201+42,l1+490,w2-201+42);
line(l1+470,w2-201+49,l1+490,w2-201+49);

/* labeling*/
setcolor(9);
outtextxy(l1+10,w1+50,"KITCHEN");
outtextxy(l1+110,w1+50,"BED ROOM");
outtextxy(l1+245,w1+50,"T&B");
outtextxy(l1+240,w1+105,"T&B");
outtextxy(l1+290,w1+70,"ROOM 2");
outtextxy(l1+325,w1+205,"GB");
outtextxy(l1+325,w1+250,"GT");
outtextxy(l1+10,w1+125,"DINNING");
outtextxy(l1+10,w1+200,"STORE");
outtextxy(l1+10,w1+250,"PRAYER");
outtextxy(l1+130,w1+250,"HALL ROOM");
outtextxy(l1+10,w1+350,"CAR PARKING");
setcolor(15);
sleep(4);
cleardevice();
}/* end of 2 bed room with swimming pool */

/* end of buildesigner */
```

PROJECT 7

PETROL BUNK SIMULATION

7.A) SYNOPSIS:

This project simulates the entire operation that can be seen in a petrol bunk. Customers arrive at the petrol bunk and they stop their vehicle at the place where the petrol is served and after that they leave the petrol bunk. When there are many customers at the same time then they form a queue. The petrol is served in the first come first serve basis.

This project consists of following modules.

1. Main module.
2. Input module.
3. Database module.
4. Introduction module.
5. Petrol filling module.
6. Animation module.
7. Timer module.
8. Thanks module.

Each of these modules and their tasks are explained below.

7.A. i) Main module.

This module displays the animation of the project heading. It also draws the basic structure to give a look for the animation that includes clouds, trees and a platform for displaying the name. then it calls all other modules included in this project one by one in the order specified. The order in which these modules are called goes like first the 'introduction' module, then 'input' module, 'database', 'timer', 'animation', 'petrol filling', again 'animation' and finally the 'thanks' module.

7.A. ii) Introduction module.

It displays a text containing information about the working of the project. The background is generated with the help of pixels drawn randomly with different color selection. The text is also displayed in different colors and styles. The normal 'outtextxy()' function is used to display the static message in the specified position.

7.A. iii) Input module.

It is used to take input regarding customer information for the subsequent execution of the project. The data like total number of customers, their name, arrival time and service time are taken from keyboard. Here there are some constraints introduced to accommodate limited screen resolution like the number of customers is restricted to 8 and other validations like it should be positive and non zero integer.

7.A. iv) Database module.

The data taken in the input module will be refined to get waiting time and cumulative waiting time for each customer according to their service time and also cumulative service time for each customer. It also calculates cumulative departure timings after serving the petrol. These data are stored in an array of structures and displayed in a tabular format with proper headings.

7.A. v) Timer module.

This module is used to display the clock that shows each customers waiting time and cumulative time of all the customers.

7.A. vi) Animation module.

Here we have designed car and made it to move to the queue. In case if the queue is empty then the car directly moves to the place where petrol is served. We have also simulated a person who serves petrol to the customers as they arrive in the queue. Once the petrol is served to a customer's vehicle it is made to leave that place.

7.A. vii) Petrol filling module.

Here the petrol serving is animated. The person standing at the petrol bunk serves the petrol. His hands are made to move along with the nozzle holding in his hand is implemented.

7.A. viii) Thanks module.

The final screen which is displayed at the end of the project execution with the "Thank you" message.

7.B) Source Code Of Petrol Bunk Simulation

```
/* This project gives the complete demonstration of petrol bunk simulation. The design of the bunk includes creation of trees, clouds, petrol bunk and the person to serve the petrol to the customers. For simplicity we are considering customers having only cars. The customer details will be taken from the keyboard which include customer name, waiting time, service time etc. for number of customers. To avoid the problem with resolution the number of customers is restricted to maximum eight. Each customer comes to the petrol bunk according to their start time and they will be served according to their service time. A timer is maintained to display the time which easily shows which customer enters next and after how much time. It also displays a screen full of information that is related to the working of this simulation system.*/

/* All the modules of this project are clubbed into a single program file that number of functions are maintained separately.*/

/* header files that are necessary */
#include <graphics.h>
#include <stdlib.h>
#include <stdio.h>
```

```
#include <conio.h>
#include <dos.h>

/* Functions declarations */
void thank();
void intro();
void introduction();
void introd();
void animate(int);
void move(int);
void move1(int);
void database();
void petrolpump();

/* Global variable declarations */
void *g,*buf,*car1;
char *b,buff[20],ch;
char name[8][8];
char buffer[10];
int yg,xg,size,h,k=0;
int ascii,scan,q1[8],dtm[8];
int gdriver=DETECT,gmode;
int midx,midy,maxx,maxy,i;//,color=4;
int  arr[8],ser[8],n=0,carr[8];
int qlen,car,deptime,wattime,idletime,j;
int q=0,l,csize;
int lo,di,r;

 /**********************************************************************/
 /* Function to display program heading. it draws trees, clouds and platform. It also animates
 project name */
 /**********************************************************************/
void thank()
{
   int poly[10];
   void *hel;
   int si,j;
   cleardevice();
   setfillstyle(6,18);
      setcolor(10);
```

```
    settextstyle(1,0,5);
    outtextxy(150,150,"PETROL BUNK ");
    setcolor(14);
    outtextxy(190,205,"QUEING SYSTEM");

        settextstyle(1,0,1);
        si=imagesize(100,128,590,260);
        hel=malloc(si);
        getimage(100,128,590,260,hel);
/* to draw the clouds */
  setcolor(1);
  setfillstyle(SOLID_FILL,5);
  pieslice(230,20,0,180,15);
  pieslice(260,20,0,180,28);
  setfillstyle(SOLID_FILL,LIGHTBLUE);

  pieslice(263,20,0,180,18);
  pieslice(290,20,0,180,15);

  setfillstyle(SOLID_FILL,10);
  pieslice(430,30,0,180,28);
  setfillstyle(SOLID_FILL,1);

  pieslice(433,30,0,180,18);
  setfillstyle(SOLID_FILL,9);
  pieslice(460,30,0,180,15);

  setfillstyle(SOLID_FILL,12);
  pieslice(100,35,0,180,15);
  pieslice(130,35,0,180,28);
  setfillstyle(SOLID_FILL,13);

  pieslice(133,35,0,180,18);
  setfillstyle(SOLID_FILL,14);
  /*End of Clouds.*/

  /*water.*/
    setcolor(LIGHTBLUE);
    setfillstyle(1,2);
    bar(0,getmaxy()-150,getmaxx(),getmaxy());
```

```
  /* movement of project heading */
    for(j=100;j>-10;j—)
      {
      sound(20);
      putimage(j-1,128,hel,XOR_PUT);
      putimage(j,128,hel,XOR_PUT);
      delay(10);
      nosound();
      }
sleep(1);
}/*END OF THANK.*/

/*****************************************************************/
/* Function to display information about the project. The different colors and text styles are used.
        */
/*****************************************************************/

void intro()
  {
  int i;
    cleardevice();
    setfillstyle(SOLID_FILL,0);
  bar(0,0,640,600);
  setcolor(4);
  settextstyle(DEFAULT_FONT,0,1);
  for(i=0;i<=100;i++)
        {
          outtextxy(random(700),random(450),".");
        }
  setfillstyle(SOLID_FILL,1);
  bar(0,0,20,500);
  bar(0,0,640,20);
  bar(610,0,640,500);
  bar(0,455,640,480);
  setcolor(14);
  settextstyle(1,0,3);
    outtextxy(180,30,"PROJECT INTRODUCTION");
    outtextxy(160,50,"* * * * * * * * * * * * * * * * ");
    settextstyle(3,0,2);
    setcolor(10);
```

```
    outtextxy(200,80,"Server Service");
    setcolor(GREEN);
    outtextxy(30,100,"Queue :");
      setcolor(12);

  settextstyle(3, HORIZ_DIR,1);
  outtextxy(135,105, "Number of people waiting for the job to be comple-");
  outtextxy(135,120,"ted sequentially . ");
  outtextxy(50,145,"Queue occurs when a group of people ask for the same job");
  outtextxy(50,165,"at a particular time.");
  outtextxy(215,185,"Single Server Service consists of a single ");
  outtextxy(50,205,"service counter.The service of this service counter is divid-");
  outtextxy(50,225,"ed into various databases. They are Arrival Time, Service Time");
  outtextxy(50,245,",Cumm.Arr.Time, Cumm.Dept.Time, Waiting Time, Idle Time, ");
  outtextxy(50,265,"Queue Length.The 1st customer's ArrTime=Cumm.Arr.Time=0");
  setcolor(9);
  outtextxy(50,305,"Cumm.Arr.Time=ArrTime(i)+Cumm.Arr.Time(i-1)");
  outtextxy(23,325,"Cumm.Dept.Time=Ser.Time[i]+Cumm.Arr.Time(i-1)+Wait.Time(i-1)");
  outtextxy(50,345,"Wait.Time=(Dept.Time(i)-Cumm.Arr.Time(i-1))if -ve");
  outtextxy(50,365,"IdleTime=(Dept.Time(i)-Cumm.Arr.Time(i-1))if +ve");
  setcolor(8);
  introduction();
  return;
  }

/****************************************************************/
/* Function to dispaly the message for proceeding the project or its termination.*/
/****************************************************************/

void introduction()
{

setcolor(14);
outtextxy(300,410,"Press S to Start simulation .");
setcolor(10);
outtextxy(100,410,"Press Ecs to exit. ");
return;
}
```

```
/**************************************************************/
/* Function to dispaly the message related to simulation */
/**************************************************************/

void introd()
{
        int i;
   clrscr();
   setfillstyle(SOLID_FILL,0);
bar(0,0,640,600);
setcolor(14);
settextstyle(DEFAULT_FONT,0,1);
for(i=0;i<=100;i++)
        {
            outtextxy(random(700),random(450),".");
        }
setfillstyle(INTERLEAVE_FILL,1);
bar(0,0,20,500);
bar(0,0,640,20);
bar(610,0,640,500);
bar(0,455,640,480);
setcolor(12);
settextstyle(7,0,4);
outtextxy(130,50,"SIMULATION PROJECT");
return;
}

/**************************************************************/
/* Function to dispaly car animation. */
/**************************************************************/
void animate(int n)
   {
   int i;
   for(i=0;i<n;i++)
   {
   if(q==carr[i])
     {
     move(qlen);
       qlen++;
       }
```

```
 /* departure animation */
 if(q==dtm[i])
    {
  qlen—;
    move1(qlen);
    }
 }
 return;
 }
/*************************************************************/
/* Function to implement movement of car */
/*************************************************************/
void move(int i)
  {
    k=1;
  xg=489;
  yg=210;
  putimage(489,210,g,XOR_PUT);
  while(k!=16-(i*6))
  {
  delay(100);
  putimage(xg,yg,g,XOR_PUT);
  xg=xg-10;
  putimage(xg,yg,g,XOR_PUT);
  k++;
  }
  return;
  }
/*************************************************************/
 /* Function to implement movement of car */
/*************************************************************/

void move1(int i)
  {
  k=0;
  setcolor(15);

  putimage(330,yg,g,XOR_PUT);
  xg=330;
```

```
  yg=210;
  i—;
  putimage(330,210,g,XOR_PUT);
  while(k!=35)
  {

  delay(200);
  putimage(xg,yg,g,XOR_PUT);
  xg=xg-10;
  putimage(xg,yg,g,XOR_PUT);
  setfillstyle(1,0);
  bar(330,210,390,235);
  k++;
  }
  setfillstyle(1,0);
  bar(400,210,450,235);

  return;
  }

/*****************************************************************/
/* Function to dispaly the customer's data base along with their arrival time, service time
needed. */
/*****************************************************************/

void database()

{
  settextstyle(0,0,1);
  setcolor(8);
  line(0,236,630,236);
  setcolor(10);
  rectangle(35,295,630,460);
  /* to make the partitions for different information of the customer.(creating the customer table)*/
  line(35,340,630,340);
  line(60,295,60,460);
  line(140,295,140,460);
  line(210,295,210,460);
  line(280,295,280,460);
  line(350,295,350,460);
```

```
line(420,295,420,460);
line(490,295,490,460);
line(560,295,560,460);

/* to give the labels to the customer table */
outtextxy(39,305,"SL.");
outtextxy(39,320,"NO.");
outtextxy(70,305,"CUSTOMER");
outtextxy(82,320,"NAME");
outtextxy(150,305,"ARRIVAL");
outtextxy(162,320,"TIME");
outtextxy(220,305,"SERVICE");
outtextxy(232,320,"TIME");
outtextxy(295,300,"CUMMU.");
outtextxy(285,310,"ARRIVAL");
outtextxy(295,320,"TIME");
outtextxy(365,300,"CUMMU.");
outtextxy(350,310,"DEPARTURE");
outtextxy(365,320,"TIME");
outtextxy(432,305,"QUEUE");
outtextxy(430,320,"LENGTH");
outtextxy(505,305,"IDLE");
outtextxy(505,320,"TIME");
outtextxy(564,305,"WAITTING");
outtextxy(576,320,"TIME");

/* to display the values from the array of customers */
   for(i=0;i<n;i++)
      {
      car=arr[i]+car;
      j=deptime-car;
         if(j>0)
          {
          wattime=j;
          idletime=0;
          }
else
         {
         wattime=0;
         idletime=abs(j);
```

```
            }
        qlen=0;
        for(j=0;j<i;j++)
        if(car<dtm[j])
        qlen++;
        deptime=ser[i]+car+wattime;
        sprintf(b,"%d",wattime);
        outtextxy(564,350+i*10,b); /* wait time */
                sprintf(b,"%d",idletime);
        outtextxy(505,350+i*10,b); /* idle time */
        sprintf(b,"%d",qlen);
        q1[i]=qlen;
        outtextxy(432,350+i*10,b); /* queue length */
        sprintf(b,"%d",i+1);
        outtextxy(45,350+i*10,b); /* serial number */
        sprintf(b,"%s",name[i]);
        outtextxy(75,350+i*10,b);        /* name of the customer */
        sprintf(b,"%d",arr[i]);
        outtextxy(170,350+i*10,b);       /* arrival time */
        sprintf(b,"%d",ser[i]);
        outtextxy(235,350+i*10,b); /* starting time */
        sprintf(b,"%d",car);
        carr[i]=car;
        outtextxy(310,350+i*10,b); /* customer number*/
        sprintf(b,"%d",deptime);
        dtm[i]=deptime;
        outtextxy(375,350+i*10,b); /*departure time */
      }
     return;
  }


/****************************************************************/
/* Function to design a petrol bunk. */
/****************************************************************/

void petrolpump()
{

/* grass lawn design */
```

```
    setcolor(2);
    setfillstyle(1,2);
    pieslice(70,165,25,20,15);
    pieslice(50,165,25,19,15);
    pieslice(40,165,155,150,15);
    pieslice(40,165,125,120,11);
    pieslice(40,165,105,110,15);
    pieslice(40,165,70,65,15);
    pieslice(55,170,60,55,15);
    pieslice(65,175,55,50,15);
    pieslice(45,173,60,65,15);
    pieslice(47,174,145,139,15);

  /* tree design */
  setcolor(7);
  setfillstyle(1,7);
  bar(41,80,59,158);
    bar(43,50,55,85);
  bar(65,50,80,57);
    bar(66,57,74,65);
    bar(60,72,65,82);
    bar(37,72,43,88);
    bar(32,66,40,76);
    bar(40,80,60,150);
    bar(27,60,35,67);
    bar(35,140,40,150);
    bar(60,140,65,145);
    pieslice(60,140,-60,-90,20);
    pieslice(33,140,-60,-90,20);
    pieslice(60,140,-90,-120,20);
    pieslice(33,140,-10,30,20);
    line(60,130,69,150);
    line(40,120,38,140);
    line(41,120,40,140);
    line(42,120,36,140);
    line(34,150,28,155);
    line(32,144,26,158);
    line(33,146,30,150);
    line(35,148,30,155);
    line(35,148,26,155);
```

```
    line(36,137,29,157);
    line(34,145,27,155);
    line(35,145,30,158);
    line(36,145,31,158);
    line(37,145,32,158);
    line(38,145,33,158);
    line(60,130,62,140);
    line(61,125,63,140);
    line(61,125,61,140);
    line(62,128,62,140);
    line(63,130,63,140);
    line(64,136,70,150);
    line(64,136,67,150);
line(64,136,68,150);
    line(22,55,37,85);
    line(19,50,36,80);
    line(8,48,32,70);
    line(17,45,40,85);
line(19,45,38,80);
    line(12,48,30,70);
line(11,38,30,70);
line(20,38,44,75);
line(21,39,42,70);
line(19,39,44,76);
pieslice(26,65,30,110,10);
    line(40,40,42,80);
    line(41,40,43,80);
        line(39,40,40,50);
    pieslice(40,50,10,35,10);
line(36,60,36,85);
pieslice(38,94,7,80,10);
line(38,85,38,91);
pieslice(71,62,45,11,7);
line(80,55,69,72);
pieslice(55,83,80,20,10);
line(56,65,56,75);
    pieslice(60,93,80,57,11);
    line(61,90,61,95);
line(59,72,59,73);
    pieslice(60,70,10,40,10);
```

```
   line(65,65,74,65);
   line(64,66,72,66);
pieslice(59,75,10,40,10);
line(60,71,65,71);
   line(74,63,63,80);
line(72,68,64,80);
   line(72,68,65,80);
   bar(27,156,75,158);
line(33,148,28,158);
   line(34,141,26,158);
   line(40,143,24,158);
   line(41,120,36,138);
   line(42,120,38,138);
   setcolor(7);
   arc(140,110,130,220,80);
   arc(-40,110,325,40,80);
   arc(-22,14,325,-20,100);
   arc(5,85,25,50,40);
   arc(-18,68,360,20,60);
   arc(-22,81,366,26,80);
   setfillstyle(1,GREEN);

   /*leaves of trees */
   setcolor(2);
   bar(2,2,105,25);
   bar(2,2,15,75);
   fillellipse(12,40,10,20);
   fillellipse(12,60,10,20);
   fillellipse(62,30,50,20);
   fillellipse(62,39,15,20);
   fillellipse(107,22,10,20);
   fillellipse(110,30,15,25);
   fillellipse(100,52,20,10);
   fillellipse(25,38,10,20);

/* moon */
   setcolor(14);
   setfillstyle(1,14);
   fillellipse(278,40,12,12);
/* clouds */
```

```
setcolor(11);
setfillstyle(1,11);
fillellipse(420,20,15,5);
fillellipse(400,35,20,10);
fillellipse(370,25,15,5);
fillellipse(350,20,15,5);
fillellipse(450,25,30,10);
fillellipse(430,35,20,10);
fillellipse(470,40,25,10);
fillellipse(500,25,25,10);
fillellipse(200,30,25,10);
fillellipse(230,35,20,15);
fillellipse(240,20,15,10);
fillellipse(250,30,25,10);

setcolor(5);
rectangle(100,70,500,200);
line(100,110,500,110);
settextstyle(8,0,1);
setcolor(15);
outtextxy(170,70,"BHARAT PETROL PUMP ");
setcolor(3);
rectangle(300,160,500,200);
rectangle(100,160,250,200);
setfillstyle(1,BLUE);
floodfill(400,190,3);
floodfill(130,190,3);

line(300,110,300,160);
line(250,110,250,160);

setcolor(RED);
setfillstyle(1,RED);
bar(340,150,360,200);
line(330,200,370,200);
setcolor(0);
rectangle(340,150,360,170);
rectangle(341,151,359,169);
rectangle(345,158,355,162);
line(350,158,350,162);
```

```
/* draw host */
  setcolor(BROWN);
  setfillstyle(1,BROWN);
  circle(375,155,5);
  floodfill(375,155,BROWN);
  setcolor(12);
  setfillstyle(7,12);
  ellipse(375,173,0,360,7,12);
  floodfill(375,173,12);
  setcolor(BROWN);
  line(370,183,367,200);
  line(380,183,384,200);
  line(370,165,360,170);
  line(380,170,364,178);

/*draw car*/
  setcolor(9);

  line(450,220,468,220);
  line(450,220,443,227);
  line(468,220,475,227);
  line(459,220,459,227);
  rectangle(435,227,483,234);
  setcolor(BROWN);
  setfillstyle(1,BROWN);
  circle(445,236,4);
  floodfill(445,236,BROWN);
  circle(472,236,4);
  floodfill(472,236,BROWN);

  /*get the image of car*/
    csize=imagesize(432,217,486,240);
    g=malloc(csize);
    getimage(432,217,486,240,g);
    putimage(432,217,g,XOR_PUT);
  }

/*****************************************************************/
/* main function */
/*****************************************************************/
```

```
void main()
{
        int d=0,m,i=200;
    char ss[10];

        int gdriver=DETECT,gmode;
        initgraph(&gdriver, &gmode, "");
        qlen=car=deptime=wattime=idletime=0;
        thank();
        intro();
        ch=getch();
        switch(ch)
        {
            case 's':
            case 'S':
            {
        cleardevice();
        setcolor(12);
        bar3d(40,100,580,150,10,10);
        setcolor(10);
        settextstyle(1,0,2);
        setbkcolor(0);
        outtextxy(100,200,"Enter the number > 0 and < 8. ");
setcolor(15);
settextstyle(1,0,1);

outtextxy(50,116,"Enter the number of customer to be consider : ");
        gotoxy(68,9);
        setcolor(7);
            settextstyle(1,0,2);
            scanf("%d",&n);

sleep(1);
/* input validation for number of customers */
if(n<1)
{
  cleardevice();
  rectangle(30,175,580,225);
  setcolor(12);
  settextstyle(1,0,2);
```

```
    outtextxy(50,200,"Invalid number of customer entered .");
    sleep(2);
    exit(0);
  }
 /* to check the number of customers */
 if(n>8)
 {
    cleardevice();
    rectangle(30,175,600,225);
    setcolor(12);
    settextstyle(1,0,1);
    outtextxy(40,190,"There is no space for that many data....Ending program.");
    sleep(3);
    exit(0);
 }
 /* when the number of customers are within the range the customer information is taken from the
 keyboard */
   else
     {
        for(i=0;i<n;i++)
   {
   cleardevice();
   setcolor(14);
   sprintf(buff,"%d",n);

   outtextxy(120,50,"The total number of customers are :::> ");
   outtextxy(528,50,buff);
   gotoxy(10,10);
   setcolor(15);
   setfillstyle(SOLID_FILL,10);
   setbkcolor(0);
   setcolor(10);
   rectangle(100,200,550,425);
   setcolor(13);
   sprintf(buff,"%d",i);
   outtextxy(598,100,buff);
   outtextxy(80,100,"Enter The Information About The Customer No:::>");
   setcolor(12);
   outtextxy(200,250,"Enter The Cust Name :");
          gotoxy(57,17);
```

```
            scanf("%s",&name[i]);
    outtextxy(200,280,"Customer Arrival Time : ");
            gotoxy(57,19);
            scanf("%d",&arr[i]);

    outtextxy(200,310,"Customer Service Time : ");
            gotoxy(57,21);
            scanf("%d",&ser[i]);

    sleep(1);
}
cleardevice();

setcolor(10);
    rectangle(198,252,400,228);
```

/* to display the progress bar before starting the simulatio of the project when it reaches 100 % project simulation starts */

```
        setcolor(15);
        outtextxy(200,270,"PROCEEDING SIMULATION...");
        for(i=200;i<=400;i+=2)
            {
                outtextxy(447,250,"%");
                setcolor(RED);
                rectangle(i,250,398,230);
                rectangle(i-1,250,398,230);
                m=d-1;
                itoa(m,ss,10);
                setcolor(0);
                outtextxy(420,250,ss);
                itoa(d,ss,10);
                setcolor(10);
                outtextxy(420,250,ss);
                delay(75);
                d++;
            }
    setcolor(0);
    setfillstyle(1,1);
    setcolor(4);
    cleardevice();
```

```
petrolpump();
database();
        q=0;
    i=0;
    qlen=0;
    while(deptime>=q)
    {
/* to implement timer to display waiting and service times */
        setcolor(9);
        setfillstyle(1,8);
        bar(560,25,630,70);
        setcolor(10);
        outtextxy(584,30,"Timer");
        settextstyle(1,0,2);
        sprintf(buf,"%d",q);
        setcolor(10);
        settextstyle(1,0,2);
        outtextxy(600,40,buf);
        animate(n);
        delay(1000);
        q++;
    }
        getch();
        cleardevice();
/* to design the final screen which displays the message "Thank You" to the user */
        for(i=0;i<500;i++)
    {
        setcolor(13);
        circle(300,200,i);
        delay(5);
    }
settextstyle(1,0,5);
    setcolor(10);
    setcolor(10);
settextstyle(4,0,20);
    outtextxy(250,250,"THANK YOU");
        break;}
    case 27: exit(0);
}
}
 getch();
}
```

PROJECT 8

DISK SCHEDULING

8.A) SYNOPSIS

In multiprogramming environment many processes may generate requests for reading and writing disk records. When these requests are faster than their service by operating system then for moving disk heads for reading and writing needs to be scheduled. There are mainly four types of disk scheduling algorithms namely,

1. FCFS
2. SSTF
3. SCAN Scheduling and
4. C-SCAN Scheduling.

This project deals with simulation of these four disk scheduling algorithms. These are explained by using certain constraints that are essential in terms of screen resolution. This project is completely menu oriented and includes sub menus whenever essential. The main menu is as follows.

1. Input Data
2. Algorithms
3. Reports
4. Help
5. Exit.

The **first menu option** simply takes the data from the user about number of cylinders, starting head and the sequence of track numbers. This data can be applied for any of the algorithms for scheduling and getting the reports. The validation of boundary values is also taken care.

The **second menu option** in turn consists of five sub menus as follows.

1. FCFS
2. SSTF
3. SCAN Scheduling
4. C-SCAN Scheduling
5. Return.

8.A. i) FCFS Disk Scheduling.

First Come First Serve is the simplest form of disk scheduling. Here the disk controller processes the I/O requests in the order in which they arrive, by moving back and forth across the surface of the disk to get the next requested location each time. Since no reordering of requests takes place the head may move almost randomly across the surface of the disk. For example,

Consider an ordered disk queue with requests involving tracks 98, 183, 37, 122, 14, 124, 65 and 67

If the read write head is initially at track 53, it will first move from 53 to 98, then to 183, 37 and so on till 67, for a total head movement of 640 tracks.

It is quite simple to implement but as the head movements are random it takes more service time.

8.A. ii) SSTF Disk Scheduling.

SSTF (Shortest Seek Time First) scheduling services all requests together depending on their position closer to the current head position. It selects the requests with the minimum seek time from the current head position. Since seek time is generally proportional to the track difference between the requests, we implement this algorithm by moving the head to the closest track in the request queue.

For the request queue mentioned above, the disk scheduling is performed as follows.

The head moves from initial position 53 to track 65, then 65 to 67. This will continue until all the tracks are processed.

8.A. iii) SCAN Scheduling.

In this type of scheduling the disk head moves either right side or left side from the initial head position. Depending on right movement or left movement SCAN Scheduling is of two types, namely R-SCAN and L-SCAN.

R-SCAN - In this SCAN Scheduling all the tracks that are greater than initial head will be processed in the order of their track numbers. The disk head reaches the right boundary and then it comes directly to the left boundary without processing any cylinders. Finally it processes all the cylinders having their track numbers smaller than initial node from left boundary to initial node.

L-SCAN - In this SCAN Scheduling all the tracks that are smaller than initial head will be processed in the order of their track numbers. The disk head reaches the left boundary and then it comes directly to the right boundary without processing any cylinders. Finally it processes all the cylinders having their track numbers greater than initial node from right boundary to initial node.

8.A. iv) C-SCAN Scheduling.

In this type of scheduling the disk head moves either right side or left side from the initial head position circularly. Depending on right movement or left movement C-SCAN Scheduling is of two types, namely RÇ-SCAN and LC-SCAN. It is also called as C-LOOK Algorithm and RC-SCAN is called as R-LOOK and LC-SCAN is called as L-LOOK.

RC-SCAN or R-LOOK - In this circular SCAN Scheduling all the tracks that are greater than initial head will be processed in the order of their track numbers. When the disk head reaches the last track in the queue then it comes directly to the smallest track in the queue without processing any cylinders. Finally it processes all the cylinders having their track numbers smaller than initial node from lowest to initial node.

LC-SCAN or L-LOOK - In this circular SCAN Scheduling all the tracks that are smaller than initial head will be processed in the descending order of their track numbers. When the disk head reaches the first track in the queue then it comes directly to the greatest track in the queue without processing any cylinders. Finally it processes all the cylinders having their track numbers greater than initial node from highest numbered cylinder to initial node.

The **third option** in the main menu gives the comparative report of performance of different algorithms in terms of number of heads processed during scheduling. It is represented in the form of horizontal bar graph with their values displayed.

The **fourth menu** option in the main menu gives the brief outline of the algorithms implemented in this project. It is achieved by displaying the text message in the graphical mode.

The **last menu** option terminates the program and takes the control back to the text mode. Apart from these modules the 'mainscreen' module is used to display the project heading with certain text animations and welcome screen.

8.B) The source code of Disk Scheduling Algorithms

8.B. i) The Main Module

```
/* This project demonstrates different disk scheduling algorithms. This is completely menu driven
program that consists of input module for taking input of data, scheduling module for demonstration
of the algorithms. The scheduling module again consists of sub modules for scan, look, FCFS, and
SSTF algorithms. The scan and look sub modules consist of the options for left scan, right scan,
circular left and circular right functions. The next options in the main menu generate reports,
display the abbreviations and display the help about algorithms. */

/* This is the main module of the project. It displays main menu and all other sub menus based on
user's selection in the main menu */

/* To include header files required */

#include<stdio.h>
#include<conio.h>
#include<dos.h>
#include<process.h>
#include<ctype.h>
#include<math.h>
#include<graphics.h>

/* the program files for different modules in this project */
```

```
#include"recbox.c"
#include"process.c"
#include"fcfs.c"
#include"sstf.c"
#include"scan.c"
#include"look.c"

/* function declarations */
void algo();
void data();
void scan();
void cscan();
void look();
void clook();
void report();
void process();

/* global variable declarations */
int n,x[30],s,sum=0;
int  s1,s2[20],s3[20],s4[20],s5[20],s6[20],s7[20],s8[20],s9[20],s10[20];

/* project execution starts from here */
void main()
{
   int i,key;
   char w;
   process(); /* to design progress bar */

   welcomescreen(); /* screens which display welcome message and project name with
animations */

/* to design the main menu of the project */
do
{
   clrscr();
   gotoxy(33,2);
   highvideo();
   textcolor(LIGHTGREEN + BLINK);
   cprintf("* MAIN MENU *");
   gotoxy(34,3);
```

```
    textcolor(LIGHTGREEN + BLINK);
    cprintf("——————————");
    textcolor(YELLOW);
    rectbox(25,4,55,18,2);
    gotoxy(28,6);
    textcolor(3);
    cprintf("1. ENTER THE DATA");
    gotoxy(28,8);
    textcolor(3);
    cprintf("2. SCHEDULING.");
    gotoxy(28,10);
    textcolor(3);
    cprintf("3. REPORT");
    gotoxy(28,12);
    textcolor(3);
    cprintf("4. ABBREVIATION");
    gotoxy(28,14);
    textcolor(3);
    cprintf("5. HELP.");
    gotoxy(28,16);
    textcolor(3);
    cprintf("6. EXIT");
    textcolor(9);
    textcolor(5);
    gotoxy(10,20);
    textcolor(9);
    cprintf("ENTER YOUR CHOICE : ");
    scanf("%d",&key);

/* based on menu option selection different modules are called */
switch (key)
{
   case 1:
              sound(456);
              delay(4);
              nosound();
              data(&x,s,&n); /* for inputting the data */
              break;
   case 2:
              sound(456);
```

```
            delay(4);
            nosound();
            algo(x,n,s); /* scheduling algorithms sub menu */
            break;
    case 3:
            sound(456);
            delay(4);
            nosound();
            report(); /* report generation */
            break;
    case 4:
            sound(456);
            delay(4);
            nosound();
            /* write the function for displaying abbreviation */
            break;
    case 5:
            sound(456);
            delay(4);
            nosound();
            help(); /* displays help */
            break;
    case 6: break;
    default:
            sound(690);
            gotoxy(23,5);
            textcolor(2+130);
            cprintf(" INVALID CHOICE ");
            getch();
            nosound();
            break;
      }
    }while(key!=6);
    }

/* function which displays sub menu for the different disk scheduling algorithms */
void algo()
{
   int key;
   char w;
```

```
clrscr();
do
 {
 clrscr();
  gotoxy(33,3);
  textcolor(GREEN+BLINK);
  cprintf("ALGORITHMS");
  gotoxy(33,4);
  cprintf("__________");
  textcolor(9);
  rectbox(25,6,50,22,2);
  gotoxy(28,8);
  textcolor(3);
  cprintf("1.FCFS SCHEDULING");
  gotoxy(28,10);
  textcolor(3);
  cprintf("2.SSTF SCHEDULING");
  gotoxy(28,12);
  textcolor(3);
  cprintf("3.SCAN SCHEDULING");
  gotoxy(28,14);
  textcolor(3);
  cprintf("4.C-SCAN SCHEDULING");
  gotoxy(28,16);
  textcolor(3);
  cprintf("5.LOOK SCHEDULING");
  gotoxy(28,18);
  textcolor(3);
  cprintf("6.C-LOOK SCHEDULING");
  gotoxy(28,20);
  textcolor(3);
  cprintf("7.MAIN MENU ");
  gotoxy(26,24);
  textcolor(18);
  cprintf("ENTER YOUR CHOICE: ");
  scanf("%d",&key);
  switch (key)
  {
  case 1: s1=fcfs(x,s,n);
        break;
```

```
    case 2: sstf(x,s,n,s2);
            break;
    case 3: scan();
            break;
    case 4: cscan();
            break;
    case 5: look();
            break;
    case 6: clook(x,s,n);
    case 7: break;
    default: clrscr();
            gotoxy(23,5);
            textcolor(2+130);
            cprintf(" INVALID CHOICE ");
            getch();
            break;
  }
}while(key!=7);

}

/* function for user input */
void data()
  {
   int i;
   clrscr();
   textcolor(9);
   rectbox(15,6,65,8,1);
    gotoxy(20,7);
    textcolor(GREEN);
    cprintf("ENTER THE CURRENT HEADER POSITION: ");
    scanf("%d",&n);
    clrscr();
    textcolor(9);
    rectbox(15,6,65,8,1);
    gotoxy(18,7);
    textcolor(GREEN);
    cprintf("ENTER NUMBER OF CYLINDERS TO R/W FOR DATA: ");
    scanf("%d",&s);
    rectbox(15,6,65,8,1);
```

```
    gotoxy(17,7);
    textcolor(GREEN);
    cprintf("ENTER THE CYLINDERS NUMBERS ACCORDING TO R/W:");
    for(i=0;i<s;i++)
    {
     gotoxy(32,10+i);
     textcolor(i+1);
     cprintf("| %d |==>",i);
     scanf("%d",&x[i]);
     }
    }

/* function to display the menu for different scan algorithms */
void scan()
{
   int key;
   do
   {
   clrscr();
   rectbox(22,6,45,15,2);
   gotoxy(28,8);
   textcolor(3);
   cprintf("1. L_SCAN");
   gotoxy(28,10);
   textcolor(3);
   cprintf("2. R_SCAN");
   gotoxy(28,12);
   textcolor(3);
   cprintf("3. RETURN");
   gotoxy(24,18);
   textcolor(4);
   cprintf("ENTER YOUR CHOICE: ");
   scanf("%d",&key);
   switch(key)
   {
     case 1: /* lscan(x,s,n,&s3); */
             break;
     case 2: rscan(x,s,n,s4);
             break;
```

```
    case 3: algo();
            break;
  }
  }while(key!=3);

}

/* sub menu for different look algorithms */
void look()
 {
  int key;
  do
  {
   clrscr();
   rectbox(22,6,45,15,2);
   gotoxy(28,8);
   textcolor(3);
   cprintf("1. L_LOOK");
   gotoxy(28,10);
   textcolor(3);
   cprintf("2. R_LOOK");
   gotoxy(28,12);
   textcolor(3);
   cprintf("3. RETURN");
   gotoxy(24,18);
   textcolor(4);
   cprintf("ENTER YOUR CHOICE: ");
   scanf("%d",&key);
   switch(key)
   {
    case 1: llook(x,s,n,s7);
            break;
    case 2: rlook(x,s,n,s8);
            break;
    case 3: algo();
            break;
   }
  }while(key!=3);
 }
```

```
/* sub menu for circular look algorithms */
 void clook()
 {
 int key;
 do
 {
  clrscr();
  rectbox(22,6,45,15,2);
  gotoxy(28,8);
  textcolor(3);
  cprintf("1. L_C_LOOK");
  gotoxy(28,10);
  textcolor(3);
  cprintf("2. R_ C_LOOK");
  gotoxy(28,12);
  textcolor(3);
  cprintf("3. RETURN");
  gotoxy(24,18);
  textcolor(4);
  cprintf("ENTER YOUR CHOICE :");
  scanf("%d",&key);
  switch(key)
  {
     case 1: lclook(x,s,n,s9);
            break;
     case 2: rclook(x,s,n,s10);
            break;
     case 3: algo();
            break;
     }
  }while(key!=3);
}

/* function for displaying sub menu of different circular scan algorithms */
void cscan()
  {
   int key;
   do
   {
   clrscr();
```

```
  rectbox(22,6,45,15,2);
  gotoxy(28,8);
  textcolor(3);
  cprintf("1. L_C_SCAN");
  gotoxy(28,10);
  textcolor(3);
  cprintf("2. R_C_SCAN");
  gotoxy(28,12);
  textcolor(3);
  cprintf("3. RETURN");
  gotoxy(24,18);
  textcolor(4);
  cprintf("ENTER YOUR CHOICE: ");
  scanf("%d",&key);
  switch(key)
  {
   case 1: lcscan(x,s,n,s5);
         break;
   case 2: rcscan(x,s,n,s6);
         break;
   case 3: algo();
         break;
  }
 }while(key!=3);
}

/* function for generating reports based on different algorithms performed*/
void report()
{
  int i,j;
  clrscr();
  highvideo();
  gotoxy(35,3);
  textcolor(BROWN+BLINK);
  cprintf("*REPORTS*");
  textcolor(RED);
  rectbox(14,5,65,20,2);
  textcolor(YELLOW);
  gotoxy(17,8);
  cprintf(" Number of Cylinders moved for FCFS = %d ",s1);
```

```
for(i=1;i<s;i++)
sum=sum+abs(s2[i]-s2[i+1]);
gotoxy(17,9);
cprintf(" Number of Cylinders moved for SSTF = %d ",sum);
sum=0;
for(i=1;i<s+1;i++)
sum+=abs(s3[i]-s3[i+1]);
gotoxy(17,10);
cprintf(" Number of Cylinders moved for L_SCAN = %d ",sum);
sum=0;
for(i=1;i<s+1;i++)
sum+=abs(s4[i]-s4[i+1]);
gotoxy(17,11);
cprintf(" Number of Cylinders moved for R_SCAN = %d ",sum);
sum=0;
for(i=1;i<s+2;i++)
sum+=abs(s5[i]-s5[i+1]);
gotoxy(17,12);
cprintf(" Number of Cylinders moved for L_C_SCAN = %d ",sum);
sum=0;
for(i=1;i<s+2;i++)
sum+=abs(s6[i]-s6[i+1]);
gotoxy(17,13);
cprintf(" Number of Cylinders moved for R_C_SCAN = %d ",sum);
sum=0;
for(i=1;i<s;i++)
sum+=abs(s7[i]-s7[i+1]);
gotoxy(17,14);
cprintf(" Number of Cylinders moved for L_LOOK = %d ",sum);
sum=0;
for(i=1;i<s;i++)
sum+=abs(s8[i]-s8[i+1]);
gotoxy(17,15);
cprintf(" Number of Cylinders moved for R_LOOK = %d ",sum);
sum=0;
for(i=1;i<s;i++)
sum+=abs(s9[i]-s9[i+1]);
gotoxy(17,16);
cprintf(" Number of Cylinders moved for L_C_LOOK = %d ",sum);
sum=0;
```

```
    for(i=1;i<s;i++)
    sum+=abs(s10[i]-s10[i+1]);
    gotoxy(17,17);
    cprintf(" Number of Cylinders moved for R_C_LOOK = %d ",sum);
    getch();
}
```

/* Designing of welcome screen, project heading that are displayed in the beginning with effective animation */

```
void welcomescreen()
{
int gd=DETECT,gm;
int i,j,x=200,y=200,p,q,s=120;
initgraph(&gd,&gm,"");
cleardevice();
i=0,j=0;
while(i!=200)
{
settextstyle(1,0,5);
setcolor(6);
outtextxy(i,j,"W");
sound(600);
delay(3);
nosound();
cleardevice();
i++,j++;
}

i=235,j=0;
while(j!=200)
{
settextstyle(1,0,5);
outtextxy(200,200,"W");
outtextxy(i,j,"E");
sound(600);
delay(3);
nosound();
cleardevice();
j++;
}
```

```
i=640,j=0;
while(i!=253)
{
settextstyle(1,0,5);
outtextxy(200,200,"WE");
outtextxy(i,j,"L");
sound(600);
delay(3);
nosound();
cleardevice();
i—;
if(j!=200)
j++;
}

i=640,j=200;
while(i!=283)
{
settextstyle(1,0,5);
outtextxy(200,200,"WEL");
outtextxy(i,j,"C");
sound(600);
delay(3);
nosound();
cleardevice();
i—;
}

i=640,j=480;
while(i!=305)
{
settextstyle(1,0,5);
outtextxy(200,200,"WELC");
outtextxy(i,j,"O");
sound(600);
delay(3);
nosound();
cleardevice();
i—;
if(j!=200)
```

```
j—;
}

i=330,j=480;
while(j!=200)
{
settextstyle(1,0,5);
outtextxy(200,200,"WELCO");
outtextxy(i,j,"M");
sound(600);
delay(3);
nosound();
cleardevice();
j—;
}

i=232,j=200;
while(i!=360)
{
settextstyle(1,0,5);
outtextxy(200,200,"WELCOM");
outtextxy(i,j,"E");
sound(590);
delay(3);
cleardevice();
nosound();
i++;
}
delay(20);
i=0;

while(i<251)
{
setcolor(WHITE);
outtextxy(200,200,"WELCOME");
setcolor(MAGENTA);
outtextxy(200+i,200+i,"WELCOME");
outtextxy(200-i,200-i,"WELCOME");
outtextxy(200,200+i,"WELCOME");
outtextxy(200,200-i,"WELCOME");
```

```
 outtextxy(200-i,200+i,"WELCOME");
 outtextxy(200+i,200-i,"WELCOME");
 i++;
 sound(s);
 delay(4);
 cleardevice();
 s++;
}
nosound();
i=305,j=200;
while(j!=440)
{

settextstyle(1,0,5);
setcolor(WHITE);
outtextxy(200,200,"WELCOME");
outtextxy(i,j,"O");
sound(350);
delay(5);
nosound();
cleardevice();
j++;
}

i=275,j=440;
while(j!=240)
{
settextstyle(1,0,5);
setcolor(WHITE);
outtextxy(200,200,"WELCOME");
outtextxy(i,j,"TO");
sound(530);
delay(5);
nosound();
cleardevice();
j—;
}
j=2;
x=590;y=50;
for(i=1;i<=6;i++)
```

```
{
setcolor(j);
settextstyle(1,0,i);
outtextxy(x,y,"DISK SCHEDULING");
outtextxy(x+75,y+60,"SIMULATION");
sound(s);
delay(200);
cleardevice();
x-=95;
y+=20;
s+=40;
}
}
```

/* This module is for indicating the process bar at the time of loading the program. This module is not mandatory to implement this project, but added with an extra interest to show animation. */

```
void process()
{
   int a=DETECT,b;
   int i,x,left,right,top,bottom;
   float color;
   char msg[80];
   initgraph(&a,&b,"");
   cleardevice();
   setcolor(YELLOW);
   settextstyle(8,HORIZ_DIR,1);
   outtextxy(235,190,"PROJECT LOADING");
   for (x=160; x<=478;x+=1)
   {
      sound(x*2);
      left = getmaxx() / 2 - 164.5;
      top = getmaxy() / 2 - 14.5;
      right = getmaxx() / 2 +164.5;
      bottom = getmaxy() / 2 + 14.5;
      /* color and border for progress bar */
      setcolor(4);
      rectangle(left,top,right,bottom);
```

/* progress bar with different colors. the size keeps on increasing as the loop proceeds and ends when progress bar reaches its border. */

```
        setcolor(x);
        rectangle(left,top+1,x+1,bottom-1);
        delay(20);
    }
    delay(200);
    nosound();
    closegraph();
}

/* To display the help related to the project */
void help()
{
    int gd=DETECT,gm;
    int x1=40,y1=40,x2=600,y2=450,color=1,i;
    initgraph(&gd,&gm,"");
    setcolor(6);
    rectangle(x1,y1,x2,y2);
    rectangle(x1+4,y1+4,x2-4,y2-4);
    setfillstyle(1,color);
    floodfill(x1+6,y1+6,6);
    line(x2,y1,x2-5,y1+5);
    line(x1,y2,x1+5,y2-5);
    setfillstyle(0,DARKGRAY);
    floodfill(x1+1,y1+1,LIGHTGRAY);
    setfillstyle(SOLID_FILL,WHITE);
    floodfill(x2-1,y2-1,LIGHTGRAY);
    setcolor(7);
    settextstyle(2,HORIZ_DIR,6);
    outtextxy(255,50,"-HELP WINDOW-");
    setcolor(YELLOW);
    outtextxy(50,100," This Simulation is designed for a disk of 256 cylinder.");
    outtextxy(50,125,"So please enter the cylinder numbers in 0-255 for perfect");
    outtextxy(50,150,"study. This is done by selecting DATA INPUT option form ");
    outtextxy(50,175,"MAIN_MENU.In DATA_INPUT it will ask for CURRENT_HEADER_ ");
    outtextxy(50,200,"POSTION means the cylinder number on which header is ");
    outtextxy(50,225,"there at end of previous scheduling. NUMBER_OF_CYLINDER ");
    outtextxy(50,250,"means no. of cylinders that contains the data to be ");
    outtextxy(50,275,"readed or data to be written there. Select SCHEDULING ");
    outtextxy(50,300,"from MAIN_MENU to switch ALGORITHMS_MENU for different ");
    outtextxy(50,325,"scheduling. Select REPORT in MAIN_MENU for number of ");
```

```
outtextxy(50,350,"cylinders moved by each schedulings. Please follow this ");
outtextxy(50,375," after all scheduling have done.");
outtextxy(50,410," Press any key ........");
setcolor(3);
setcolor(RED);
settextstyle(3,HORIZ_DIR,1);
getch();
closegraph();
}
```

8.B. ii) The Rectangle Module

/* This module is used to draw rectangle boxes for each of the menus and reports used in this project. It takes four parameters for top left corner and bottom right corner of the rectangle and fifth parameter is to indicate the type of rectangle such as rectangles for main menu, sub menus and reports etc. It makes use of pre processor directives. */

```
#ifndef _rectbox_h
#define _rectbox_h
void rectbox(int x,int y,int xx,int yy,int type)
{

  int sline=196,top_right_corner=218,top_left_corner=191;
  int bottom_right_corner=192,bottom_left_corner=217;
  int vline=179;
  int i,tx,ty,txx,tyy;
  tx=x;
  ty=y;
  txx=xx;
  tyy=yy;
  if(type==2)
  {
    sline=205;
    top_right_corner=201;
    top_left_corner=187;
    bottom_right_corner=200;
    bottom_left_corner=188;
    vline=186;
    }
    for(i=x;i<xx;i++)
    {
```

```
            gotoxy(i,y);
            cprintf("%c",sline);
            gotoxy(i,yy);
            cprintf("%c",sline);
    }
    for(i=y;i<yy;i++)
    {
            gotoxy(x,i);
            cprintf("%c",vline);
            gotoxy(xx,i);
            cprintf("%c",vline);
    }
    gotoxy(tx,ty);
    cprintf("%c",top_right_corner);
    gotoxy(txx,ty);
    cprintf("%c",top_left_corner);
    gotoxy(tx,tyy);
    cprintf("%c",bottom_right_corner);
    gotoxy(txx,tyy);
    cprintf("%c",bottom_left_corner);
}
#endif

/* This module is used for arranging the given data in ascending order. It makes use of reference
parameter for passing values. It takes two parameters one for array of numbers and the other one is
for total number of elements in the input array. */
void sort(int *X,int N)
{
   int tmp,i,j;
   for(i=0;i<N;i++)
   for(j=i;j<N;j++)
    if(X[i]>X[j])
    {
      tmp=X[i];
      X[i]=X[j];
      X[j]=tmp;
    }
}
```

8.B. iii) The FCFS Module

/* This module demonstrates the algorithm based on first come first serve disk scheduling. It makes use of small circles to represent the disk cylinders. The parameters indicate the user input in an array and the array size. */

/* This module returns the sum of cylinders that are processed for reporting purpose */

```
int fcfs(int x[],int s,int n)
{
  int gd=DETECT,gm,sum=0;
  float x1,x2,y1,y2;
  float dx,dy,a,b,xi,yi;
  int i,j,steps,k=0,l=5;
  initgraph(&gd,&gm,"");
  cleardevice();
  printf("\n%5d",n);
  if(n==0)
  {
  x1=45;
  y1=65;
  }
  else
  {
  x1=45+(2.155*n);
  y1=65+n;
  }
  /* for rectangular area of the demo */
  setcolor(6);
  rectangle(601,61,41,451);
  rectangle(600,60,40,450);
  /* for displaying the inputted data */
  setcolor(CYAN);
  outtextxy(45,35,"0|....");
  outtextxy(541,35,"...|255");
  setcolor(LIGHTRED);
  circle(x1,y1,4);
  circle(x1,y1,3);
  delay(2000);
  /* for demonstrating the algorithm */
  for(i=0;i<s;i++)
  {
```

```
    x2=45+(2.155*x[i]);
    y2=65+l;
    printf("%5d",x[i]);
    k++;
    l+=40;
    if(k==9) l=0;
    setcolor(CYAN);
    circle(x2,y2,3);
    circle(x2,y2,4);
    setcolor(5);
    if(i==0)
    sum=sum+abs(n-x[i]);
    else
    sum=sum+abs(x[i-1]-x[i]);
    line(x1,y1,x2,y2);
    delay(1000);
    x1=x2;
    y1=y2;
  }
  delay(2000);
  closegraph();
  return sum;
}
```

8.B. iv) The SSTF Module

/* This module demonstrates SSTF algorithm. It shows the starting header position and then proceeds to all specified cylinders one by one in the order of the shortest unprocessed cylinders from the header position. */

```
#include<stdio.h>
#include<conio.h>
#include<graphics.h>
#include<math.h>
void sstf(int x[],int s,int n,int *s2)
{
  int D[20],i,key,j,no,B=0;
  int gd=DETECT,gm;
  float x1,x2,y1,y2;
  float dx,dy,a,b,xi,yi;
```

```
int steps,k=0,l=5;
initgraph(&gd,&gm,"");

/* Making inputted data absolute after taking their distance from the header. */
for(i=0;i<s;i++)
D[i]=abs(n-x[i]);
cleardevice();
s2[B]=n;
printf("\n%6d",n);
B++;
if(n==0)
{
x1=45;
y1=65;
}
else
{
x1=45+(2.155*n);
y1=65+n;
}

/* for border */
setcolor(6);
rectangle(601,61,41,451);
rectangle(600,60,40,450);

/* for cylinder heads */
setcolor(CYAN);
outtextxy(45,35,"0|....");
outtextxy(541,35,"...|255");
setcolor(LIGHTRED);

/* starting header position */
circle(x1,y1,4);
circle(x1,y1,3);
delay(2000);

/* processing all other cylinders in the order of their distance from the header */
for(i=0;i<s;i++)
{
```

```
   key=999;
   for(j=0;j<s;j++)
   {
          if(D[j]<key)
          {
          key=D[j];
          no=j;
          }
   }
   D[no]=999;
   x2=45+(2.155*x[no]);
   y2=65+l;
   s2[B++]=x[no];
   k++;
   l+=40;
   if(k==9)
          l=0;
   setcolor(CYAN);
   circle(x2,y2,3);
   circle(x2,y2,4);
   printf("%4d",x[no]);
   setcolor(5);
   line(x1,y1,x2,y2);
   delay(1000);
   x1=x2;
   y1=y2;
  }
 delay(2000);
 closegraph();
}
```

8.B. v) The Circular Scan Module

```
/* This module demonstrates circular scan algorithm that makes a loop from right to left. */

void lcscan(int x[],int s,int n,int *s5)
{
   int q[20],r[20],i,j,d,m=0,h=0,B=0;
   int gd=DETECT,gm;
   float x1,x2,y1,y2;
   float dx,dy,a,b,xi,yi;
```

```
int steps,k=0,l=5;
initgraph(&gd,&gm,"");

/* for counting the left side cylinders and right side cylinders from header position in separate
variables */

for(i=0;i<s;i++)
{
 if(x[i]<n)
 q[m++]=x[i];
 else
 r[h++]=x[i];
}

 /* for sorting each of sub lists that hold the left side cylinders and right side cylinders */
 sort(q,m);
 sort(r,h);
 highvideo();
 cleardevice();
 s5[B++]=n;
 printf("\n%5d",n);
 if(n==0)
 {
 x1=45;
 y1=65;
 }
 else
 {
 x1=45+(2.155*n);
 y1=65+n;
 }

  /* for border */
  setcolor(6);
  rectangle(601,61,41,451);
  rectangle(600,60,40,450);

 /* for cylinder positions */
 setcolor(CYAN);
```

```
    outtextxy(45,45,"0|....");
    outtextxy(541,45,"...|255");

    /* for representing cylinders with small circles */
    setcolor(LIGHTRED);
    circle(x1,y1,4);
    circle(x1,y1,3);
    delay(2000);

    /* processing of all the cylinders from header position to its left */
    setcolor(GREEN);
    for(i=m-1;i>=0;i--)
      {
      x2=45+(2.155*q[i]);
      y2=65+l;
      s5[B++]=q[i];
      k++;
      l+=40;
      if(k==9) l=0;
      setcolor(CYAN);
      circle(x2,y2,3);
      circle(x2,y2,4);
      printf("%4d",q[i]);
      setcolor(5);
      line(x1,y1,x2,y2);
      delay(1000);
      x1=x2;
      y1=y2;
      }
  /* whenever there are no cylinders on the right side of header position */
  if(h>0)
  {
  s5[B++]=0;
  printf(" 0");
  y1=y1+8;
  line(x1,y1-8,43,y1);
  setcolor(4);
  setlinestyle(2,1,4);
  s5[B++]=255;
  printf(" 255");
```

```
line(43,y1,600,y1);
x1=600;
}
```

/* for processing all the cylinders that are present on the right side of the header will be processed from right most border to the left border one by one */

```
for(i=0;i<h;i++)
{
 x2=600-(2.155*r[i]);
 y2=65+l;
 s5[B++]=r[i];
 k++;
 l+=40;
 if(k==9) l=0;
 setcolor(CYAN);
 circle(x2,y2,3);
 circle(x2,y2,4);
 printf("%5d",r[i]);
 setcolor(5);
 line(x2,y2,x1,y1);
 delay(1000);
 x1=x2;
 y1=y2;
}
delay(2000);
closegraph();
}
```

/* This module demonstrates circular scan algorithm that makes a loop from left to right */

```
void rcscan(int x[],int s,int n,int *s6)
{
 int q[20],r[20],i,j,d,m=0,h=0,B=1;
 int gd=DETECT,gm;
 float x1,x2,y1,y2;
 float dx,dy,a,b,xi,yi;
 int steps,k=0,l=5;
 initgraph(&gd,&gm,"");
```

```
/* separating inputted cylinder information into to two arrays for cylinders that fall in left side of
the header and right side of the header */
    for(i=0;i<s;i++)
    {
     if(x[i]<n)
     q[m++]=x[i];
     else
     r[h++]=x[i];
    }
    sort(q,m);
    sort(r,h);
    highvideo();
    cleardevice();
    s6[B++]=n;
    printf("\n%7d",n);
    if(n==0)
    {
    x1=45;
    y1=65;
    }
    else
    {
    x1=45+(2.155*n);
    y1=65+n;
    }
    /* for drawing a border */
    setcolor(6);
    rectangle(601,61,41,451);
    rectangle(600,60,40,450);
    /* to display cylinder information */
    setcolor(CYAN);
    outtextxy(45,45,"0|....");
    outtextxy(541,45,"...|255");
    setcolor(LIGHTRED);
    circle(x1,y1,4);
    circle(x1,y1,3);
    delay(2000);
    /* processing all cylinders that fall on right side of the header */
    setcolor(GREEN);
    for(i=0;i<h;i++)
```

```
{
  x2=45+(2.155*r[i]);
  y2=65+l;
  s6[B++]=r[i];
  k++;
  l+=40;
  if(k==9) l=0;
  setcolor(CYAN);
  circle(x2,y2,3);
  circle(x2,y2,4);
  printf("%4d",r[i]);
  setcolor(5);
  line(x1,y1,x2,y2);
  delay(1000);
  x1=x2;
  y1=y2;
 }
 if(m>0)
  {
  line(x1,y1,600,y1+8);
  y1=y1+8;
  s6[B++]=255;
  printf(" 255");
  setcolor(4);
  line(600,y1,43,y1);
  s6[B++]=0;
  printf(" 0");
  x1=43;
 }
/* processing all the cylinders that fall on left side of the header */
 for(i=0;i<m;i++)
 {
  x2=45+(2.155*q[i]);
  y2=65+l;
  s6[B++]=q[i];
  printf("%4d",q[i]);
  k++;
  l+=40;
  if(k==9) l=0;
  setcolor(CYAN);
```

```
    circle(x2,y2,3);
    circle(x2,y2,4);
    setcolor(5);
    line(x1,y1,x2,y2);
    delay(1000);
    x1=x2;
    y1=y2;
   }
  delay(2000);
  closegraph();
}

/* this module demonstrates the right scan algorithm */

void rscan(int x[],int s,int n,int *s4)
{
  int q[20],r[20],i,j,d,m=0,h=0,B=0;
  int gd=DETECT,gm;
  float x1,x2,y1,y2;
  float dx,dy,a,b,xi,yi;
  int steps,k=0,l=5;
  initgraph(&gd,&gm,"");
  for(i=0;i<s;i++)
  {
  if(x[i]<n)
  q[m++]=x[i];
  else
  r[h++]=x[i];
  }
  s4[B++]=n;
  sort(q,m);
  sort(r,h);
  highvideo();
  cleardevice();
  printf("\n%7d",n);
  if(n==0)
   {x1=45;y1=65;} else{
   x1=45+(2.155*n);
   y1=65+n; }
   setcolor(6);
```

```
rectangle(601,61,41,451);
rectangle(600,60,40,450);
setcolor(CYAN);
outtextxy(45,45,"0|....");
outtextxy(541,45,"...|255");
setcolor(LIGHTRED);
circle(x1,y1,4);
circle(x1,y1,3);
delay(2000);
setcolor(5);
for(i=0;i<h;i++)
 {
 x2=45+(2.155*r[i]);
 y2=65+l;
 s4[B++]=r[i];
 k++;
 l+=40;
 if(k==9) l=0;
 setcolor(CYAN);
 circle(x2,y2,3);
 circle(x2,y2,4);
 printf("%4d",r[i]);
 setcolor(5);
 line(x1,y1,x2,y2);
 delay(1000);
 x1=x2;
 y1=y2;
 }
if(m>0)
{
setcolor(5);
line(x1,y1,600,y2);
x1=600;
s4[B++]=255;
printf(" 255");
}
for(i=m-1;i>=0;i—)
{
 x2=45+(2.155*q[i]);
 y2=65+l;
```

```
    s4[B++]=q[i];
    k++;
    l+=40;
    if(k==9) l=0;
    setcolor(CYAN);
    circle(x2,y2,3);
    circle(x2,y2,4);
    printf("%4d",q[i]);
    setcolor(5);
    line(x1,y1,x2,y2);
    delay(1000);
    x1=x2;
    y1=y2;
    }
    delay(2000);
  closegraph();
}
```

8.B. vi) The Look Algorithm Module

/* This module demonstrates different look algorithms namely left look, right look, circular right look and circular left look */

/* This module checks all the cylinders by looking left side of the header */

```
void llook(int x[],int s,int n,int *s7)
{
  int q[20],r[20],i,j,d,m=0,h=0,B=0;
  int gd=DETECT,gm;
  float x1,x2,y1,y2;
  float dx,dy,a,b,xi,yi;
  int steps,k=0,l=5;
  initgraph(&gd,&gm,"");
  for(i=0;i<s;i++)
  {
  if(x[i]<n)
  q[m++]=x[i];
  else
  r[h++]=x[i];
  }
  s7[B++]=n;
  sort(q,m);
```

```
sort(r,h);
highvideo();
cleardevice();
printf("\n%5d",n);
if(n==0)
{
x1=45;
y1=65;
}
else
{
x1=45+(2.155*n);
y1=65+n;
}
setcolor(6);
rectangle(601,61,41,451);
rectangle(600,60,40,450);
setcolor(CYAN);
outtextxy(45,45,"0|....");
outtextxy(541,45,"...|255");
setcolor(LIGHTRED);
circle(x1,y1,4);
circle(x1,y1,3);
delay(2000);
setcolor(GREEN);
setlinestyle(SOLID_LINE,3,4);
for(i=m-1;i>=0;i—)
  {
  x2=45+(2.155*q[i]);
  y2=65+l;
  s7[B++]=q[i];
  printf("%4d",q[i]);
  k++;
  l+=40;
  if(k==9) l=0;
  setcolor(CYAN);
  circle(x2,y2,3);
  circle(x2,y2,4);
  setcolor(5);
  line(x1,y1,x2,y2);
```

```
    delay(1000);
    x1=x2;
    y1=y2;
    }
    for(i=0;i<h;i++)
    {
     x2=45+(2.155*r[i]);
     y2=65+l;
     s7[B++]=r[i];
     printf("%5d",r[i]);
     k++;
     l+=40;
     if(k==9) l=0;
     setcolor(CYAN);
     circle(x2,y2,3);
     circle(x2,y2,4);
     setcolor(5);
     line(x1,y1,x2,y2);
     delay(1000);
     x1=x2;
     y1=y2;
    }
   delay(2000);
   closegraph();
}
```

/* This module checks all the cylinders right side of the header first the checks the cylinders that fall on the left side of the header position */

```
void rlook(int x[],int s,int n,int *s8)
{
   int q[20],r[20],i,j,d,m=0,h=0,B=0;
   int gd=DETECT,gm;
   float x1,x2,y1,y2;
   float dx,dy,a,b,xi,yi;
   int steps,k=0,l=5;
   initgraph(&gd,&gm,"");
   for(i=0;i<s;i++)
   {
    if(x[i]<n)
```

```
q[m++]=x[i];
else
r[h++]=x[i];
}
s8[B++]=n;
sort(q,m);
sort(r,h);
highvideo();
cleardevice();
printf("\n%5d",n);
if(n==0)
{
x1=45;
y1=65;
}
else
{
x1=45+(2.155*n);
y1=65+n;
}
setcolor(6);
rectangle(601,61,41,451);
rectangle(600,60,40,450);
setcolor(CYAN);
outtextxy(45,45,"0|....");
outtextxy(541,45,"...|255");
setcolor(LIGHTRED);
circle(x1,y1,4);
circle(x1,y1,3);
delay(2000);
setcolor(GREEN);
setlinestyle(SOLID_LINE,3,4);
for(i=0;i<h;i++)
  {
  x2=45+(2.155*r[i]);
  y2=65+l;
  s8[B++]=r[i];
  printf("%4d",r[i]);
  k++;
  l+=40;
```

```
    if(k==9) l=0;
   setcolor(CYAN);
   circle(x2,y2,3);
   circle(x2,y2,4);
   setcolor(5);
   line(x1,y1,x2,y2);
   delay(1000);

   x1=x2;
   y1=y2;
   }
  for(i=m-1;i>=0;i—)
  {
   x2=45+(2.155*q[i]);
   y2=65+l;
   s8[B++]=q[i];
   printf("%4d",q[i]);
   k++;
   l+=40;
   if(k==9) l=0;
   setcolor(CYAN);
   circle(x2,y2,3);
   circle(x2,y2,4);
   setcolor(5);
   line(x1,y1,x2,y2);
   delay(1000);
   x1=x2;
   y1=y2;
  }
 delay(2000);
 closegraph();
}
```

/* This module demonstrates processing of all cylinders circularly left to right from the header position. */

```
void lclook(int x[],int s,int n,int *s9)
{
  int q[20],r[20],i,j,d,m=0,h=0,B=0;
  int gd=DETECT,gm;
```

```
float x1,x2,y1,y2;
float dx,dy,a,b,xi,yi;
int steps,k=0,l=5;
initgraph(&gd,&gm,"");
for(i=0;i<s;i++)
{
 if(x[i]<n)
 q[m++]=x[i];
 else
 r[h++]=x[i];
 }
 s9[B++]=n;
 sort(q,m);
 sort(r,h);
 highvideo();
 cleardevice();
 printf("\n%5d",n);
 if(n==0)
  {
  x1=45;
  y1=65;
  }
  else
  {
  x1=45+(2.155*n);
  y1=65+n;
  }
  setcolor(6);
  rectangle(601,61,41,451);
  rectangle(600,60,40,450);
  setcolor(CYAN);
  outtextxy(45,45,"0|....");
  outtextxy(541,45,"...|255");
  setcolor(LIGHTRED);
  circle(x1,y1,4);
  circle(x1,y1,3);
  delay(2000);
  setcolor(5);
  setlinestyle(SOLID_LINE,3,4);
```

```
    for(i=m-1;i>=0;i—)
      {
      x2=45+(2.155*q[i]);
      y2=65+l;
      s9[B++]=q[i];
      printf("%4d",q[i]);
      k++;
      l+=40;
      if(k==9) l=0;
      setcolor(CYAN);
      circle(x2,y2,3);
      circle(x2,y2,4);
      setcolor(5);
      line(x1,y1,x2,y2);
      delay(1000);
      x1=x2;
      y1=y2;
  }

  for(i=h-1;i>=0;i—)
  {
   x2=45+(2.155*r[i]);
   y2=65+l;
   s9[B++]=r[i];
   printf("%4d",r[i]);
   k++;
   l+=40;
   if(k==9) l=0;
   setcolor(CYAN);
   circle(x2,y2,3);
   circle(x2,y2,4);
   setcolor(5);
   line(x1,y1,x2,y2);
   delay(1000);
   x1=x2;
   y1=y2;
 }
 delay(2000);
 closegraph();
}
```

```
/* This module demonstrates circular scan algorithm that makes a loop from left to right */
void rclook(int x[],int s,int n,int *s6)
{
 int q[20],r[20],i,j,d,m=0,h=0,B=1;
 int gd=DETECT,gm;
 float x1,x2,y1,y2;
 float dx,dy,a,b,xi,yi;
 int steps,k=0,l=5;
 initgraph(&gd,&gm,"");
 /* separating inputted cylinder information into to two arrays for cylinders that fall in left side of
the header and right side of the header */
 for(i=0;i<s;i++)
 {
   if(x[i]<n)
   q[m++]=x[i];
   else
   r[h++]=x[i];
  }
  sort(q,m);
  sort(r,h);
  highvideo();
  cleardevice();
  s6[B++]=n;
  printf("\n%7d",n);
  if(n==0)
  {
  x1=45;
  y1=65;
  }
  else
  {
  x1=45+(2.155*n);
  y1=65+n;
  }
  /* for drawing a border */
  setcolor(6);
  rectangle(601,61,41,451);
  rectangle(600,60,40,450);
  /* to display cylinder information */
  setcolor(CYAN);
```

```
outtextxy(45,45,"0|....");
outtextxy(541,45,"...|255");
setcolor(LIGHTRED);
circle(x1,y1,4);
circle(x1,y1,3);
delay(2000);
/* processing all cylinders that fall on right side of the header */
setcolor(GREEN);
for(i=0;i<h;i++)
 {
  x2=45+(2.155*r[i]);
  y2=65+l;
  s6[B++]=r[i];
  k++;
  l+=40;
  if(k==9) l=0;
  setcolor(CYAN);
  circle(x2,y2,3);
  circle(x2,y2,4);
  printf("%4d",r[i]);
  setcolor(5);
  line(x1,y1,x2,y2);
  delay(1000);
  x1=x2;
  y1=y2;
 }
if(m>0)
  {
   line(x1,y1,600,y1+8);
     y1=y1+8;
   s6[B++]=255;
   printf(" 255");
   setcolor(4);
   line(600,y1,43,y1);
   s6[B++]=0;
   printf(" 0");
   x1=43;
  }
/* processing all the cylinders that fall on left side of the header */
for(i=0;i<m;i++)
```

```
{
 x2=45+(2.155*q[i]);
 y2=65+l;
 s6[B++]=q[i];
 printf("%4d",q[i]);
 k++;
 l+=40;
 if(k==9) l=0;
 setcolor(CYAN);
 circle(x2,y2,3);
 circle(x2,y2,4);
 setcolor(5);
 line(x1,y1,x2,y2);
 delay(1000);
 x1=x2;
 y1=y2;
}
delay(2000);
closegraph();
}
```

APPENDICES

APPENDIX A

'C' GRAPHICS FUNCTIONS

The graphical functions that are available in C programming language in the header file 'graphics.h' are listed below with their syntax and description.

1. **initgraph( );** Initializes the graphics system.

   Declaration: void far initgraph (int far *graphdriver, int far *graphmode, char far *path to driver);

   Remarks: To start the graphics system, we must call initgraph( ) first. It initializes the graphics system by loading graphics driver and mode and then puts the system into graphics mode.

2. **setbkcolor( );** It sets the current background color using palette.

   Declaration: void far setbkcolor (int color);

   Remarks: setbkcolor sets the background color specified by 'color'. Color can be specified by either its code from 0 to 7 or by color name specified in capital alphabets.

3. **setcolor( );** setcolor sets the current drawing color.

   Declaration: void far setcolor (int color);

   Remarks: It sets the current drawing color to 'color', which can range from 0 to getmaxcolor( ). Color ranges from 0 to 15.

4. **rectangle( );** Draws a rectangle (graphics mode)

   Declaration: void far rectangle (int left, int top, int right, int bottom);

   Remarks: rectangle( ) draws a rectangle in the current line style, thickness and color between the co-ordinates specified by the points (left, top) to (right, bottom).

5. **settextstyle( );** Sets the current text characteristics.

   Declaration: void far settextstyle (int font, int direction, int charsize);

   Remarks: It sets the text font, the direction in which text is displayed and the size of the characters.

6. **putimage( );** putimage outputs a bit image onto the screen.

Declaration: void far putimage (int left, int top, void far *bitmap, int op);

Remarks: putimage puts the bit image previously saved in a variable with getimage back onto the screen, with the upper left corner of the image placed at (left, top)

7. **getimage ( );** getimage saves a bit image of the specified region into memory.

   Declaration: void far getimage (int left, int top, int right, int bottom, void far * bitmap);

   Remarks: getimage copies an image from the screen into memory variable.

8. **floodfill( ):** fills a bounded region.

   Declaration: void far floodfill (int x, int y, int border);

   Remarks: fills an enclosed area on bitmap devices. The area bounded by the color border are flooded with the current fill pattern and fill color.

9. **closegraph( ):** closes the graphics system.

   Declaration: void far closegraph(void);

   Remarks: It deallocates all memory allocated by the graphics system and takes the progZram control back to the text mode.

10. **cleardevice( ):** It clears the graphics screen.

    Declaration: void far cleardevice(void);

    Remarks: It erases the entire graphics screen and moves the current position (CP) to home(0, 0).

11. **line( ):** draws a line between two specified points.

    Declaration: void far line(int x1, int y1, int x2, int y2);

    Remarks: draws a line from (x1, y1) to (x2, y2) using the current color, line style and thickness. It does not update the current position (CP)

12. **arc():** draws a circular arc

    Declaration: void far arc(int x, int y, int stangle, int endangle, int radius);

    Remarks: draws a circular arc in the current drawing color.

13. **circle():** draws a circle

    Declaration: void far circle(int x, int y, int radius);

    Remarks: draws a circle in the current drawing color.

14. **pieslice():** draws and fills a circular pie slice

    Declaration: void far pieslice(int x, int y, int stangle, int endangle, int radius);

    Remarks: draws a pie slice in the current drawing color, then fills it using the current fill pattern and fill color.

15. **bar():** Draws a bar

Declaration: void far bar(int left, int top, int right, int bottom);

Remarks: draws a filled-in, rectangular, two-dimensional bar. The bar is filled using the current fill pattern and fill color. bar does not outline the bar.

16. **bar3d():** Draws a 3-D bar

Declaration: void far bar3d(int left, int top, int right, int bottom, int depth, int topflag);

Remarks: draws a three-dimensional rectangular bar, then fills it using the current fill pattern and fill color.

17. **clearviewport():** Clears the current viewport

Declaration: void far clearviewport(void);

Remarks: erases the viewport and moves the CP (current position) to home (0,0), relative to the viewport.

18. **detectgraph():** Determines graphics driver and mode to use by checking the hardware.

Declaration: void far detectgraph(int far *graphdriver, int far *graphmode);

Remarks: detects your system's graphics adapter and chooses the mode that provides the highest resolution for that adapter.

19. **drawpoly():** draws the outline of a polygon

Declaration: void far drawpoly(int numpoints, int far *polypoints);

Remarks: draws a polygon using the current line style and color.

20. **fillpoly():** draws and fills a polygon

Declaration: void far fillpoly(int numpoints, int far *polypoints);

Remarks: draws the outline of a polygon using the current line style and color, then fills the polygon using the current fill pattern and fill color.

21. **ellipse():** draws an elliptical arc

Declaration: void far ellipse(int x, int y, int stangle, int endangle, int xradius, int yradius);

Remarks: draws an elliptical arc in the current drawing color.

22. **fillellipse():** draws and fills an ellipse

Declaration: void far fillellipse(int x, int y, int xradius, int yradius);

Remarks: draws an ellipse, then fills the ellipse with the current fill color and fill pattern.

23. **sector():** draws and fills an elliptical pie slice

Declaration: void far sector(int x, int y, int stangle, int endangle, int xradius, int yradius);

Remarks: sector draws and fills an elliptical pie slice in the current drawing color, then fills it using the pattern and color defined by setfillstyle or setfillpattern.

24. **getmaxx():** Returns maximum x screen coordinate

Declaration: int far getmaxx(void);

Remarks: getmaxx returns the maximum x value (screen-relative) for the current graphics driver and mode.

25. **getmaxy():** Returns maximum y screen coordinate

Declaration: int far getmaxy(void);

Remarks: getmaxy returns the maximum y value (screen-relative) for the current graphics driver and mode.

26. **imagesize():** Returns the number of bytes required to store a bit image

Declaration: unsigned far imagesize(int left, int top, int right, int bottom);

Remarks: imagesize determines the size of the memory area required to store a bit image.

27. **moveto():** moves the CP to (x, y)

Declaration: void far moveto(int x, int y);

Remarks: moves the current position (CP) to viewport position (x, y).

28. **moverel():** moves the current position (CP) a relative distance

Declaration: void far moverel(int dx, int dy);

Remarks: moves the current position (CP) dx pixels in the x direction and dy pixels in the y direction.

29. **outtext():** displays a string in the viewport (graphics mode)

Declaration: void far outtext(char far *textstring);

Remarks: display a text string, using the current justification settings and the current font, direction, and size. outtext outputs textstring at the current position (CP)

30. **outtextxy():** displays a string at the specified location (graphics mode)

Declaration: void far outtextxy(int x, int y, char far *textstring);

Remarks: display a text string, using the current justification settings and the current font, direction, and size. outtextxy displays textstring in the viewport at the position (x, y)

31. **getpixel():** gets the color of a specified pixel

Declaration: unsigned far getpixel(int x, int y);

Remarks: gets the color of the pixel located at (x,y).

32. **putpixel():** plots a pixel at a specified point

    Declaration: void far putpixel(int x, int y, int color);

    Remarks: plots a point in the color defined by color at (x,y).

33. **getfillpattern():** copies a user-defined fill pattern into memory

    Declaration: void far getfillpattern(char far *pattern);

    Remarks: copies the user-defined fill pattern (set by setfillpattern) into the 8-byte area *pattern.

34. **setfillpattern():** selects a user-defined fill pattern

    Declaration: void far setfillpattern(char far *upattern, int color);

    Remarks: sets the current fill pattern to a user-defined 8x8 pattern.

35. **setfillstyle():** Sets the fill pattern and color

    Declaration: void far setfillstyle(int pattern, int color);

    Remarks: sets the current fill pattern and fill color.

36. **setlinestyle():** Sets the current line style and width or pattern

    Declaration: void far setlinestyle(int linestyle, unsigned upattern, int thickness);

    Remarks: sets the style for all lines drawn by line, lineto, rectangle, drawpoly, etc.

37. **setviewport():** Sets the current viewport for graphics output

    Declaration: void far setviewport(int left, int top, int right, int bottom, int clip);

    Remarks: establishes a new viewport for graphics output.

38. **graphdefaults():** Sets all graphic settings to default values.

    Declaration: void graphdefaults(void);

APPENDIX B

GRAPHICAL CONSTANTS

In graphical functions number of constants is used to represent the parameter values. The graphical constants such as color names and their corresponding codes, font names and their corresponding codes, line style names and their codes etc. are given below.

Constants Related to Colors

The COLORS constants are used by the text mode functions like textattr, textbackground textcolor and graphics mode functions like setallpalette, setbkcolor, setcolor, setpalette, putpixel, floodfill, settextstyle, setfillstyle etc.

Valid Colors Depend on the Current Graphics Driver and Current Graphics Mode

Constant	*Value*	*Background?*	*Foreground?*
BLACK	0	Yes	Yes
BLUE	1	Yes	Yes
GREEN	2	Yes	Yes
CYAN	3	Yes	Yes
RED	4	Yes	Yes
MAGENTA	5	Yes	Yes
BROWN	6	Yes	Yes
LIGHTGRAY	7	Yes	Yes
DARKGRAY	8	No	Yes
LIGHTBLUE	9	No	Yes
LIGHTGREEN	10	No	Yes
LIGHTCYAN	11	No	Yes
LIGHTRED	12	No	Yes
LIGHTMAGENTA	13	No	Yes
YELLOW	14	No	Yes
WHITE	15	No	Yes

Fill Patterns

Fill Patterns are Used for Getfillsettings and Setfillstyle Etc.

Names	*Value*	*Means Fill With...*
EMPTY_FILL	0	Background color
SOLID_FILL	1	Solid fill
LINE_FILL	2	—
LTSLASH_FILL	3	///
SLASH_FILL	4	///, thick lines
BKSLASH_FILL	5	\\\, thick lines
LTBKSLASH_FILL	6	\\\
HATCH_FILL	7	Light hatch
XHATCH_FILL	8	Heavy crosshatch
INTERLEAVE_FILL	9	Interleaving lines
WIDE_DOT_FILL	10	Widely spaced dots
CLOSE_DOT_FILL	11	Closely spaced dots
USER_FILL	12	User-defined fill pattern

Font Names

Name	*Value*	*Meaning*
DEFAULT_FONT	0	8x8 bit-mapped font
TRIPLEX_FONT	1	Stroked triplex font
SMALL_FONT	2	Stroked small font
SANS_SERIF_FONT	3	Stroked sans-serif font
GOTHIC_FONT	4	Stroked gothic font

Line Styles

Line Styles for Getlinesettings and Setlinestyle

Name	*Value*	*Meaning*
SOLID_LINE	0	Solid line
DOTTED_LINE	1	Dotted line
CENTER_LINE	2	Centered line
DASHED_LINE	3	Dashed line
USERBIT_LINE	4	User-defined line style

Line Widths

Line Widths for Getlinesettings and Setlinestyle

Name	*Value*	*Meaning*
NORM_WIDTH	1	1 pixel wide
THICK_WIDTH	3	3 pixels wide

Putimage Operators

Constant	*Value*	*Meaning*
COPY_PUT	0	Copies source bitmap onto screen
XOR_PUT	1	Exclusive ORs source image with that already onscreen
OR_PUT	2	Inclusive ORs image with that already onscreen
AND_PUT	3	ANDs image with that already onscreen
NOT_PUT	4	Copy the inverse of the source

Text Justification Constants

Horizontal and Vertical Justification for Settextjustify

Argument	*Constant*	*Value*	*Meaning*
horiz	LEFT_TEXT	0	Left-justify text
	CENTER_TEXT	1	Center text
	RIGHT_TEXT	2	Right-justify text
vert	BOTTOM_TEXT	0	Justify from bottom
	CENTER_TEXT	1	Center text
	TOP_TEXT	2	Justify from top

Horizontal and Vertical Direction Constants

Defines the Direction While Displaying the Text in Graphics Mode

Name	*Value*	*Direction*
HORIZ_DIR	0	Left to right
VERT_DIR	1	Bottom to top (rotated 90 degrees counterclockwise)